Foreign Investment and Corporate Governance in China

Also by Yanni Yan

INTERNATIONAL JOINT VENTURES IN CHINA

Foreign Investment and Corporate Governance in China

Yanni Yan

palgrave
macmillan

First published 2005 by
PALGRAVE MACMILLAN
Houndmills, Basingstoke, Hampshire RG21 6XS and
175 Fifth Avenue, New York, N.Y. 10010
Companies and representatives throughout the world

PALGRAVE MACMILLAN is the global academic imprint of the Palgrave Macmillan division of St. Martin's Press, LLC and of Palgrave Macmillan Ltd. Macmillan® is a registered trademark in the United States, United Kingdom and other countries. Palgrave is a registered trademark in the European Union and other countries.

ISBN 1–4039–4362–1

This book is printed on paper suitable for recycling and made from fully managed and sustained forest sources.

A catalogue record for this book is available from the British Library.

Library of Congress Cataloging-in-Publication Data
Yan, Yanni, 1958–
Foreign investment and corporate governance in China / Yanni Yan.
p. cm.
Includes bibliographical references and index.
ISBN 1–4039–4362–1
1. Investments, Foreign—China. 2. Corporate governance—China.
3. Corporate governance—Law and legislation—China. I. Title.

HG5782.Y33 2005
332.67'3'0951—dc22

2004052230

10 9 8 7 6 5 4 3 2 1
14 13 12 11 10 09 08 07 06 05

Printed and bound in Great Britain by
Antony Rowe Ltd, Chippenham and Eastbourne

Contents

List of Figures

List of Tables

Preface

This book reports on foreign investments in transitional economies and the corporate governance of international strategic alliances in China. Foreign investments in China have caused a remarkable shift in the competitiveness of its economy to the extent that it has dramatically increased exports of labour intensive products. The long-standing central issues of FDI in transitional economies have added new dimensions to conventional Western management practice and highlighted new relationships that must be considered when choosing the right form of market entry strategy. Corporate governance, namely the relationship between the ownership and control of firms, takes on new dimensions in the case of international strategic alliances operating in the special context of China. The book contributes an insightful examination of foreign investment in transitional economics and its strategic roles played in international business. Key findings provide implications for understanding strategic, managerial and operational matters.

The book is intended to offer new academic perspectives and insights to illustrate corporate investment in transitional economies. This book discusses the dichotomies faced by most international firms that include: whether to tightly integrate international investment to the implementation of their own strategic and financial control or to relinquish equity authority to host country managers; whether market orientation should be dependent mainly upon non-equity based investments using an international branding approach or should be more focused on local market conditions; whether ongoing development of organizational culture, learning and corporate governance should strictly adhere to corporate standards or be developed with local conditions in mind. In a transitional economy, the foreign investments pursued through international strategic alliances create great challenges for the host government.

This book throws new light on the foreign investment process and provides an overview of corporate governance in China. It draws on investigations into over a thousand international strategic alliances. The creation of a sound market environment requires primarily an understanding of how a host country's economic, socio-cultural and political institutions influence a firm's governance. Such influence is believed to affect the competitiveness of the national economy as it dictates how strategic alliances can be run more effectively within a given society. The book draws important conclusions for theory and practice on the basis of original empirical research conducted with the co-operation of strategic alliance managers. The construction of market environments that facilitate the effective use of a host country's overall investments is essential. It appears that western theory can usefully be applied to China, despite the contextual differences.

The book examines FDI in transition economies and develops the conceptual and theoretical basis of the significant research that has been undertaken. Because of FDI policy work with nationa1 and international organizations, this book is able to offer a first-hand perspective of corporate governance activities in international strategic alliances. As a result, this book lays the foundation for an understanding of the rise of transition economies through the explanation of overall patterns of international trade and the role that China plays in international business, especially as a host for foreign investment.

This book not only offers a strong theory base on building blocks for corporate governance but also fully reflects the managerial concerns of those who work on the frontline in the business world. The assessment and management of foreign investment is an integral element of a firm's corporate governance. The corporate governance of an international strategic alliance in China may involve different forms of political patronage, privileged access to markets, or development opportunities.

This book offers the perspective of the corporate governance in international strategic alliances. In-depth attention is paid to the role of FDI, cultural issues, corporate governance and organizational learning. It provides a good understanding on how and why governments intervene in markets and suggests alternatives for working with governments to achieve corporate goals. The book also addresses key issues associated with the management of foreign investments. Achievement of an optimal balance of foreign investment inputs and the associated corporate governance in an international strategic alliance is bound to be dependent upon the local investment conditions and technical requirements. Applying a research framework on international strategic alliance to formation, foreign investment, corporate governance, organizational culture and learning has derived key findings and implications. Specific experiences in international strategic alliances have stimulated research and discussion into a number of issues of wider interest to international business. The research evidence shows that China's economy is developing rapidly with the assistance of considerable diversification in the sources and destinations of investment. The political and economic evidence in China on increases in foreign trade, international investment and international production have generated significant attention from researchers who wish to examine the subsequent effects on FDI and foreign trade flows.

YANNI YAN

Acknowledgements

First and foremost I wish to express my appreciation to those individuals, companies and employers who have made significant commitments of time, effort and financial resources. I am most grateful for their dedication, support and assistance in helping me in my endeavours to complete the book. This study has benefited significantly from the encouragement and support generously given by my colleagues in the Marketing Department of the City University of Hong Kong. I would like to thank all of them sincerely.

I must acknowledge the valuable collaboration of a large number of international strategic alliances in China who have had the courage to air their foreign investment decisions and corporate governance publicly. In preparing this book, I have been significantly assisted by many strategic alliances and their managers who have provided me with many examples. My thanks go to the numerous expatriates and Chinese managers of these international strategic alliances in China who have provided the data on which this study is based. Without their co-operation, there would have been no research findings to report. The areas of foreign investments and corporate governance in international strategic alliances have long intrigued me as I am deeply impressed by the investment strategies that are formulated and the efficiency of the alliances' corporate governance. Throughout this book, I have made reference to what I have learned from managers during the interviews I conducted. This book not only provides readers with a strong pragmatic base but also fully reflects the managerial concerns of those who work on the front line.

Colleagues in the China project team contributed ideas about international strategic alliances and their fieldwork methods, as well as assisting with access to such alliances. My deep gratitude goes to Professor John Child, who has given me continuous guidance and support throughout the four years that I have worked in Hong Kong. The final writing of this book gained a great deal from support generously given by Professor Yang Shu Quan from the Ministry of Electronics, and Shirley Yeung, my research assistant, who has worked diligently with me at the City University of Hong Kong after successfully completing her BA in Chinese

Business. She brought great insight to research projects and continues to engage in stimulating discussion with me on the subject.

I would like to express my thanks to my current employer for allowing me the time to complete this book. The City University of Hong Kong has been most generous in its research grants in support of all my research activities. I have also benefited from opportunities to pursue research for the book sponsored by a competitive earmarked research grant (a grant from the Hong Kong government), a direct allocation grant (a grant from the City University), and a strategic research grant (also from the City University). I have been fortunate to receive eight research project awards over four years resulting in grants of more than HK$1.5 million which has definitely enhanced my general understanding of the subject of foreign direct investment, corporate governance, corporate culture and organizational learning within international strategic alliances. I am also very grateful to various institutions including the Research Grant Committee of the Hong Kong Government for their sponsorship of this study. United Distillers Asia Pacific, Rothmans Charitable Trust, the School of Business at Hong Kong University, Churchill College and Cambridge University have all provided further funds to cover research costs and conference travel.

Within the university community, I have been fortunate to work with a series of postgraduate students who have become research assistants. I wish to thank those students at the City University of Hong Kong, members of the City University Executive Master of Business Administration (EMBA) in the Management of International Joint Venture courses of 2000 and 2002, the Hong Kong Polytechnic University's Doctor of Business Administration (DBA) in Management of International Joint Venture courses of 2001 and 2002, and undergraduate students for the Chinese Multinational course 2004 who have let me try my new material on them. My colleagues are thanked for their constant insights and contributions in the departmental seminars that have helped me to develop my own ideas and have provided valuable comments on an earlier draft of the book. Both undergraduates and postgraduates have generously supplied an untold number of insightful comments and helpful suggestions.

A number of people have assisted in bringing this book to print. I appreciate the encouragement and support received from Dr John Richard Fawn who has been a constant source of assistance and advice throughout the publishing process. Dr Fawn has contributed in many ways to this book through his insights in discussions and I have benefited greatly from his help during the evolution of this book. My thanks also go out to Keith Povey, the book editor, and Jacky Kippenberger, the editor of Palgrave Macmillan; they offered considerable help in directing my efforts in the book. In addition, I give special thanks to Geff Heathman, Shirley Hockins and Easther Lam for their helpful suggestions. Last but not least, I could not have completed the task without the forbearance and sympathetic support of my family. During the time in which this book has taken shape, I have been the fortunate beneficiary of constant support from my family, especially the love and encouragement of my parents, Gongxin Yan and Liqin Lin. My brother, Keguo Yan, sister, Mingxia Yan, and uncle, Professor Gongbiao Yan, also gave their encouragement. In particular, Rungang Zhang, my husband, and Zichao Zhang, our son, have demonstrated their patience, tolerance, and above all love throughout my studies in Birmingham, Cambridge, Essex and at the City University of Hong Kong.

List of Abbreviations

CJV	co-operative joint venture
EJV	equity joint venture
FDI	foreign direct investment
GDP	gross domestic product
H–O	Heckscher–Ohlin
HRM	human resources management
IJVs	international joint ventures
OLI	ownership, location, internalization
PLC	product life cycle
R&D	research and development
SEZs	special economic zones
SOEs	state-owned enterprises
WOS	wholly-owned subsidiary
WTO	World Trade Organization

Part I

Foreign Investment in Transitional Economies

1
The Rise of the Transitional Economies

Introduction

This chapter presents an overall view on available market entry strategies, organizational configurations and the alternative methods by which firms may structure their international investment and international production in foreign countries. It has become increasingly important for business practitioners and researchers to examine the trends in foreign direct investment (FDI) in China. Although the World Trade Organization (WTO) indicates that major foreign investments have successfully changed key economic indicators in transitional economies, most foreign firms in China still find it a challenge to select an effective market entry strategy for an international investment in production facilities. This chapter identifies the principal issues and outlines the content of the book.

Outlook of the transitional economies

The process of structuring foreign investments in transitional economies in a way that will satisfy market demands and the overall strategic objective of achieving a more efficient global trading system based upon international investment and production is complex. The scale of FDI ultimately defines the types of advanced technology, product innovation and international management created in a given country. Foreign investments in China have caused a dramatic shift in the competitiveness of other national economies to the extent that they have increased China's exports of labour-intensive products and taken market share from companies with a higher labour cost base. The emerging Chinese market economy has also developed its industries in areas where more technology-intensive production methods can be combined with lower labour costs. The long-standing central issues of foreign investment in transitional economies have added new dimensions to the conventional Western investment approach by introducing new relationships for evaluation when choosing the most appropriate form of market entry strategy, ownership resources, corporate governance, corporate culture and organizational learning. Issues of particular importance to transitional economies are discussed with respect to their possible primacy on FDI policies in countries such as China.

As an illustration of foreign investment in transitional economies, this chapter presents the dichotomies faced by most foreign firms in China, which include strategic issues such as technological intensity, investment location and ownership arrangements. The writer provides a detailed discussion as to whether to tightly link international investment and international production with the implementation of foreign firms' strategic and financial control or relinquish their equity authority to a host country's managers; whether market orientation should be dependent mainly upon foreign firms' non-equity based investments through the use of an international branding approach or more focused on local market conditions; whether on-going development of foreign firms' corporate culture, organizational learning and corporate governance should strictly adhere to Western management standards or should be developed with local conditions in mind.

Host governments in transitional economy countries may wish local firms to maintain some control over their subsidiaries even if these local firms are not in a financial position to contribute the majority of equity capital. Their strategic rationales are to minimize possible exploitation by powerful foreign firms through the manipulation of controls on technology transfer whilst encouraging local participation in joint equity ownership such as international joint ventures (IJVs) in a form that facilitates international technology transfer. One of the primary driving forces behind the long-term upturn in the Chinese economy is the dramatic increase in the growth of foreign investment, the transformation of the technology base, potential market demand and business internationalization. The more upbeat current economic forecasts suggest that China is ranked as the top FDI recipient amongst the developing countries and has the highest ranked current overall gross domestic product (GDP) growth rates in the world. China has continuously achieved an average growth rate of 8 per cent for three decades. There are strong indications that the increasing rate of FDI in China is due to the government's economic policy which prioritizes expansion of its domestic market demand. China's economic growth is also dependent upon economic liberalization based upon overall industrial development. Thus the increase in foreign investments in China reflects not only domestic market demand, but also an overall industrial ability to meet the needs of primary international markets.

Strategic profile of foreign investment

China is the largest host country for FDI amongst developing countries and provides an important venue for the study of market entry strategies from both a theoretical and practical perspective. With a long-standing and unique cultural tradition, China is still a nominally socialist country whose government plays an active role in business affairs. Central government intervention, infrastructure changes, specific targeted plans for political institution development, technology transformation and economic liberalization are mainly used to justify government authority and the formal right to manage the economy. The diversity of overall trade development allows a multifaceted analysis that sheds significant light on how the Chinese economy performs. There is no doubt, however, that the Chinese economy has been able to benefit from its improved international competitive position, which in turn has primarily been derived from its economic transformation based upon FDI-led increases in foreign trade.

Increases in FDI have raised significant concerns within China about heightened market competition from international businesses which now dominate certain industrial sectors with highly profitable operations in China at the expense of some domestic firms which used to service provincial markets. Some foreign firms have found that the provision of local capacity in specific industrial sectors establishes the opportunity for market expansion throughout broader-based Chinese nationwide markets. There are growing numbers of international strategic alliances in China where equity joint ventures and co-operative ventures are fully capable of managing exogenous factors which can impact business performance achievement, such as quality of local resources, labour, the supply of components and administrative intervention by the central government. Despite the overall positive FDI environment established in China, government attention still needs to be directed towards the reforms necessary in its political institutions and economic infrastructure. The formal propaganda that concentrates on the positive indicators of

China's economic growth shows that the government may be complacent in its attitude towards the formulation and implementation of economic reforms, including FDI policies.

China has been able to capitalize on its improved economic competitiveness only when its economic and political reforms are properly codified. FDI flows are positively influenced by increasing the level of certainty affecting those strategic factors that determine a host country's market performance, especially if they ensure that superior performance from better-quality high-technology operations is available in a transparent and predictable political and legal environment. For example, the establishment of IJV bankruptcy laws and the operational procedures that provide a legal framework for an IJV's management functions are essential prerequisites, including areas such as the appointment of the board of directors, the requirements for accounts to be drawn up according to international conventions, and international auditing procedures and operational regulations. The regulations, procedures and policies relating to foreign investments that were introduced encouraged foreign firms to generate more investments and increased the rate of establishment of international strategic alliances in China. This new regulatory framework was accompanied by specific short-term regional tax benefit policies that provided incentives for targeted FDI activities.

The Chinese government pursues a macroeconomic policy that includes an emphasis on maintaining steady economic growth with low inflation and a stable currency. Whilst evaluating the effectiveness of a strategic profile on overall foreign investments in China, attention has been generally focused on the goodness of fit between foreign firms' resources, knowledge and capabilities and the relevant control priorities they adopted to achieve effective market entry. The management of foreign investments in a transitional economy poses even greater challenges in the proper exploitation of strategic benefits which can accrue from FDI consistent with the determinants of foreign firms' investment profile and the level of control achieved over their intellectual property rights. Increasing economic activity in international production and foreign trade has driven Chinese markets to become more transparent, particularly in sectors that have opened up as WTO agreements have been successfully implemented. With China's accession to the WTO, foreign capital, advanced technology and international management have increasingly flowed into the country to take advantage of the lower cost production activities that are a result of low labour costs and cheap component resources.

Economic profile of foreign investment

China's industrial economics and overall industrial performance at the national level have been and will continue to be affected by shifts in tax policy, changes in the regimes that formulate regulations and the creation of incentive policies that direct foreign investments. With a population of 1.3 billion, China represents the largest potential market in the world. The establishment of effective economic institutions in China to regulate import tariffs, tax breaks, exchange rates and foreign currency controls has been driven by the need for many foreign firms to tap into the market that has the largest potential growth rate in the world. Most foreign firms find that China has a combination of cheap labour, cheap resources and tax incentives which compares well with other developing countries. This combination also establishes China as an attractive 'manufacturing' base from which to serve world markets. The Chinese authorities have effectively developed FDI policy to prioritize high-technology product exports whilst scrapping the traditional tax credit schemes. Economic liberalization has pressured the government to favour international trade and economic progress, even where this means that the market has become more open and more transparent.

China is adapting to the new business environment induced by heightened market competition, infrastructure changes and technological transformations. Strong domestic Chinese industries built with support from foreign investments seem to be establishing sound economic bases. FDI-oriented economic legislation has enabled technologically-based companies and the necessary industrial infrastructure to become properly entrenched in China. Favourable economic policies have positively impacted market performance, and economic reforms have become important conduits for the implementation of other national legislation that increases overall economic and political liberalization. However, there are still some protectionist pressures on the government to restrict market access agreements for strategically important projects which could significantly affect international trade regulations, corporate governance and market competition policies.

Socio-cultural profile of foreign investment

An in-depth knowledge of the Chinese socio-cultural background is helpful for expatriate managers operating in modern industries in China. It is important for foreign firms who do business there to integrate the necessary international business experience with an appreciation of local cultural traditions, national values, business conventions and the social welfare system. Many foreign firms are attracted by the market potential but, after their investments have been committed, they encounter difficulties in facing the challenges posed by the complexities of operating a business there. Most foreign firms lack knowledge of local management culture. China has a large population with rapid economic growth and strong socio-cultural traditions embedded in its national institutions, business systems, national values and social norms. Purchasing power, cultural traditions and local management practices vary greatly in different regions. However, it is perfectly possible for foreign companies to acquire sufficient knowledge relating to government policies, regulations and procedures, distribution systems and supply chains to manage their investment profiles and achieve an excellent business performance in China.

The use of an international strategic alliance as a vehicle for increasing foreign firms' resource commitments may also be an attractive proposition to a local firm, as it may trigger international business activities in addition to the creation of more direct production activities and new marketing service involvement that would otherwise be unavailable. Within the context of Chinese government economic and trade liberalization, the most attractive mechanism for introducing FDI in the Chinese market is through the formation of international strategic alliances. Foreign firms may perceive the market risk in China as high due to the under developed market infrastructure, and may prefer to make non-equity investments in the form of technology-based investments that are likely to provide earlier positive returns on their capital. However, equity-based investment is perceived as providing flexibility in both international investments and international production because the establishment of formal contracts can protect investors.

More recent studies of international management practices in the context of international strategic alliances have emphasized the need to integrate indigenous national culture into operational practices to meet the demands of the new economic environment. A few studies specifically explain the dilemmas faced by local managers when accepting roles in a strategic alliance where they have unaccustomed responsibility for achieving superior performance. Chinese managers often confuse their professional role in an objective, rational organizational system with expectations of conformity and paternalism from their local firms. Only by exposure to modern management philosophies and performance practices over the years do local managers come to consider international management practices as important dimensions of performance. Even where such practices are established within a strategic alliance, socio-cultural influences in traditional management culture and decision-making, together with the strategic importance ascribed to traditional management practices, may deter initiatives on progressive performance changes migrating to local firms. The FDI surge in China has brought with it a rapid socio-cultural improvement and economic development since the government adopted new industrial policies associated with economic reform, but only in specific demographic sectors.

The central business drive for the internationalization of domestic firms is leading to increasing levels of interest in technology, innovation and managerial techniques. The consequence of an increase in local firms' business awareness of international market potential is the realization that their resources, knowledge and capabilities need updating, and they achieve this through the formation of international strategic alliances. The establishment of an international strategic alliance is significantly influenced by the socio-cultural background, information, experience, and perception of management that in turn is shaped by local firms' motivation and their strategic intentions. Overall, Chinese government policy encourages the development of international strategic alliances and other efficient production facilities.

Foreign investment in the industrial sector

The pattern of industrial sector distribution of FDI in China has changed substantially. The investment pattern is significantly shifting from service activities to manufacturing. Foreign investment and production have made important contributions to the development of the service and manufacturing sectors. There are some indications that, in the manufacturing sector, investment in China is heavily concentrated on heavy machinery and equipment (with a small portion also going to the specialized food processing industry). Investments in the manufacturing sector tend to be widely distributed according to strategic, economic and technological factors. This reflects not only a wider range of Chinese national interests, but also a broader spectrum of foreign firms' investments. The cost of establishing a new company in China is often prohibitive and the time needed too excessive for the domestic industries to contemplate, even with government help. Foreign investments and their associated production capabilities are perceived by the Chinese government as an effective way to enhance and diversify the host country's industrial base and thereby increase its overall technological capital and production strength.

The sectoral distribution of foreign investments and associated production in China have undergone significant change. Foreign firms now contribute over 10 per cent of the country's total investment in fixed assets in a period where the total industrial output value has increased dramatically. The Chinese government is encouraging foreign investments in production, technology and export-oriented projects, infrastructure and basic industries such as new materials. Recently, China has opened several new service industries to foreign investments including domestic retail, banking and insurance. Foreign investment in agriculture and infrastructure remains small. Despite all the changes in the industrial sector investment mix, approximately 60 per cent of total FDI in China is still in the manufacturing sector. Within the manufacturing sector much of the foreign investment is in labour-intensive and relatively low-technology industries such as textiles, clothing, and assembly of mechanical and electronic products. The strong performance of the manufacturing sector in China reflects the success of specific FDI policies and other measures adopted to encourage foreign firms' investments.

Geographical distribution of foreign investment

The geographical distribution of foreign investment inflows indicates that 80 per cent of all foreign investment activities are concentrated in coastal cities and provinces. These easily accessible areas are economically better developed and able to provide supporting infrastructure facilities, production components and other necessary production inputs. The flow of foreign investments into coastal cities is also encouraged by the existing strong local production base, a relatively highly-educated workforce and good infrastructure. It is the coastal areas that have been favoured by government policies which have opened up specific new market regions and this development has been reinforced by strong promotion from local provincial governments aimed at attracting foreign investments. The availability of raw materials such as coal, oil, electricity, gas and other components in these areas is also an advantage to foreign firms establishing themselves in China. FDI inflows are attracted by the comparative advantage of the combination of cheap labour and good local supply chain resources. The non-capital resources offered by foreign firms are based on the quality of technology and productivity of labour. These firms will seek to form strategic alliances in the most developed regions, as this will make it easier to implement the technology and managerial knowledge that provide their competitive advantage. Lack of infrastructure, noticeably with transportation and communication, still seriously constrain many provincial governments' ability to attract foreign capital and technology.

The Chinese government has recently started to encourage the redirection of FDI from coastal cities to western regions or inland cities. Foreign investment policy in China may to a certain degree help to divert FDI to less attractive areas, but the coastal areas still remain the chief recipients. Incentives have been established that direct and encourage new foreign investments to flow to the central and western regions, although companies that have already invested in the eastern coastal regions are not disadvantaged in the active development of capital-intensive, technology-intensive and export-oriented firms. The central and western regions in China include 19 provinces, municipalities and autonomous regions, which together offer vast land resources, rich mineral resources, a large population, low labour costs and a large market potential. Moreover, there are many important industrial cities with educational, scientific and research centres in the central and western regions. With geographic isolation, fragile environmental conditions, historical problems and unbalanced economic development policies, the central and western areas in China have only relatively recently opened their local markets and are having to play catch-up in the FDI game.

Recently, the Chinese government has adopted policies to encourage foreign investments in the central and western regions and it is expected that domestic funds will also be increased to support foreign firms investing in these regions. Currently the host country's government loans and credit services are mainly used to finance key infrastructure and environmental protection projects. Previous studies on investment locations have suggested that foreign firms favour areas with an established industrial base and well-developed physical infrastructure, and until the infrastructure is in place it will be difficult to attract FDI despite the opportunities for foreign firms to increase their market share by taking advantage of regional gaps in supply and demand.

Overview of the Chinese domestic investment profile

The competitiveness of indigenous Chinese industries depends on the progress of national institution building, technological development and modern corporate systems being applied to local firms. The government has undertaken the logistically necessary move of 'taking hold of the large and letting go the small' by concentrating mainly on state-owned enterprises (SOEs). This policy successfully adjusts the industrial infrastructure by achieving corporate governance efficiencies. Economic transition and FDI in China have given birth to a diversity of new organizational forms that have enabled more new markets to be opened. State-owned enterprises have relative advantages in access to scarce resources, materials, capital, information and investment infrastructure in comparison with other types of domestic firms in China. Moreover, it is fairly common for SOEs to have privileged access to 'government-associated' distribution channels and financial support from the central government.

China's industrial reform and economic liberalization have made significant progress over the last three decades. However, the government has to become very much more active in tackling the problems of inefficient SOEs and must facilitate industrial restructuring. No doubt the responsibility for the business of re-engineering at the national level will be devolved to local governments and this will generate many opportunities for creative collaborations with foreign firms. The superior performance of foreign firms is highly associated with the possession of advanced technologies, sophisticated means of production, competitive skills and sufficient amounts of capital. It is argued that the performance of SOEs in China is continually affected by restrictive government investment policies and the ownership structure. Sceptics of the 'state-owned enterprise' argument present abundant evidence to suggest that SOEs face significant challenges concerning FDI, ownership configuration, motivation issues, organizational governance and performance evaluation. Foreign investments in China have successfully forced the implementation of the concept of 'modern corporatization' in SOEs by using international strategic alliance structures to ensure that international corporate governance structures are adopted for 'international production'.

SOEs must be transformed to embrace a commercial approach that starts by replacing state-owned property rights with commonly shared rights implying ownership by the 'whole nation'. The improvement of macro-institutional infrastructure may induce foreign firms to invest or operate in China. However, managers in SOEs often lack the information that would enable them to acquire new product designs or new service offerings that fulfil market demands. The structure of SOEs may not be easily transformed to assimilate modern corporate systems which consciously reward innovation or savagely punish failure. The modernization of SOEs' resources, knowledge and capabilities has to involve the acceptance by these firms of new management frameworks.

Experimentation in China with a 'shareholding system' indicates that the shareholding structure of an SOE can be reformulated to build effectively on international experience of corporate governance. An assessment of the general advantages of SOEs to the Chinese industrial infrastructure suggests that policies will be implemented by the government to ensure that many SOEs will be able to operate effectively. The policies will be based upon actions such as the promotion and adoption of a shareholding system in large enterprise groups, encouraging banks and other financial institutions to hold enterprise shares, abolishing the bureaucratic overhead of ministries and bureaus, establishing institutions in which shareholders make boards of directors legally responsible for their actions, imposing strict conditions on firms that experiment with the shareholding system and developing management and employee compensation schemes in shareholding firms. However, the strategic impact of foreign investments and their production activities has given rise to higher expectations across the population and strategic alliances often are expected to assume leadership roles in comparison with other types of domestic firms due to their financial, managerial and technological strength.

A plant established by a foreign firm will automatically assume a built-in positive stereotype or image for product quality and there is widespread expectation that foreign trade, international investments and international production facilities will lead to local technological diffusion and enhanced economic activity. Because the improvement of China's investment environment may seriously challenge those local firms that have dominant local market positions, such firms may work to inhibit the development of FDI policy transparency and openness. There are examples where local taxation and foreign exchange availability factors have been manipulated and where the tendency of local governments to engage in competitive bidding for FDI inflows has encouraged them to undertake some uncompetitive strategic alliance investments through local firms under their jurisdiction. It is believed that failures arising from the manipulation of markets will eventually lead to the development of an open and transparent market. Figure 1.1 shows the strategic investment profile of SOEs, collective owned-enterprises (COEs), private-owned enterprises (POEs) and foreign-owned firms (FOFs) in China.

Market entry modes of foreign investment

There are various types of business financing schemes that can be employed by foreign firms investing in China which require different levels of

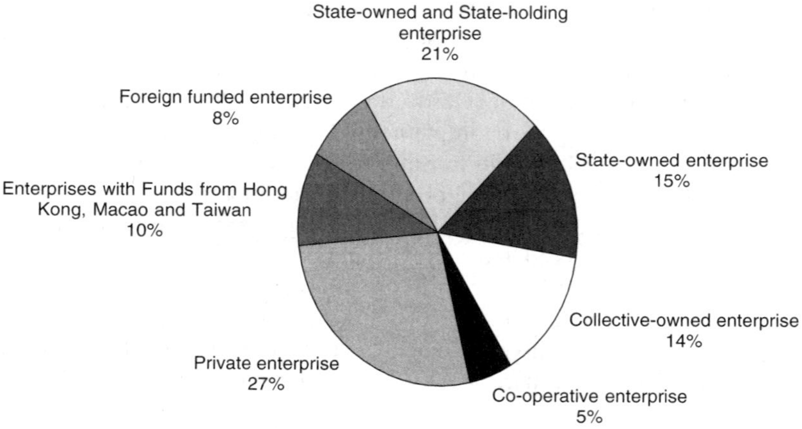

Figure 1.1 Strategic investment profile in China
Source: *China Statistical Yearbook* (2003).

financial commitment. This allows foreign firms to utilize various alternatives for raising capital in China, and enables them to develop working relationships with local people and gain confidence that they can use local resources, knowledge and capabilities to their advantage. The government has committed to various economic measures to facilitate foreign firms' development. These include the development of institutional infrastructure and the adoption of laws to regulate the legislative, administrative and judicial operations of government. Special tax incentive zones and generous tax incentive policies are offered to attract foreign investments to China, and are framed to ensure that the choice of foreign firms' ownership investments will meet the investment demands of the local market. Six main types of foreign investment in China can be identified.

Representative office

Foreign firms have been permitted to set up branch offices in China to enable them to engage in international business activities. Many foreign firms establish a representative office to develop their local networks and explore investment opportunities. Although representative offices are not functionally limited to particular industrial sectors, there are formidable restrictions on how the representative office may conduct business. In particular, a representative office is prohibited from engaging in direct business activities, such as production activities.

Franchising

Franchising is the granting of the right associated with a franchiser's non-capital resources to another independent franchisee to do business in a prearranged manner. The rights of the franchisee include selling the franchiser's products and services, using its brand name, production technology and marketing techniques, and employing its general business practices, expertise and skills. The franchiser must offer unique products or distinctive marketing services that are rare, inimitable and tacit in nature to achieve a superior performance in international franchising. In China, the experience is that when a franchiser's non-capital resources are offered and unique comparative advantages are real, a new market can be secured and sustained. The advantages of taking a 'franchise' as a foreign investment across national borders focuses on achieving a firm's business expansion, such as increasing economic scale for the achievement of its product or service potential, reducing business risks by implementing a proven concept, improving financial gain by taking advantage of transfer pricing, increasing economic scope by avoiding saturated markets, and reducing costs by generating outflows of foreign currency. Generally, the franchiser needs to spend significantly on product promotion, servicing and training in order to enable the franchisee to understand the franchiser's product and service specification.

Licensing

Licensing is when a licensor issues an agreement including a property contract, innovation patents, trademarks, brand name, company logo and copyright to allow the licensee to produce and market products and services in a specific geographical area. The recipient firm is known as the licensee, and is granted this status by the licensing agreement. The licensee is obliged to pay to the licensor compensation that is designated as a royalty. There are advantages of using licensing as a method to gain international market entry because the licensee can gain benefits from the reduction in the risk of expropriation, the avoidance of a host country's regulations, the ability to monopolize a market before the entry of competition, and the provision of a mechanism for corporations from industrialized countries to capitalize on their technology. These advantages are available through adopting the licensing agreement only when the licensor offers its product knowledge and managerial expertise to the licensee.

The deal on offer by the Chinese government is intended to attract foreign capital and superior technology up front in return for its supplying labour, land, plant and facilities. It is assumed that the advanced technology in question can be successfully licensed even though there may be a significant proportion of tacit knowledge involved. It is generally believed that licensing is efficient in transferring 'old types' of technology. The foreign licensor needs to specify input parameters and, if possible, arrange an established supply of materials that demonstrate quality and endurance. The licensor is generally responsible for providing the technology, equipment, training, and service covered by warranty in addition to other basic support, such as the supply of spare parts. The foreign licensor generally receives progress payments or royalties as output is sold. The local firm will also expect the foreign licensor to help market and sell its products nationwide, regardless of whether the locally managed products will compete with the licensor's own products. If the licensor is willing to accept progress payments rather than a lump-sum user fee, payment will typically be made through a letter of credit issued by the Bank of China. Generally speaking, royalty rates are around 3 per cent of the end product's sales price.

Licensing is not a favoured option for licensors from developed countries as such firms prefer internal transfers to their subsidiaries. Licensing is generally discouraged as such arrangements are normally costly due to haggling over complicated terms and conditions and enforcing the agreements, particularly if the opportunity cost of capital is higher in the recipient country than in the potential licensor's country. The technology licensor needs to make sure that its equipment and/or process can perform under adverse conditions. Contractual details related to output or production rate must allow for energy shortages and delays in the delivery of materials and components. Foreign licensors must be careful to protect their patents and copyrights. The cost of the technology transfer in licensing is known in advance, and hence the risk borne by the licensor is reduced. Normally, the licensor can dispense with any examination of the licensee's accounts. A royalty arrangement can be viewed as a profit/return sharing rule between the parties, and its economic value should be calculated and compared with that of an alternative arrangement. In some cases, licensors have an incentive to lower the perceived volatility of the project but, if they do so, the licensee may be required to pay higher variable royalties.

Co-operative joint venture

A co-operative joint venture (CJV) refers to the co-operation between two separate economic entities who reach an agreement or a contract on specific matters such as the provisioning of investment conditions, the earnings on products, the sharing of profit and loss, the operating procedure and the ownership of the property. There are many reasons why foreign firms in China favour CJVs, such as the ability to take a strategic position to make good use of their specific advantages when they invest in a host country. A CJV is perceived as a less risky investment mode but requires more mutual trust and co-operation from investing firms. Foreign firms are able to act more rationally in markets that are characterized by a high level of uncertainty. CJV investment status enables foreign firms to gain preferential treatment from the host country's government in terms of profit distribution. The provisions of a foreign firm's 'co-operation terms' or 'partner conditions' are not only based on the amounts of resources invested by both sides, but also depend on the terms of the contract drawn up between the local and foreign firm.

A CJV offers both local and foreign partners opportunities on a contractual basis to pursue mutually beneficial ends. A CJV that is registered as a legal entity is a limited liability company. The proportion of investments contributed by the foreign partner cannot be less than 25 per cent of the registered capital and a CJV firm's liquidity is critical to operations because it directly affects the firm's ability to pay off short-term financial obligations. Most CJVs in China depend heavily on government-supported short- and long-term financial loans that are not normally available to local firms and are thus vulnerable to strategic changes in governmental monetary policy for their own business operations. Profit sharing in a CJV is determined by discussions that occur on a yearly basis between the relevant partners. The duration of a CJV is decided by mutual consent of the local and foreign partners and must be clearly stated in the contract.

Equity joint venture

An equity joint venture (EJV) is perceived as a quasi-independent 'child' organization, which is defined as two or more parent firms investing in a separate legal business entity in which each firm contributes assets and shares profits as well as risks. An EJV, according to the Chinese definition, is a limited-liability joint venture that is financed and managed by firms with shared responsibilities regarding profit and risk proportional to their respective equity investments. The partners' contributions typically include capital funds, technology, plant and people. An EJV has its own independent assets and liabilities and it pays taxes to the host country. In an EJV, all partners contribute capital and non-capital resources and knowledge, with profits shared according to the proportion of the contribution invested by the partners. By drawing on sets of resources, knowledge and expertise from partner firms, EJV investment costs can be reduced. It may offer a partner firm the opportunity to sell its product in another country in a way that can integrate resources forwards or backwards. The process of such integration may require considerable investment by a partner in learning the other partner firms' business practices, customs and expertise.

An EJV is perceived to generate opportunities for partners to take an active role in decision-making activities. As each partner will receive a proportionate share of the dividend for its investment, the investments are protected by representation on the EJV's board of directors. An EJV is hybrid in nature, but has its own strategic objectives, identifiable organizational systems, working procedures, risk and cost structures, management control, learning, managerial staff and technical personnel. An EJV's objectives are usually derived from a combination of the partners' strategic objectives. An EJV links organizational systems as a means by which two or more parent firms can establish a partnership. Within an EJV, partners can contribute and exchange either tangible resources, such as assets, and/or intangible properties such as knowledge, skills, training, and information. The value of the partnership lies in having a control mechanism through which parent firms endeavour to create a synergistic context and within which the EJV can draw upon their organizational systems and resources.

Management control of an EJV is often fraught with problems because of complications, which are embedded in both the inter-partner and the parent–EJV relationships. Each partner may have non-congruent working procedures and the criteria for evaluating the EJV's performance may diverge. In addition to the formal definition of control rights, differences in the partners' management styles, cultures, and managerial perceptions are also likely to mould the EJV's behaviour. An EJV in China takes the form of a limited liability firm in which each party is liable for the capital subscribed to it and is formed by foreign firms or individuals that wish to engage in a partnership with a local firm. A minimum of 25 per cent of the EJV's registered capital needs to come from both participating parties and while there is no law stipulating the upper limit, profits can only be released according to the proportion of initial investment in the project. There are certain basic requirements necessary before a foreign firm can apply to form an EJV. Compared with other forms of investment, an EJV operates in a fairly well developed regulatory environment.

Wholly-owned subsidiary

The wholly-owned subsidiary (WOS) is considered important internationally as one of the most significant methods of market entry since it gives an investing company control over its financial and managerial performance achievement. A WOS is owned 100 per cent by its parent firm. Full ownership of a subsidiary is desirable when a foreign firm possesses the necessary resources, technological capital and management expertise, and has strong linkages with its suppliers and customers. A WOS is perceived as an effective market entry method if its management can be granted rights to secure absolute autonomy over business operations in the specific country being considered. Many foreign firms tend to use a WOS approach as it can increase profit by selecting only those local personnel who are competent.

Establishing a WOS in foreign markets needs a high degree of control and standardized technology in the running of business operations. There are advantages to investing in a WOS in that a company can safely transfer advanced technology and management experience to the foreign market in a way that strengthens its competitive ability. For the Chinese government, the benefit of adopting a WOS investment is that it encourages local firms to increase their performance and provides more foreign exchange revenue through income tax, free land use, rent, and payments for raw materials. The foreign company has the benefit of controlling employment, guaranteeing greater strategic consistency across management structure and protection of their own intellectual property, and these are perceived as the primary advantages for making a WOS investment.

The WOS has become an increasingly popular investment, which testifies, *inter alia*, to the growing confidence that firms feel about establishing a market presence *vis-à-vis* competitors in a very different foreign market. A WOS is an autonomous legal entity where the ownership resides with the parent organization but is instituted in a host country by foreign firms using foreign capital and adhering to local laws. It is registered as a legal entity and independently performs production and operation activities subject to the conditions of the registered business licence. The net gains from WOS contributions largely depend on the management of fixed and inventory assets. In recent years, asset efficiency has become particularly important for the evaluation of WOS performance because a WOS primarily exists to exploit intellectual property rights. A WOS provides much higher autonomy in allocating and utilizing various assets than other forms of investment in China.

The level of asset management mirrors the degree of sophistication of managerial skills and the extent of effectiveness of corporate administration in the use of advanced technology and equipment. The duration of a WOS is fairly open and amenable to revision. Any foreign firm in China is required to pay the full price of the equity, and asset transfer must take place within three months of the relevant government authority issuing the foreign firm's business licence for the establishment of a WOS. If a foreign firm intends to transfer cutting-edge technology, it is better done in a WOS because, by having full control over management, the transferor has a free hand to design working procedures and organizational structures which facilitate the interaction of technical personnel.

Principal issues identified

A stream of research within international business studies has focused on the impact of FDI where foreign firms take equity investments in return for capital and non-capital resources and then leverage these resources. However, there is still far more speculation than sound research into the management of an international strategic alliance in order to understand the challenges faced in overcoming distance-related problems between the partners that occur due to geographical, cultural and institutional factors. The objective of this book is to make a contribution in the relatively unexplored conceptual territory concerning international business and investment, strategic management and organizational studies. It seeks to cover the following five main aspects: the formation of an international strategic alliance; the assessment of ownership configuration on international technology transfer; the institution of corporate governance; the management of corporate culture and organization in transitional situations; and the achievement of organizational learning.

The formation of an international strategic alliance is often used as an effective vehicle to enter the Chinese market. Foreign firms can provide knowledge regarding technology, management and capital while the local partner can provide knowledge regarding host-country markets, infrastructure and political institutions. By pooling these firms' resources, it is possible to increase a strategic alliance's long-term business presence *vis-à-vis* competitors. The successful exchange of a strategic alliance's resources is important in the achievement of increases in overall resource effectiveness. A successful strategic alliance's resources, knowledge and capabilities exchange relies on the management of all participating firms being involved in the effective exchange of relevant information.

The assessment of ownership configuration on international technology transfer centres on questions of who should have rights and powers to allocate corporate resources and returns, the appropriate mechanisms to support those rights and powers, and the impact of such mechanisms on the performance of the strategic alliance firm. A firm with the majority equity share usually has more rights and power to appoint members to the board of directors and also possesses the right to nominate key managerial staff in a new business venture. The most important organizational control gained for these majority owners is associated with what has become known as the 'three rights': the right to appoint the general manager; the right to determine organizational structure; and the right to appoint personnel to critical functional areas. Equity investment in a strategic alliance constitutes the source of ownership power for the owner and this in turn contributes to its organizational control. Ownership determinants have been identified as some of the major factors in explaining organizational control. A firm's ownership provision is perceived as a major lever for exercising control over its capital and non-capital resource investment. The balance of a firm's equity between its capital and non-capital resources is also pivotal in the organizational control it has over its business investment.

The institution of corporate governance and the creation of a sound institutional environment primarily require an understanding of how a country's economic, socio-cultural and political institutions influence a strategic alliance's corporate governance. Such influence is believed to affect the competitiveness of national economies as they dictate how a strategic alliance can be run more effectively within a given society. The construction of a national institution that facilitates the effective use of a country's overall investments is essential. Several theoretical explanations on corporate governance are expounded, mainly relating to new institutional economics in emerging business environments with China used as the main example. Analyses of corporate governance systems encompass both the macro-institutional environment at the national level and the micro-institutional context at the organizational level. National institution and taxation systems in China are still at the developmental stage. If a host country creates a favourable financial environment or provides an infrastructure of supporting industries, foreign firms will have an increased confidence in that country. With the appropriate establishment of financial institutions, corporate financing and national taxation, international strategic alliances operating in

China are able to effectively execute their capital and non-capital investments across nationwide markets.

The management of corporate culture and organization in transitional situations requires the exploration of the development of indigenous approaches essential to the understanding of corporate culture's influence in the management of an international strategic alliance. Traditional Chinese culture is heavily dependent upon relationships, informality, trust in the group, and respect for the internal hierarchy. This last characteristic is particularly important in Chinese society. National culture has evolved into a paradigmatic dualism that includes value, norm, organizational principles, diffused network structures and qualitative judgement.

The achievement of organizational learning has generated considerable research interest, focusing on the identification of factors that influence business configuration by participating firms. Prior research incorporates organizational learning activities conducted within the operational support systems and strategic contexts by participating firms and identifies factors that may influence each level of strategic alliance management.

Plan of the book

The book is divided into four parts. The first part introduces the impact of foreign investment in transitional economies; the second part focuses on the theoretical foundations of building blocks for foreign investments and corporate governance; the third part concentrates on the management of an international strategic alliance; and the final part is a contribution to the implications for research and practice (see Figure 1.2).

Part I: foreign investment in transitional economies

International strategic alliances in China provide insights into the dynamics of foreign investment decision-making and the unique corporate governance processes used. The chapters in Part I concern FDI in transition economies (Chapters 1–2) and develop the conceptual and theoretical basis of the significant research that has been undertaken. This chapter has laid the foundation for an understanding of the rise of the transition economies through the explanation of overall patterns of international trade and the role that China plays in international business, especially as a host for foreign investment. Chapter 2 discusses the main characteristics of foreign investment and economic development in the Chinese context. In particular, the theory of FDI, geographical distribution and sectors of FDI are highlighted.

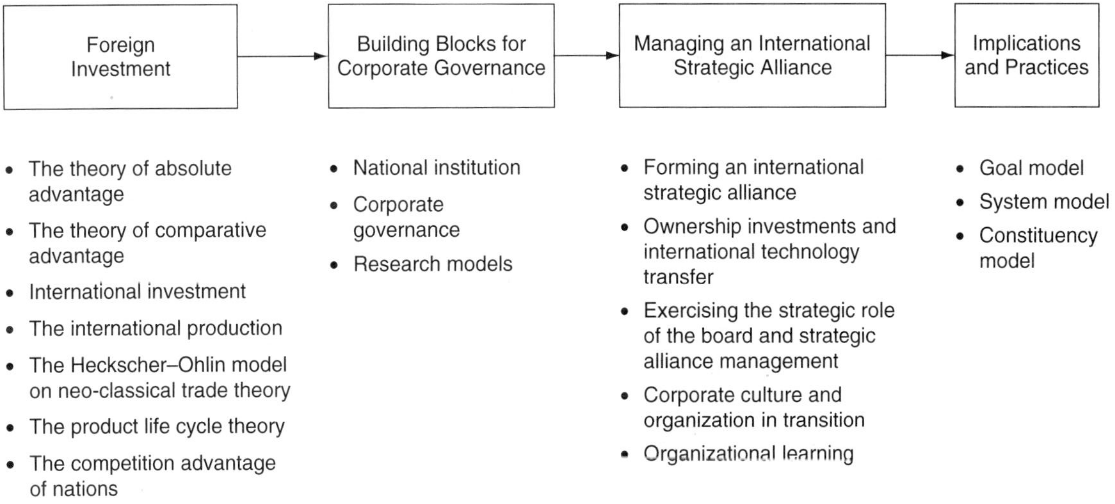

Figure 1.2 Foreign investments and corporate governance

Part II: building blocks for corporate governance

The issues relevant to corporate governance are the central points of this section. The assessment and management of the political environment is an integral element of a firm's corporate governance. Political constraints can often make the best economic strategy infeasible. The corporate governance of an international strategic alliance in China may involve different forms of political patronage, privileged access to markets, or procurement opportunities. The task of managing foreign investments sympathetically in China is critically important. Part II considers building blocks for corporate governance (Chapters 3–5) and focuses on three major aspects: (1) building blocks for macro institution and economic changes; (2) building blocks for corporate governance; and (3) the available materials for an empirical study and the justification of the methodology used. Chapter 3 draws upon available literature to consider the specific business context for FDI in China, including reform of corporate finance, reform of national institutions and reform of national taxation policies. Chapter 4 presents an overview of corporate governance that encompasses both the macro-institutional environment at the national level and the micro-institutional context at the organizational level. Chapter 5 outlines the available research methods employed in the study.

Part III: managing an international strategic alliance

This part addresses key issues associated with the management of foreign investments. Achievement of an optimal balance of foreign investment inputs and the associated corporate governance in an international strategic alliance is bound to be dependent upon the local political conditions and technical requirements. Part III discusses the management of an international strategic alliance in five chapters (Chapters 6–10). Chapter 6 examines how to undertake a feasibility study for the formation of an international strategic alliance. Chapter 7 provides empirical evidence of ownership configurations and international technology transfer. Chapter 8 then profiles possible strategic roles for the board and management. Chapter 9 focuses on the management of corporate culture and organizations in transition, while Chapter 10 outlines organizational learning issues.

Part IV: implications for research and practice

Part IV examines the implications for research and practice in chapter 11. Applying the research framework on international strategic alliance to formation, foreign investment, corporate governance, organizational culture and learning has derived key findings and implications. It shows a consistent picture of significant factors that are perceived to shape foreign investments and their corporate governance. There are a number of recent developments within China that have obliged foreign firms to reconsider their international strategic position. In a transitional economy, the foreign investments pursued through international strategic alliances create great challenges for the host government. Specific experiences in international strategic alliances have stimulated research and discussion into a number of issues of wider interest to international business.

Summary

This chapter is concerned with managing foreign investments in transitional economics such as China and the identification of relevant principal issues identified in this book. The research evidence shows that China's economy is developing rapidly with the assistance of foreign investments and international production. There are still some uncertainties remaining in China's infrastructure changes but there is no doubt that China's economy is moving towards being more open and more transparent. The political and economic evidence in China on increases in foreign trade, international investment and international production have generated significant attention from researchers who wish to examine the subsequent effects on FDI and foreign trade flows. This chapter also examines various dimensions such as the strategic, economic and socio-cultural profiles of foreign investments associated with the rise of the transitional economy of China.

2
Foreign Direct Investment

Introduction

This chapter provides an account of systematic research undertaken into FDI in China, which highlights an overview of its source determinants and foreign development trends. It offers a summary of FDI theory in terms of the absolute advantage explanation, the theory of comparative advantages, international production, the Heckscher–Ohlin model, the product life cycle and the competitive advantages of nationals. The literature review offers a logical and comprehensive examination of a host country's market-related factors that impact upon foreign trade, international investment and international production. China is assuming an increasingly prominent position in global economies and is projected to become one of the world's largest recipients of FDI. In this chapter, the theory of FDI is introduced and followed by a review of the Chinese government's investment policies and regulations together with the overall utilization of foreign trade and foreign investment.

The theory of foreign direct investment

The development of FDI is traced by how the growth of foreign trade, international investment and international production in both products and services are facilitated in a particular country. The rise in FDI is based upon a combination of both 'technology push' and 'market pull' factors. As the world economy grows, the increase in the size of worldwide markets has enabled many international firms to set up new businesses in foreign countries that achieve similar cost structures to those achieved in their own countries. Studies of the effectiveness of firms' international investment and international production are based upon a number of assumptions such as the traditional arguments of 'how' and 'why' international trade improves the overall welfare of all countries using a variety of theories including the absolute advantage theory from the work of Adam Smith (1961), the return on investments for examining comparative advantage from the work of David Ricardo (1951), international investment, international production, and the theory of factor proportions from the work of Ohlin (1933), product life cycle from the work of Vernon (1966), and the competitive advantage of nations from the work of Michael Porter (1990). See also Table 2.1.

Table 2.1 Theoretical contributions on foreign direct investment

The theory of FDI	Theoretical implications
The theory of absolute advantage	Absolute advantage is defined by general efficiency in the use of resources, knowledge and capabilities in a country's production and its ability to produce a good or service more cheaply than its rivals.
The theory of comparative advantage	This is when a country possesses absolute advantage in the production of two or more products but is relatively more efficient in the production of one of those products.
The theory of international investment	A firm's 'equity-based investment' (including the purchasing of equity shares in foreign firms across a national boundary, the acquisition of foreign bonds, the obtaining of foreign debt instruments and the acquisition of government-based loans).
The theory of international production	A firm's 'equity-based production' whereby the firm extends its ownership investments, operations and management across its national borders into foreign countries. The enhancement of the international production comprises the effective grouping of its capital stock, know-how, human resources, technology and physical plant.
The Heckscher–Ohlin model	The Heckscher–Ohlin theory considers two factors of production, namely labour and capital. Technology determines the way it combines to form a product. Factor intensities of 'labour' and 'capital' depend on the state-of-the-art technology, and different products may require different proportions of these production factors.

Table 2.1 (Continued)

The theory of FDI	Theoretical implications
The product life cycle theory	PLC[1] is used to measure perfect market competition for marketing new products. The PLC model is based upon the product life cycle of introduction, growth, maturity and decline for a firm's business investment.
The theory of the competitive advantage of nations	Michael Porter categorizes four major components of 'the diamond of national advantage' that a firm must avail itself of to compete in new markets. The diamond of national advantage includes factor conditions, demand conditions, related and supporting industries and firm strategy, structure and rivalry.

1 PLC = product life cycle

The theory of absolute advantage

Adam Smith, the father of economics, published a famous book entitled 'The Wealth of Nations' in 1776. He explained the process by which markets and production actually operate in a country. Adam Smith's major contribution was to introduce the concepts of 'absolute advantage' and 'the division of labour', terms that are perceived as fundamental to international trade theory. Following Adam Smith's explanation of 'absolute advantage', the primary tenet suggests that each country will specialize in the production of the finished products and services for which it is uniquely qualified and thus more will be produced. In other words, production of specific products or services may require the use of a country's primary element of resources, knowledge and expertise.

Some countries that possess a bundle of natural resources, superior knowledge and better capabilities can produce the same products or services as other countries with fewer labour-hours. Such industrial efficiency is termed 'the absolute advantage' for a country acknowledged as specializing in the production of specific products or services. On the whole, a country will exchange what it has produced for products or services in which it does not have absolute disadvantage. Advantage is defined by general efficiency in the use of resources, knowledge and capabilities in a country's production. With regard to the 'division of labour', Adam Smith states that industrial efficiency can be achieved by separating the production process into distinct 'stages' or 'areas' that are known in industrial economics circles as the division of labour. Adam Smith believed that specialization increased the production of entire industries. The absolute advantage and the division of labour are identified as the most important efficiency factors for foreign trade, international investment and international production.

The theory of comparative advantage

David Ricardo published a book entitled 'On the Principles of Political Economy and Taxation'. In this book, David Ricardo explains 'comparative advantage' by saying that even if a country possesses absolute advantage in the production of two products, one of those products must enjoy a relatively greater advantage than the other. Although a competitor country may also possess an absolute advantage in the production of the same two products, it may be that in one of its products the absolute advantage is greater than that enjoyed by the competitor country, and for the other product their absolute advantage is less than the other country. Each country will then possess comparative advantage in the production of one of the two products, and both countries will then benefit by specializing completely in one product and trading for the other. The law of comparative advantage concentrates on country differences in 'relative' efficiencies. In other words, the comparative advantage indicates that a country with an absolute advantage in the production of both products in a perfect world should specialize in the production and export of the product in which its absolute advantage is greatest. Hence the theory of comparative advantage offers a fundamental explanation of how nations can improve the welfare of their populations through international trade. This is because a country can actually achieve consumption levels beyond what it can produce by itself.

The theory of international investment

Foreign investment represents a primary component of the international business flow. Two types of economic activity are regarded as critical determinants for foreign investment. The first refers to a firm's 'equity-based investment', including the purchasing of equity shares in foreign firms across national boundaries, the acquisition of foreign bonds, the establishment of foreign debt instruments and the acquisition of government-based loans. The second type of foreign investment deals mainly with a firm's 'equity-based production' whereby the firm extends its ownership investments, operations and management across its national borders. For the latter, the major objective of a firm's investment is to establish a new business presence in foreign markets and to gain ownership control over the core resources and technologies involved in its investment projects. The economic rationale for the rise in equity-based production is generally decided by the market-related elements of 'technology push' and 'market pull'. As the world economy has become more globalized, technology transformation and further simplification of trade barriers have driven many firms to establish their business presence in those foreign countries where they can attain transfer price benefits, lower cost organizational structures, cheaper labour and low-cost component sourcing.

The theory of international production

The most efficient market entry strategy for the dissemination of a firm's technology, innovation and managerial expertise is strongly associated with international production. The enhancement of international production comprises the effective grouping of capital stock, know-how, human resources, technology and physical plant. Levels of capital can also influence a firm's international productivity technology and the managerial skills possessed. Effective international productivity is achieved by promoting a firm's advanced technologies in combination with local firms' business practices and their relevant supply management. International production is perceived as one of the effective means for firms to deliver their products and services to foreign markets. The discussion of international production is strongly related to the identification of the main determinants of a firm's 'production-based' factors, the 'market-based factors' and performance outcomes in the foreign market where the firm's production is sited.

The Heckscher–Ohlin Model

Two Swedish economists, Heckscher and Ohlin, developed the neo-classical theory of international trade known as the 'factor proportion theory'. The Heckscher–Ohlin theory considers two factors of production, namely labour and capital. Technology determines the way they combine to form a product. Factor intensities of 'labour' and 'capital' depend on the state-of-the-art technology that different products may require. The theory states that factor prices will determine the cost structure of a particular product. These prices are determined by the endowments of labour and capital the country possesses. A country should specialize in the production and export of those products that intensively use the factor that it has in relative abundance. Such products fall into the general categories of 'labour-intensive' products or 'capital-insensitive'.

The standard Heckscher–Ohlin (H–O) model suggests that a country must have a comparative market advantage in the production of those goods and services that can be effectively produced. The simple equation of H–O theory is based upon a country exporting those products and services that can be effectively produced, and importing those commodities that are influenced by factors in which they are comparatively poorly endowed. Given that related market factors differ in different countries, each country must have a comparative advantage in their factor endowments within some market sector. The country's comparative advantage can be used to identity factor endowments such as the achievement of economies of scale, economies of scope, perfect competition, and differences in technological changes. These factors suggest ways of enhancing international productivity within the global market.

A firm may require market access to non-capital resources from a country which is comparatively well endowed in those specific resource advantages. International production promotes the move of production facilities to other locations as the relative costs of production in the home country rise. Foreign firms may undertake international production as a response to capacity shortfalls, which are the consequence of rapid expansion into new markets that have relatively low trade barriers. If there are substantial differences in the host country's factor endowments of human capital, technology and managerial expertise, international production activity in foreign markets will be encouraged. A firm's international investment and international production activities are guided by the attraction of market location advantages where the host country may offer a sufficient wealth of resources and an appropriate incentive policy to attract foreign investments. International production may lead a foreign firm to produce at low-cost production sites, as ownership investments are generally motivated by the firm's need to upgrade its products and services to achieve superior economic performance. The explanatory power of the basic H–O model can identify the characteristics of a host country's comparative advantages in relation to the investment activities of foreign firms. Transportation costs are perceived as inevitable when undertaking international operations in a global market, but it is important for firms to have familiarity with the foreign market and investment conditions before they commit to the costs of international investment in production facilities.

The product life cycle theory

Perfect market competition can be measured by the product life cycle (PLC). The PLC model is based upon the product life cycle of introduction, growth, maturity and decline for a firm's business investment. Vernon (1966) proposed that an analysis of a firm's PLC be used to assess perfect market competition for predicting the success of new products in a specific market. The PLC model is used to trace a product over a period of its development. When a firm's product is introduced or launched into a new market, it will gain more and more customers as the market grows until eventually the market stabilizes and the product becomes mature. After a period of time, the product is overtaken by the development and the introduction of superior products by competitors. Eventually, the market goes into decline and the product is eventually withdrawn. One variant of this is the cyclical maturity phase which occurs when the market for the product enters the decline phase, the product is upgraded and promoted to regain existing (and attract new) customers. It must always be remembered that most products fail in the introduction phase.

The length of each prescriptive PLC varies enormously. Managers may delay the move of the PLC from maturity to decline by price-cutting. Not all products go through each stage: some go directly from introduction to decline. The PLC model is used to identify which stage the product is at in order to identify an appropriate strategy for the specific stages of the PLC. At the 'product introduction' stage, the product is promoted to create market awareness as the need for immediate profit is not a pressure. If the product has no or few competitors, a skimming price strategy will be employed. A limited number of products are introduced to selected channels of distribution. In the market 'growth' stage, competitors offering very similar products will be attracted. As the products become established and more profitable, firms will be encouraged to form new international strategic alliances. Advertising costs in this stage are high and focused upon building brand image as this establishes market share, which tends to stabilize towards the end of this phase. Market share is important because the highest volume producer normally has the lowest unit costs.

Those products that survive the earlier stages tend to spend longest in the 'maturity' phase. Sales growth decreases and then stabilizes. It is at this stage that a firm attempts to differentiate products, and brands are crucial to product development activity. Price wars and intense competition occur and eventually the market reaches saturation forcing some firms to leave the market due to poor profit margins. Promotions become more widespread and use a greater variety of media. Finally, at the point of decline there is a downturn in the market, which is often predicated by more innovative products being introduced (or it may be that consumer tastes have fundamentally changed). There is intense price-cutting and many more products are withdrawn. Profits can be significantly improved by reducing marketing spending and cutting costs. Economies of scale are important at this stage and the global producers will have the advantage of low cost production in combination with high volume. The foreign firm can maintain its bargaining power locally by developing a support system through local financing, sourcing procurement and business contracts. In this way, it can maintain control over access to existing technology and markets.

The theory of the competitive advantage of nations

Michael Porter published a book that is entitled 'The Competitive Advantage of Nations'. He hypothesized that a nation's competitiveness depends on the capacity of its industry to innovate and upgrade. Innovation is regarded as the primary source of competitiveness that reflects an increased focus for the industry and new product creation, because innovation can be treated as a motivation factor that encourages factor conditions such as cost components, demand conditions, factor proportions and product life cycle management. The competitive advantage of nations is created and sustained through a highly localized process. Porter categorized four major components as 'the diamond of national advantage' that a firm must use to succeed in the market it faces. The diamond of national advantage includes factor conditions, demand conditions, related and supporting industries and firm strategy, structure and rivalry.

Factor conditions include natural resources, climate, capital, infrastructure, labour skills, resources, and technical and managerial knowledge. Demand conditions consist of the composition of the home market and its size compared to overall global market demand. It also specifically takes into account the local existing market demands from home customers. The existence of market competition is related to the infrastructure of support industries and this suggests that a committed supply chain will boost the competitiveness of firms who are using their products and services by offering better support than that available to their competitors. Firm strategy, structure and rivalry are commonly used to identify the importance of a firm-related variable such as ownership, investment, management and operational strategies that can be employed to enhance its overall competitiveness. In this way, the four factors identified as 'the diamond of national advantage' can be mutually reinforced to create a country's overall competitiveness. A nation's competitiveness in an exacting area will be enhanced if favourable demand conditions co-exist with these four important factors.

Foreign investment and economic liberalization

The encouragement of FDI has been ground breaking for Chinese economic liberalization and has opened local markets to the outside world. Economic liberalization based on the Chinese government's FDI policies has been employed to lower trade barriers for foreign firms wishing to invest. The welcome that China offers to such foreign firms has led to many Western business executives enthusiastically embracing the advantages that China offers, including its cheaper workforce and its huge market. The opening of the market based upon China's vast population of 1.3 billion and its growing global economic muscle offers long-term economic opportunities according to a growing number of executives, economists and officials.

The potential size of the Chinese market has made it very hard for foreign firms to ignore, particularly as the economy is being transformed to a state-of-the-art, hi-tech producer. On the downside, its transition from a planned economy to a form of capitalism seems to make it especially susceptible to economic boom and bust cycles. So far, China's national institutional system has been able to adapt to the social tensions brought to the surface by its rapid economic development.

Several factors have contributed to the economic liberalization policies. Designing an effective investment regime allows the pursuit of industrial and economic reform at a measured pace. The Chinese government has taken great care to create a healthy business environment in which the positive effects on international technology transfer and the benefits of other intangibles such as modern management systems and Western management practices can be efficiently integrated. Economic liberalization has taken place at a speed compatible with the capability of the institutions and political processes involved to adapt. In manipulating Chinese markets, the government has responded to the need to adjust relevant investment and trade policies. FDI relies on proactive policies that seek to enhance China's attractiveness through the appropriate improvement of its investment infrastructure. The physical infrastructure provision, size of the domestic market and labour costs will directly affect foreign firms' economic activities. There are six major challenges that face the government in its efforts to develop its economic liberalization of FDI policies, and these are discussed in Figure 2.1.

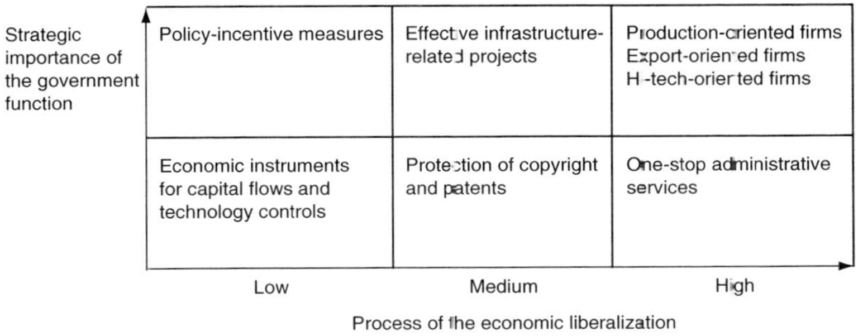

Figure 2.1 The strategic importance of the influence of governance and economic liberalization in China

The FDI policy-incentive measures devised by the Chinese government have had a significant impact on its economic liberalization. China has expressed concern over the possible political and negative economic impact of foreign investment policy, especially in areas of capital flows, technology controls and market competition. The activities of foreign firms are susceptible to pressure from their home governments, who wish to use them to be used as economic/political policy instruments, and also from the host government, in trying to win concessions from other governments. Host governments insist on deals in which FDI is contingent on adherence to specified requirements. The decision to open the Chinese economy to the outside world marked a very important turning point in China's history of economic development. Upon the advent of FDI, China experienced large inflows of foreign capital and advanced technology to the extent that it has now become one of the major host recipients of FDI in the world. The increase in its share of FDI allows China to play a significant role in international trade. The ideologically left-wing government has decided to transform its internal socialist economy into one it defines as a 'market economy with socialist characteristics'. China is the only country to exhibit a constant increase in its FDI for a continuous 30-year period, and most foreign firms are now positive about the experience of managing their investment and production there. Chinese political institutions can be understood by examining the government's role in the opening of its markets to the outside world in the process of building government influence through the stipulation of rules, regulations and policies.

FDI has been found to exert significant influence in the regulation of the host country's market. The policy-incentive measures have been defined broadly to preclude not only the threat of political upheaval but also the likelihood of arbitrary government action that will detrimentally affect the financial, technological and economic gains of firms. The Chinese government's control over its industrial organizations will vary depending on the policies concerning corporate ownership, the establishment of strategic objectives and the generation of investment conditions. Recent research into inward FDI indicates that the stability of the economic environment is perceived as one of most important determinants in defining the development pattern of foreign trade. The Chinese government has taken action recently to control foreign investment by imposing tax increases, setting ownership control limits, local content requirements, remittance restrictions and export requirements.

The facilitation of effective infrastructure-related projects has been typified by attempts to ensure sufficient availability of market information about commercial products and moves to decrease the transaction costs of establishing new institutional arrangements. The need to increase domestic firms' industrial competitiveness requires managerial development and the use of modern products and process technologies. All of these are facilitated by a policy of encouraging investment from foreign firms. One of the major issues restricting the adoption and diffusion of these 'incoming technologies' in China is the establishment of an effective legal system that enforces intellectual property rights. Copyright infringement can easily damage foreign firms' profits and investment confidence. It deters both innovation and the transfer of state-of-the-art technology from foreign firms to local firms. Although the government has made significant efforts to control piracy, the development of an effective system for protecting intellectual property still needs reinforcement. The biggest worry facing the government is its vulnerability to acute setbacks such as a banking failure, an inflationary spiral or even a temporary economic downturn.

The Chinese government has attempted to prevent the vertical integration of organizational activities of subsidiaries and the foreign parent where those subsidiaries are dominated by foreign parent firms. The Chinese government has taken steps to exclude or limit foreign ownership participation in certain strategic sectors of local industry and to encourage active local participation in the ownership and management of those international strategic alliances already established. The extent of local management participation in corporate governance will vary by industrial sector, depending on how much overall foreign investment is needed by the host economy. The discriminatory policies on FDI include setting 'local content' requirements, technology standards and export requirements. Under such investment regimes, the government has the power to limit foreign payments, control the repatriation of dividends, and specify minimum levels of technology transfer, or the sophistication and level of operation that is engaged in. Currently, its strategic priorities are to continue to attract high-technology in order to pursue effective industrial restructuring or foster import-substitution investments.

Economic reform in China, in its attempt to provide a significant improvement in market conditions, has aimed at significant deregulation for production, export and high-technology-oriented firms by the provision of a structure for the implementation of specific incentive-based market mechanisms. There are still contradictions in Chinese economic reforms between the conceptual virtues of taxes and trading mechanisms that are intended and the practical implementation which is dealt with on a day-to-day basis by local government officials. Economic liberalization in China does not necessarily translate into appropriate concrete incentive measures that encourage corporate governance modernization by the introduction of new management systems. Changes in the Chinese market are aimed at putting in place competition mechanisms which allocate resources effectively among domestic and foreign firms, but the incentive-based market conditions necessary for markets to flourish in relation to products and services are not easy to regulate. Economic liberalization in China means that its market distribution system needs to create well-defined rights that safeguard a firm's products and services.

The Chinese government has used economic instruments for capital flows and technology controls that affect how a foreign firm's capital and non-capital resources are managed. Given major differences in foreign firms' ownership investments and their technical complexity of market operations, more empirical research is necessary to identify the circumstances under which firms adjust their corporate activities. The implementation of regulatory reforms can slowly reorient local firms towards the achievement of sustainable development. In contrast, foreign firms are able to rapidly change their business investment behaviour where appropriate host government incentives and directions exist. The introduction of foreign capital may compensate for a shortage of capital in China's domestic economic construction but the introduction of advanced technology, equipment and management skills is equally important. FDI in China can help existing local firms to upgrade their technology base and to create new production, technology and export-oriented firms that will change the overall industry structure. Higher quality products from production, technology and export-oriented firms will ultimately lead to increased business prosperity.

The upgrading of the law governing areas such as the protection of copyrights and patents to international standards has increased foreign firms' confidence in the Chinese market. The government updated a variety of legal issues, including legislation, incentive policies, bureaucratic deregulation and the restructuring of foreign exchange. The downsides deterring potential foreign investing firms include inflated labour costs, unreliable supplies of component parts and raw materials, and bureaucratic decisions, as these can represent a significant start-up cost to them. The high degree of local government autonomy in controlling business deals may confuse foreign firms who are often unclear as to what investment regime will actually apply once their investments have been made. Examination of how the potential incentive policies and investment rewards offered by the Chinese government are implemented at local level is therefore very important. The Chinese government tries to harmonize the implementation of FDI policies, but interpretation is always at the local level.

Part of the harmonization of encouraging FDI in China has been the creation of 'one-stop administrative services' to improve operational efficiencies. Foreign firms perceive the quality of economic liberalization as the acid test as to whether the host government is genuinely friendly towards their international investment. Provision of a 'one-stop' administrative service for foreign investments is fully implemented in China, but the quality of the facilitation of market entry varies significantly between cities and provinces. In theory, the governmental 'one-stop' agency does have discretion to grant a variety of business licences and the permission which is necessary to operate legally in the country; but, in China, responsibilities overlap between local agencies and the central government's departments. Public regulation is an essential part of developing a policy conducive to foreign investment and production but for foreign firms to increase their overall investments in China they must be able to position their products and services for easy access to growth in this huge potential market. There is mounting pressure on the government to lift restrictions on equity options and open up protected industrial sectors to foreign investments. In pursuit of a national policy for all firms, the Chinese government announced the removal of duty-free status for capital goods imported by foreign firms. Import substitution, export earnings, and subsidized imports of technology and management have already assisted the government in encouraging foreign trade and improving the balance of payments.

The implications of opening Chinese markets

The market transition in China has been closely associated with a number of aspects, a key factor being the development of special economic zones and the special designation of 14 coastal cities. Opening up the Chinese market has improved administrative efficiency and reduced the cost of doing business even in the coastal cities and relevant provinces. Improvements in corporate governance will increase the quality of inward investment by making it easier for foreign firms to make the right decisions based on an accurate appraisal of the long-term economic benefits and political factors involved. The Chinese economy has recorded major growth, especially in coastal areas, where foreign investments have helped to spur the output of both domestic and export products and services. The phasing-out of special investment privileges is based on the strategic vision of the size of the market, the rate of economic growth, the relevant costs, the availability of resources and skills involved as well as the market investment infrastructure. The decentralization of government power to the local provincial level has ensured the stability, transparency and effectiveness of the regulatory framework for foreign firms in their investments and operational procedures. A steady opening of the Chinese market in conjunction with a managed FDI policy will create a robust and transparent institutional framework.

The establishment of an institutional and regulatory environment at the national level is conducive to foreign investments. The central government's governance power must be used flexibly in order to attract FDI and will need to be redefined and articulated further as its strategic vision develops. There will still be plenty of opportunity for the government to facilitate inward investment in ways that reduce the perceived risk of investments in a given location preference but do not interfere with market competition. The enforcement of international investment laws in China has significantly facilitated an increase in foreign trade, international investment, international production and the development of flourishing privately-owned enterprises. The introduction of bankruptcy laws and intellectual property rights protection has enhanced FDI, as have improved labour laws and relevant regulations which primarily serve as protection for foreign firms. China has consistently encouraged involvement by foreign investors in industrial sectors that are export-oriented or that involve new and advanced technology-oriented firms entering the local market.

The government has begun to introduce special incentives to channel foreign investment into particular sectors of the local market. Foreign firms that have invested in the various industrial sectors have helped domestic industries to reduce business transaction costs. For many foreign firms, success in business depends not just on their products and their technological efficiency in each part of the value chain but also on how effective they are in their dealings with the government. The government is aware of how important it is to continuously reappraise policies as an integral part of its investment strategy formulation. Business network systems and national institutions in China allow local firms to retain some influence over a strategic alliance in an environment where foreign firms tend to exert a dominating influence in the strategic direction of overall business development. One of the main decisions facing foreign firms in managing strategic alliances is whether to introduce Chinese so-called 'local management standards' of corporate governance or import Western governance practices that are deeply embedded in their own national traditions.

The Chinese institutional environment is becoming distinctive in providing effective rules, regulations and procedures which encourage many foreign firms to conduct business at the operational level by employing international business standards and practices. This can provide foreign firms with the opportunity to exercise more extensive control and power over their strategic alliance operations. In emerging business environments, foreign firms may have the opportunity to exercise new forms of corporate governance because the institutional environment is still in the process of evolving rules, regulations and procedures to encourage a strategic alliance's business development. The Chinese government is pressing hard to encourage its industry to use the most up-to-date technology from foreign countries and is achieving this by offering legally-encouraged incentive and reward policies to foreign firms to increase 'local content' or 'local sourcing'. This means that foreign firms have to work closely with their local partners in the alliance in order to ensure that technological quality standards are met. At the same time local firms need to develop or improve their operational standards in order to meet foreign firms' original equipment and technology specifications.

Given the significant development of international trade, FDI (together with domestic industrial investments) has created significant per capita income growth. China is now the largest FDI host country in the developing world and is ranked second only to the USA as a global destination for FDI. Foreign firms account for 27 per cent of the nation's total industrial output value and by 2003 were responsible for 44 per cent of China's exports and 48 per cent of its total foreign trade. Successful accession to the WTO has eased the brake on international investments and international production activities for products and services. Local Chinese firms have been encouraged to set up production facilities abroad in order to get a foothold in international markets. One of the implications of China joining the WTO is the political and economic stimulus to promote its national industries, foreign trade and international production in foreign countries.

Given the heightened market competition triggered by central planning economies moving to free trade market economies, the development of foreign investments actively encourages the regulation of market reform through its industrialization plans. Foreign firms are showing their great interest in the Chinese market, as confirmed by the significant scale of investment and the relative GDP growth at the national level. The attraction of China's market is enhanced by a series of economic incentives and favourable FDI polices which are closely linked to a series of finance mechanisms including tax breaks, allowances, grants, rebates to permit the repatriation of profits and the improvement of national infrastructure. The government encourages foreign firms with their perceived superiority in resources, sufficient capital, advanced technologies, production facilities and innovations to become involved in key Chinese industries with the objective of improving the efficiency of local firms through market competition. Such strategic actions will in turn spur on Chinese industrial performance by encouraging domestic and foreign firms to seek wider market access to increase their investments and production activities.

Figure 2.2 shows those developments of FDI that have an important impact on the Chinese economy. China is increasingly participating in

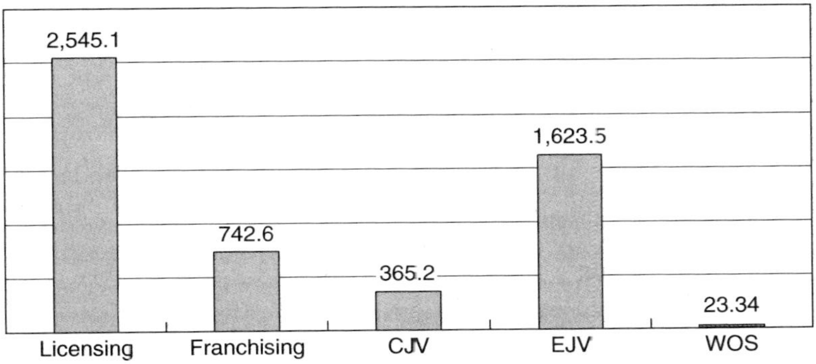

Figure 2.2 An overview of foreign investments in China (US$ million)

the world economy and it has become an important source of outward direct investment with a total stock value of US$30 billion in 2003. The choices involved in making an international market entry are related to a foreign firm's resources and its strategic plan for business expansion. Most FDI in China has come from neighbouring Asian countries and this has surged to a record $50 billion. Overall, the FDI inflow has resulted in the establishment of 145,000 foreign firms realizing $216 billion in capital investments. Industrial estimates suggest that this investment provides 40 per cent of China's economic growth. Firms under foreign ownership account for 23 per cent of industrial production with manufacturing concentrated in hi-tech products and other high value-added labour-intensive sectors. A large number of factors associated with China's implementation of FDI can be examined by analysing their impact on foreign trade, market competition, and political and economic reforms. Evidence suggests that foreign firms' objectives can be achieved more quickly through the acquisition of local firms to obtain local market outlets or by setting up international strategic alliances than through creating start-ups on their own.

FDI may intensify competition to the benefit of the local economy and international consumers, through increased productivity and possibly lower prices. Market competition typically introduces new techniques, products and services and new innovative ideas to the market, and may improve existing foreign investment patterns. There is mounting evidence that competition in domestic, regional and international markets is increasing. In China, it is widely acknowledged that the major challenges are primarily investment decisions related to labour-intensive, capital-intensive or technology-intensive projects. A given foreign investment in China has to be registered as belonging to a certain category and this defines the level of benefits in the local market, the tax it should pay, the import duty levied and the valuation method for depreciation. For a given product, the higher the advanced technology content achieved, the larger the proportion of the products that can be sold in China, the greater the tax benefits.

New forms of international investment and international production have accompanied the upsurge in global FDI. The worldwide surge of international investment has given foreign firms new impetus to purchase the existing assets of Chinese firms or to form many international strategic alliances. It is Chinese government policy to improve its competitive advantage by attracting substantial FDI inflows. The unique feature of FDI in China is that ethnic Chinese have contributed the majority of inward investment. Most foreign investment in China has come from Asian economies such as Hong Kong, Taiwan, Macao, Singapore, Korea and Japan. Changes in the organizational structures of foreign firms have been driven by the pressures of international competitiveness and have in turn stimulated the overall growth in FDI. The increasing global integration and the internationalization of investment portfolios have facilitated financial capital flows into and out of developing countries (such as China) as firms have become more willing and able to invest in businesses internationally.

China has adopted a policy of further opening its markets to the outside world. Hong Kong is in a dominant investment position due to its geographical advantage, similar cultural background, close economic relations and family ties with Mainland China. Hong Kong is becoming the largest investor and has undertaken large-scale trade activity based upon its familiarity with the economic system, market environment and business practices in China. Taiwan is also one of the important investors in Mainland China. Many studies state that one major attraction for Taiwan-based firms transferring operations to Mainland China is that of production efficiency resulting from lower labour costs. Japan tends to favour an export approach rather than direct investment. Japanese firms believe exporting can be an effective way of penetrating the Chinese market. Through exporting, Japanese firms have been able to provide relatively high quality products to the Chinese market. South Korea has recently emerged as a major source of FDI inflow to China. Economically, higher costs of production at home, particularly labour costs, have forced them to shift labour-intensive production to lower-cost countries in the region. US investments in China are strong and the USA has become the third largest investor. The Chinese trade surplus with the USA has soared, quintupling in the last decade to $124 billion in 2003. For European countries such as the UK, Germany, the Netherlands, France and Italy, their share of total investment in China has gradually increased. Inward FDI and relevant investment policies guiding various phases of Chinese industrial development are shown in Table 2.2.

Summary

Foreign firms that operate in technology-intensive industries in China usually want to concentrate on marketing the products developed from their research and development (R&D) efforts, especially their basic research. The foreign firm can assist the host country's economic development with its international technology transfer, but this may leave

Table 2.2 FDI policies in China and their outcomes

Policy	Outcome
1978	
The guiding principle in FDI, i.e., 'relying mainly on our own efforts', is adopted.	Limited acquisition of technology and equipment from foreign firms. Establishing IJVs in China in order to learn technology and management skills from foreign firms. The idea of self-sufficiency is still rooted in China's industrialization.
The third plenary session of the Eleventh Central Committee of the Chinese Communist Party is convened and the 'four modernizations' are adopted.	The term 'four modernizations' (i.e., the modernization of agriculture, industry, science and technology, and national defence) is formally introduced, leading to a fundamental shift in China's political institution and economic policy.
The most senior government organization responsible for FDI is established.	The following ministries are formed to reinforce these policies on FDI: (1) Import and Export, the Ministry of Foreign Trade; (2) Ministry of Foreign Economic Relations and the Administrative Committee of Foreign Investment form the Ministry of Foreign Economic Relations and Trade (MOFERT). 1. Popular forms of foreign investments are associated with imports, licensing and compensation trade. 2. IJVs are limited. 3. A limited amount of FDI is introduced into four small special economic zones (SEZs): Shenzhen, Zhuhai, Shantou and Xiamen.

1979	
The Law of the People's Republic of China on Chinese–Foreign Joint Ventures is implemented.	Provinces are responsible for their own fiscal revenues and expenditures, sharing with the central government the foreign exchange incomes augmented. The central government also allows Guangdong and Fujian Provinces to adopt special policies.
1980	
Income Tax Law of the People's Republic of China concerning Chinese–Foreign Joint Ventures is passed.	IJVs are encouraged to increase exports instead of having revenues assigned and allocated by the State. Establishing SEZs marks the beginning of the new era of China's opening-up to the outside world.
The 15th Session of the Standing Committee of the 5th National People's Congress approves the Regulations on Special Economic Zones in Guangdong Province.	The SEZs are used to provide the 'window' necessary to attract FDI and the transfer of know-how. Construction of the four SEZs (i.e. Shenzhen, Zhuhai, Shantou and Xiamen) is established.
Non-convertibility of Chinese currency is introduced.	By experiencing FDI in SEZs the Western capitalist system could be used to benefit China's development goals while Chinese socialism and sovereignty would not be undermined. Accommodation of capitalist elements is established in China's socialist economy.
1981	
The Income Tax Law for enterprises with Foreign Investment and Foreign Enterprises.	Economic conditions are stable and allow for expansion. SEZs and Shanghai's Pudong New Area are established. Macroeconomic readjustment realizes a number of important achievements. IJVs with foreign investment not only absorb foreign capital but also adopt advanced technology and management. Fourteen open coastal cities (OCCs) and three open economic zones (OEZs) are established.

Table 2.2 (Continued)

Policy	Outcome
The Central Committee of the Communist Party and the State Council decide to open fourteen coastal port cities.	A provision that EJVs, CJVs and WOSs in these cities should pay only 80 per cent of the current enterprise-income tax applied to local firms is approved.
	EJVs, CJVs and WOSs located in the economic and technical development districts within these cities enjoy a tax rate of only 15%.
	The importance of FDI in the capital formation of Chinese industry (i.e., Dalian, Qinhuangdao, Tianjin, Yantai, Qindao, Lianyungang, Natong, Shanghai, Ninbo, Wenzhou, Fuzhou, Guangzhou, Zhanjiang and Beihai) is recognized.
	Industrial production results in 23% growth, and increases exports to 40%.
	The use of foreign funds, technology and markets, and the updating of existing enterprises' technology, aids the strengthening of the competitive ability of their products in world markets.
	These coastal cities, which were regarded as the next layer of China's opening-up to the outside world after SEZs, are expected to help in other areas of economic development.

1985	
The State Council turns the Changjiang (Yangtze River) Delta, the Zhujiang (Pearl River) Delta and the South Fujian Triangle area into 'Open Economic Zones'.	The OEZs are the next layer of China's opening-up to the outside world after the SEZs and the OCCs, and they are also expected to promote economic development of the interior. Zhujiang Delta develops first in order to gain experience for the development of other areas in the Deltas.
1986	
'Provisions of the State Council of the People's Republic of China for the Encouragement of Foreign Investment' (also known as the 22 Articles) are adopted.	Readjusting the structure of FDI in China offers particularly favourable treatment by encouraging foreign businessmen to invest in technically advanced enterprises and export-oriented enterprises, as well as in the so-called 'basic industries' and infrastructure. China opens up more areas to foreign investors.
1987	Shandong Peninsula and East Liaoning Peninsula are added to the OEZs; Hainan province is granted full SEZ status.
1989	Shanghai's Pudong New Area is set up and some cities in the interior are opened up to the outside world.
1995	
Interim Regulations on FDI Directions and the Industrial Catalogue Guiding Foreign Investment are formulated.	The *Regulations* and the *Catalogue* categorizes the industrial projects into four types (items to be encouraged, items to be permitted, items to be restricted and items to be forbidden) and clearly state the 'rules' for the investor.
1995	
Interim Procedures on Establishing Pilot Sino–Foreign Joint Ventures and Wholesale Business are introduced.	China expands its opening-up into other areas such as finance, insurance, transportation, international freight forwarding, legal service, tourism, advertising, medical care and public health, accounting, assets appraisal, education, leasing, engineering design, consulting and real estate.

Table 2.2 (Continued)

Policy	Outcome
1997	
State Development Planning Commission, State Economic and Trade Commission together with the Ministry of Foreign Trade and Economic Cooperation begin to revise the *Industrial Catalogue Guiding Foreign Investment* and put it into enforcement.	The revision highlights priority industries alongside the principles which accord with structural adjustment, contributing to the introduction of advanced technology, and fully embodies encouragement to invest in central and western areas.
	The revised text reflects an expansion in the investment scope encouraged by the State. The Industrial Catalogue gives encouragement to foreign investing firms on establishing export-oriented enterprises.
Category of Encouragement and Category of Restriction.	The Category indicates that all the equipment imported for self-use within the aggregated investment shall be exempted from tariff and import stage value added tax.
2001	
Circular from the State Council's general office on the distribution of suggestions on the implementation of policies and measures pertaining to the development of the Western Region.	The State Council approves the suggestions on the implementation of policies and measures pertaining to the development of the Western Region.
	The scope of application of policies and measures include 70 suggestions. With regard to increasing investment in the western region, the circular specifies that the proportion of funds in the central budget that are earmarked for the Western Region should

	be increased, including central funds for capital construction and funds raised through treasury bonus. In the allocation of loans from state policy-mandated banks and concessionary loans from international financial organizations and foreign governments in accordance with lending terms, vigorous efforts should be made to direct as much capital as possible towards projects in the Western Region and increase the proportion of loans taken by the Western Region.
2001–10	
Circular from the State Council's general office concerning the distribution of suggestions on the implementation of policies pertaining to the development of the Western Region.	The corporate income tax of enterprises in government-encouraged sectors that are financed by either domestic or foreign investment in the Western Region will be collected at a reduced rate of 15% during the period of 2001–10.
2002	
Provisional measures on administration of domestic securities investments of qualified foreign institutional investors.	China's Securities Regulatory Commission and People's Bank of China issue decree no. 12 with 39 articles. It covers (1) general provisions; (2) qualifications, criteria and approval procedures; (3) custody, registration and settlement; (4) investment operations; (5) fund management; (6) regulatory issues and (7) supplementary provisions. This decree comes into effect from 1 December 2002.

the host country dependent on flows of new and updated technology. Foreign investments come in many forms and their strategic impact on the needs of the local firms varies. In this chapter, a series of FDI theories has been introduced and the Chinese investment policies and regulations on opening the Chinese market have been traced. Finally, the overall utilization of foreign trade and economic liberalization have been thoroughly discussed.

Part II

Building Blocks for Corporate Governance

3
Building Blocks for National Institutions

Introduction

This chapter provides an overview of the Chinese national institutions that have brought significant economic liberalization and rapid change to the market environment. It concentrates on those economic reforms that have lessened the costs of the Chinese government's trade policies and diminished regulation barriers for foreign investments. This chapter also highlights how the proper management of foreign investments may enhance business opportunities for foreign firms which operate overseas. The reforms, together with the appropriate establishment of national financing, political institutions and taxation, aims to provide a clear guidance for foreign firms about how to invest and conduct production activities, and to enable most foreign firms operating in China to manage their investments more effectively. This study offers an essential understanding of a foreign firm's investment activities through the use of macro-institution analysis.

As part of the appraisal of alternative investment opportunities in China, most foreign firms devote considerable resources to calculating the potential profitability of each business. Over time, foreign firms also revise the expected value of their current capital and non-capital investments as well as potential profitability in the light of falling local production costs stemming from the impact of new regulations introduced by the Chinese government. The reform of national institutions is primarily shaped by changes undertaken by the Chinese regulatory authorities. Properly functioning capital markets will enable the operation of free market fiscal policies, investment mechanisms and corporate operations in China. Market-based regulations, a predictable tax structure and a stable monetary system are expected to determine supply and

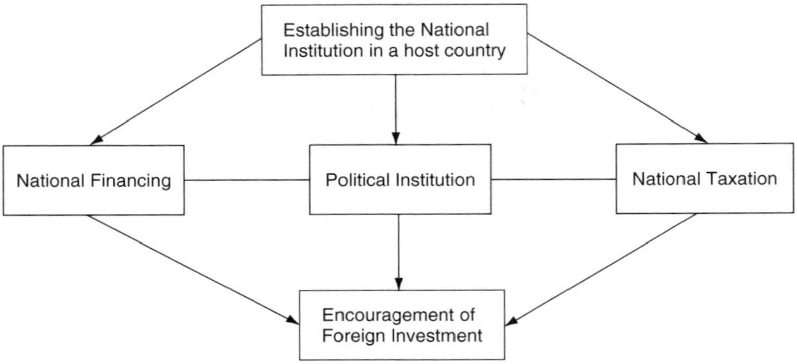

Figure 3.1 Building blocks for national institutions in China

demand pricing signals that are communicated to the firms operating in those markets. Figure 3.1 shows that constitution of the Chinese national institutions is aimed at increasing both local and foreign firms' investment confidence as these aspects have always had an important influence on national financing, political institutions and national taxation.

Reform of national financing

Reform of fiscal and monetary policies in China has been used to replace the traditional revenue remittance system as it allows foreign firms with different national financial systems, market entries and ownership arrangements to compete in a local market on a more equal footing. The transformation of fiscal and monetary policies in China will reduce the extent and the scope of Chinese government involvement in a specific industrial sector. The actual impact of reform is to decentralize the national financial system by granting local government and regions greater autonomy, responsibility and flexibility in the collection of revenues and to leave appropriate corporate investment decisions to the companies themselves. Nevertheless, several issues can be identified that have a significant impact on the co-ordination between the central government and local fiscal government bodies, especially where the national financial system needs to control regional or local financing resource disparity and to co-ordinate the management of extra budgetary funds from the central government. The fiscal and monetary policies that have recently been applied to foreign firms show that the central bank is exercising a leading role in the direction of foreign investments and international production activities in China.

It is common knowledge that decisions relating to China's commercial banks' current domestic firms' business investments are coloured by the fact that they are overburdened by the large volume of lower performing loans made to local firms such as state-owned enterprises. It has been argued that one motive for creating an international strategic alliance is to wrest control of a local Chinese firm's finances from local banking constraints. International corporate financial services enable a foreign firm to manage its business portfolio within a globally integrated framework. However, moving funds from a foreign firm's subsidiaries in China to another within its organization is strategically challenging because there are many barriers hampering the international movement of funds.

Importantly for China, such movements may affect the foreign firm's willingness to commit overall resources, knowledge, favourable transfer pricing, accounting procedures and financial obligations to its local firms and their operational strategies. Reform of national financial procedures and regulations in China has positively contributed to the growth of foreign investment that was attracted in the first place by tax incentives, GDP growth and potential markets. Deregulation of the financial services sector, coupled with technological advances in ownership control, has significantly stimulated foreign firms' investments in China. The institutional framework that is the basis of China's capital markets is crucial to the building of competitive products and production capacities in domestic industries. The availability of financial information ensures that an efficient national financial environment can be built and healthy capital markets established. These are an essential platform for the management of China's foreign trade, business investments and international production. Financial information regarding foreign firms' overall performance has emerged as a salient factor in all investment calculations.

At the macro economic level, financial loans from the government have different impacts upon firms operating in China. The preferential availability of these financial loans can be used to encourage particular styles of market development by financing market entry into a new combination of business opportunities with controlled risks at the national level. The financial institutions established in China offer various types of loans. If the financial performance of a particular project is deemed to be sound, a loan may be provided without any debentures to guarantee repayment. The Chinese government has made significant efforts to improve its financial loan efficiency in order to maintain its domestic firms' business growth. The improvement of a firm's financial capabilities can ensure its strategic and long-term business presence and thus enables it to consider on-going capital investment, technological development and sourcing commitments to facilitate increased localization. The provision of guaranteed medium and long-term debt directly influences a firm's ability to invest in capital projects, fulfil financial commitments and disperse financial resources.

The provision of a Chinese government loan not only enables a firm to establish an optimal equity structure that will minimize its costs and risks, but also affects its profitability, liquidity, working capital structure and cash balance, all of which influence a firm's financial position. An analysis of the operation of banking and the financial loan system structured in China can provide insights into how to take advantage of such favourable financial services. When foreign firms initiate new investments, they may apply for Chinese government financial guarantees for their business working capital needs. With such financial guarantees in place, many financial options become available to raise external funding for the investment project through their own channels or through local financial institutions. Qualifying firms may obtain foreign exchange by borrowing from local or foreign banks. The demand for financial guarantees has increased rapidly in line with the growth of foreign firms' business activities in China, and Chinese financial institutions are being forced to provide quality services to international standards in order to compete.

Capital markets are fundamental to international investment and production activities as well as the foreign trade that underpins economic activities in modern society. Reform of national financial services has promoted a financial structure that should produce an efficient and effective means for managing foreign firms' investment and production activities which is sustainable in the long term and can stabilize Chinese markets. A burgeoning interest in the economic aspects of fiscal and monetary regulation has also played an important role in China's capital market, international production and foreign trade activities. Although there is uncertainty in China regarding the viability of fiscal and monetary systems, foreign firms need to increase their local debt facilities as part of their overall commitment to international investment. Foreign firms in China may bring about economic change not only in the way their resources and capabilities are to be employed, but also through the products and services they require for day-to-day business operation. The foreign firm will therefore create a profound impact through the non-capital resources they deploy which require technology, managerial and service infrastructures and which are then available to other local industries.

The opening of China's banking and security industries to more and more local and foreign firms is aimed at reducing the transaction costs in the financial markets. China has achieved significant progress through the implementation of market-oriented reforms of national financial systems. Most Chinese banks, particularly the state-owned commercial banks, have established a reasonable network of banking services throughout the country. Having achieved this, state-owned commercial banks are also able to offer domestic residential loans and deposit accounts which in turn will increase local capital reserves and this diversification will reduce their overall business risk. State-owned commercial banks are not allowed to extend long-term credit on market terms because of the restrictions on ownership and this leaves space for foreign banks operating in China to play a significant role in the development of efficient capital markets.

The financial institutions in China are now developing services that include fixed-asset loans, buyer credit, syndicated loans, working capital financing, mortgage loans and reserve loans as vehicles to help firms to run their business in China. A firm's cost structure is often dependent on its financial situation and an analysis of cost structure can help improve its investment analysis, financial policy, accounting and budgeting, tax avoidance, liquidity control, debt management and cash flow balances. Forming an effective 'cost centre' for a firm directly affects expense reduction, asset allocation and working capital management. These financial attributes become important if a firm is concerned with minimizing these costs.

Market expansion is of particular importance to the Chinese government as a firm's investment is normally only permitted if it includes plans to export products to international markets. New fiscal and monetary policies plus favourable export loan guarantees in China are expected to improve the investment environment, as they are critical to the ease of entry of foreign investments. More recently, Chinese foreign investment restrictions on many service industries including financial services, insurance and securities and so on have been relaxed. Foreign firms may attempt to reduce costs by expanding output to maximize the benefits available. For domestic companies, obtaining market growth through the formation of an international strategic alliance may be one way to achieve cost reduction benefits based upon their partners' resource complementarities. The capital structure of a nation has to be perceived not just as a function of exogenous industry, regulatory and product market factors, but also of strategies that produce market competition within an industry.

Reform of political institutions

Foreign firms, with their superior product offerings and marketing expertise, may stimulate competition in a host country's market and encourage local entrepreneurship. There is much evidence to suggest that local Chinese firms seek not only to rely on foreign firms' investments for their superior technologies and resources, but also wish to upgrade their own knowledge and expertise by working in more up-to-date environments. Many studies confirm that reform of political institutions in China may result in more foreign investments and internationally competitive operating production businesses being created that build efficient infrastructure, based upon an incentive investment policy that structures FDI in such a way as to accelerate the transformation of China's economy. The government's incentive policies are aimed at creating effective ways to structure and guide FDI into the national financial system. One of the purposes of such policies is to ensure that the government itself gets a return on its investment.

Political institutions are used to secure the flows of enormous amounts of national funds to firms and this in turn results in repatriation of profits to the government through the provision of national financial services and taxation, which is further boosted by the multiplier effect. Effective distribution of capital funds at the national level includes capital structure, cash flow management and foreign exchange control. The growing interaction between a firm's investment strategies is most visible in the case of corporate takeovers, restructuring and the formation of international strategic alliances. Many firms are now using foreign market entry strategies as one of the major instruments in balancing their business expansion between global integration and local responsiveness. A firm's resources, knowledge and capabilities are important not merely to its localization strategies but also to the implementation of global-based corporate strategies. The choice of investment strategy represents a foreign firm's decision on how to access international markets to get the best possible terms and seek windows of opportunity for further expansion of the firm's business. The creation of effective resource distribution involves a financial appraisal of a firm's investment including product competition, market factors and the integration of financial markets.

The creation of effective resource distribution can be used to facilitate a firm's investment opportunities in China through the exploitation of pricing in financial markets, reduction of taxes and mitigation of investment risks. An appropriate distribution system for the resources at the national level can bring strategic benefits to a firm, generate managerial incentives and reduce costs incurred from low working capital. Foreign firms in China are commonly required to obtain local firm-specific resources. For example, a domestic firm which maintains a relationship with its local financial institutions usually knows the best ways to secure financing from a Chinese commercial bank. Foreign firms that wish to exploit a local market have to choose the right local partner firm in order to get access to appropriate local resources, knowledge and capabilities.

The theory of economic change indicates that selecting appropriate political institution governance requires extensive consideration of the 'strategic fit' between a participating firm's market expansion requirements and their local partner's ability to access resources and knowledge. The formation of an international strategic alliance with a local firm is particularly subject to political constraints, which will dictate how the foreign firm enters the market. A large investment without any partner may stretch the ability of a foreign firm to run its business effectively in China. An international strategic alliance will allow a firm to pool its capital resources, especially if its objective is to draw together the complementary skills and abilities of each partner. Foreign firms need to understand the nature of the legal infrastructure of a host country that underlies and protects specific corporate governance systems as they are economic mechanisms and legal institutions that can be altered through the political process. Market competition will force firms to increase economic efficiency and to minimize costs if they are to be profitable at competitive prices. Most foreign firms in China need to create effective access to trained technicians and other personnel if they are to take advantage of the cheap labour that drew them to China in the first place. Research into what makes companies successful in China suggests that investment in physical resources, human capital and R&D all enhance business performance.

Research indicates that it is a combination of technology, R&D and human capital accumulation that triggers economic growth. Generally speaking, the creation of an effective resource distribution infrastructure in China enhances the case for investment in these factors by enabling foreign trade and FDI, and is perceived to have an endogenous influence on a firm's business as it defines the type of access to the market and suppliers to which a firm may be exposed. There is a strong association between external macro-market institutions and the internal organizational strength that facilitates a firm's products and services. The academic, Dunning (1980), suggests that the capability of a firm to explore market opportunities usually arises from an advantageous combination of ownership, localization and internalization. The choice of ownership vehicle for engaging in a new business investment is determined by a firm's investment preferences exerted with respect to the extent and focus of products and services within the organization.

A firm that invests in a new business needs to ensure that the relevant supporting industries will be able to offer the products and services needed to complement the high value-added activities of the company itself. If a foreign firm is in a market-making situation in the host country's market, it needs to know what it can do through the legal system to protect its intellectual property, such as brand names, proprietary knowledge and designs. One of the informal ways they can influence the situation is by taking an active role in the local political institution governance.

The evaluation of a foreign firm's investments is especially difficult in volatile business markets, especially in an emerging market situation influenced by 'local conditions'. The decision as to whether to use 'localization' strategies constitutes a key factor for foreign firms who must weigh the new opportunities against costs posed to international investments and operations. This decision, which will define the future style of operations, must be taken right at the start of a new venture. Firms must operate in dramatically changing business competition and international landscapes as the rise of new industrial centres and trade blocs creates new supply and distribution infrastructures. The local political infrastructure will press hard for foreign firms to increase 'local content' for raw materials, components, product technology, processing and marketing. Business opportunities for many foreign firms depend upon being accepted in local markets, and increasing the local content of a strategic alliance's products will favourably incline the local political system to open new routes to market and provide other competitive advantages. Foreign firms must be able to certify the level of 'localization' in their business developments in order to increase the influence they exert to ensure that the local political system makes strategic decisions that are to their benefit.

The implementation of a strategic alliance investment strategy also requires certain decision activities that will increase the predictability of a local partner's involvement. The contractual view of a firm developed by Schultz (1961) indicates that firms need to be sure that their nominated manager's specialized human capital is able to generate sufficient return on their investments. This requires that an investing firm must have the right to make some decisions in circumstances that are not fully predicted by the contract. As most future contingencies are hard to describe and forsee, complete contracts are not technologically possible. Firms need to make sure that their investments are not expropriated or wasted and, as foreign partners in a strategic alliance cannot expect to rely on the quality of resources and capabilities that they obtain from their local partners, they must have contingency plans for access to alternatives.

The Chinese government may restrict access to certain strategic resources as a competitive weapon to safeguard their domestic industries. Although foreign managers appear to make investment decisions based on local market analysis, certain market-related activities are reliant upon the local partner's ability to guarantee access to distribution channels, copyright and regulatory protection. In addition any investment strategy comprises multidimensional areas at the national institutional level that are concerned with regulatory variables such as price controls, governmental regulation and legal terms of foreign investment policies and economic trade. A foreign firm must do due diligence at the formation of an international strategic alliance to ensure that the local firm will not be called on to contribute more capital than it can comfortably afford. One motivation for a local company to engage in an international strategic alliance is to improve its performance. A successful strategic alliance will be able to create capital resources of its own and the local company will hope that it will have access to these funds. If the local firm is dissatisfied with the benefits they are receiving or if material circumstances of the local company change, a foreign firm cannot guarantee that their local partners will always be willing to meet all future resources and potential knowledge contributions.

Forming an international strategic alliance involves sharing resources, knowledge and capabilities between partner firms and before entering a strategic alliance in China it is advisable to create a clear checklist, agreed by all partners, of the types of capability each partner will be encouraged to invest. In forming an international strategic alliance the initial investment is unlikely to be the main business cost. To be successful, each partner must have equivalent levels of resources committed to the new organization. A strategic alliance must recognize the importance of technological and managerial co-operation in furthering its objectives but the resulting management participation will also ensure that the investing partners' own particular objectives will be met. One of the reasons that firms enter strategic alliances is to have access to the right resources to be truly globally competitive. The Chinese government prefers to encourage this option rather than wholly-owned subsidiaries in its territory because it allows more influence over industrial affairs and thus, despite the inherent risks, it is often necessary for foreign firms to enter into a strategic alliance to gain access to markets. The choice of partner is guided by factors such as resource complementarities and goal congruence, but FDI in China is regarded as a financially lower risk option. A strategic alliance's ability to optimize cash flow and capital budgeting is critically important and, since these capabilities are highly influenced by business location, it is crucial that a strategic alliance is able to understand what is the most effective allocation of its investment within the country. With regard to possible expropriation of firms' investments, foreign firms may decide to reduce the amount of resources that they are willing to provide up front to finance these firms, to reduce the misallocation of funds provided and thus to induce firms to provide more funds for future projects.

It is critical that an investing firm specify business contracts in great detail, laying out terms and conditions at the creation of an international strategic alliance, as this will limit opportunities for misappropriation by its strategic alliance or local partner managers, especially if these contracts are negotiated with poorly motivated partner firms. Managers need to be able to gauge the total costs of their strategic alliances' investments and to develop appropriate 'discount rates' to be used in assessing their investments. A strategic alliance's ability to evaluate a host country's investment opportunities properly will contribute directly to its business growth. Most foreign firms judge the performance of a strategic alliance by observing their output measures. A strategic alliance is well advised to avoid integration wherever the supplier market is competitive, because it is then that the strategic alliance can receive a high return at low costs. Making an FDI in China as part of a global business operation does expose a firm to risk, but an international strategic alliance can be perceived as an ideal form of hedging and risk sharing that creates a particular type of financial/intellectual gearing which can generate high levels of growth. The ability to undertake proper investment assessment and capital budgeting is critical to a firm that is undertaking international expansion. Table 3.1 shows the summary of some research evidence pointing to how an analysis of a host country's political institution might be undertaken.

Table 3.1 Summary of some research evidence pointing to a host country's political institutions

Theoretical contribution	Research questions	Strategic impact on political institutions
Standard model of agent–principal relationship	(1) With regard to the large impact of a host country's actions on values of firms, how are investment incentive mechanisms used? (2) Is their use limited by less than optimal design and distribution of investment incentives by political institutions?	National governance deals with the ways in which suppliers of capital to the national financing system, which lends money to corporations, ensure a return on their investment. The political governance system has assured the flows of enormous amounts of national financing to firms and actual repatriation of profits to the national providers of finance.
Theory of economic change (Demsetz 1991; Williamson 1996; Macaulay 2000)	(1) What is the nature of the legal protection of investors that underlines China's corporate governance system?	Corporate governance mechanisms are economic and legal institutions that can be altered through the political process.
	(2) Do evolutionary legal rules appear to play a key role in corporate governance?	Market competition will force firms to increase economic efficiency and to minimize costs at a competitive price.
Reputation-building in the capital market (Galbraith 1973; Hakansson and Johanson 1988)	(1) What are the costs and benefits of concentrated ownership? (2) Can investing firms' intellectual property be granted legal protection from expropriation by managers? (3) What are the protection of investors' rights and legal prohibitions against managerial self-dealing?	Concentrated ownership refers to matching significant control rights with significant roles of legal protection.

Table 3.1 (Continued)

Theoretical contribution	Research questions	Strategic impact on political institutions
Contractual view of the firm developed (Schultz 1961; Badaracoo 1991; Corones 2000)	(1) How can the investing firms ensure the manager's specialized human capital is able to generate return on their funds? (2) How are the returns to be divided between the investing firm and the managers who look after its investments? (3) How can the investing firm specify the rights to make decisions in circumstances that are not fully foreseen by the contract?	As most future contingencies are hard to describe and foresee, complete contracts are not technologically possible. The agency problem in this context refers to the difficulties investing firms have in ensuring that their investments are not expropriated or wasted on unattractive projects or activities.

Reform of national taxation

The rate of tax and the timescales within which it must be paid will have a significant effect on how a firm manages its net income, cash flow, capital structure and operational growth. Heightened market competition in China has put the Chinese government under pressure to match the lowest tax burden obtainable by any firm in the same industry anywhere in the world in order to attract businesses to locate in China. The taxation system across China is gradually being harmonized as different provinces have different tax burdens and this will make it easier for strategic alliances operating in markets across China to co-ordinate their business activities. Relative to local firms, foreign companies are generally in a better position to create financial synergies from transfer pricing and internal 'transaction costs' because of their ability to operate across national borders. This capability is essential to the prosperity of a firm intent on international expansion and the taxation policy of the Chinese government is to maximize the value added in China.

While some of the financial synergies in a strategic alliance occur through transfer pricing of real inputs and outputs, the pricing of inter- or intra-subsidiaries' financial transactions can provide opportunity and flexibility for a company to minimize its total taxation burden. Furthermore, a local firm may minimize taxes through internal structuring of inter- or intra-subsidiaries' commercial and financial dealings as well as hedging the risks of individual firms through external business transactions. A local firm will try to minimize its costs and financial risks such that if any of its financial components experience losses the Chinese tax system will allow these losses to be offset by other operations in the group.

Preferential tax

Preferential tax can be used as one of the Chinese government's economic instruments for regulating FDI. Research evidence states that government subsidies associated with local Chinese firms' investments may subvert the viability of fiscal tax instruments as a means of economic reform. The efficient design of fiscal taxes must lie within politically acceptable tax norms in China and this requires that the overall competitiveness of the tax structure is effectively addressed but still allows tax reductions in targeted industrial sectors, regions and modes of ownership investment. A foreign firm may have few choices as how to protect its investments without establishing unique tax standards. As a consequence, China adopts a low tax policy towards foreign investments and at the same time grants preferential tax to certain industrial sectors and regions where there is a policy to promote foreign investment. Thus tax instruments are not only used for industrial modernization purposes, but also in providing an institutional framework to facilitate the involvement of the tax services in controlling foreign investments and their production activities.

Preferential tax includes enterprise income tax, personal income tax, turnover linkage tax tariff, land value added tax, resource tax and city real estate tax. The costs of tax servicing can affect cash flow at the organizational level. The Chinese government has recently reformed tax institutions to better regulate its tax policy associated with types of local and foreign firm developments. China has increased the opening of its local markets through the progressive lowering of tax barriers to foreign investments and their production. This economic liberalization of domestic markets and the removal of restrictions on capital movement and corporate governance structure for an international strategic alliance are a key component of this process. The creation of appropriate tax regulatory regimes has secured stability and reduced uncertainty for most foreign firms in China.

Preferential income tax policies toward foreign firms have been adopted in China. The income tax rate is 15 per cent in economic zones, hi-tech industrial zones and economic and technological development zones. The enterprise income tax rate is 24 per cent in coastal areas and provincial capital cities. Tax reduction and exemption policies for foreign firms have been introduced that provide the benefit of income tax exemption for the first two years after generating profit, and income tax is reduced by half in the following three years. Foreign firms in the hi-tech sector can enjoy the benefit from income tax exemption in the first two years after making profits, and income tax reduced by half in the following six years. In addition, the export-oriented firms will enjoy income tax reduced by half so long as the volume of their annual exports accounts for more than 70 per cent of the general sales of the firm. If foreign firms purchase domestically made equipment within the volume of the total investment, these foreign firms are entitled to a special category of tariff exemption and will enjoy tax credits that depend upon certain requirements being met.

The implementation of a unified value added tax, consumption tax and business tax has recently replaced industrial and commercial consolidated taxes. Foreign firms receive exemption from business tax when they undertake international technology transfer. The Chinese government so far has reduced its import tariff rate eight times. It has moved the average tariff level downward to 17 per cent with a comparatively large-scale lowering of the overall tariff level. The implementation of a tariff exemption policy for the importation of equipment, for both local and foreign firms, has been implemented. Preferential tax treatments are granted to foreign firms in China that are engaged in production-oriented, export-oriented or technology-oriented firms.

The Foreign Income Tax Law offers the following three savings to a foreign firms. First, the law does not distinguish capital gains from ordinary income: both are taxed in the same way. An IJV can save a great deal of income tax in China although it must be aware of many restrictions. In order to enjoy the lowest income tax rate, it will be confined to a special zone and 70 per cent of its business activities must be production, technology and export-oriented projects.

Second, if a foreign firm is engaged in certain sectors such as agriculture, forestry or animal husbandry, or established in the remote economically underdeveloped areas, the income tax can be reduced to between 15 and 30 per cent following the initial five-year tax exemption and reductions. Finally, if a foreign firm is engaged in the construction of energy, seaport or transportation projects with a life expectancy greater than 15 years of operation, it is exempt from income tax in the first five years commencing from the first profit-making year, and its tax liability is reduced by 50 per cent from the sixth through to the tenth year. If a foreign firm sustains losses in the early years, the loss can be carried forward to offset the gains in the next five years, but not backwards. The so-called 'first profit-making year' means the year in which the firm begins to make a profit after the previous losses have been offset. These so-called 'five-year tax exemption and reductions' are counted consecutively from the first profit-making year and cannot be deferred due to the losses incurred during this five-year period.

Tax incentives and rewards

The Chinese government has a wide range of different authorities able to offer additional tax incentives (see Appendix I). This provides foreign firms with a great deal of bargaining power. The designations of production-oriented, export-oriented and technology-oriented firms are essential in a business plan because they involve a great deal of tax savings. However, some local governments are reluctant to issue advance approval, though the central government has given permission for them to do so. The Chinese government treats foreign firms differently from local firms. The lowest income tax rate of 15 per cent is granted only to foreign firms, but they must be one of the 'production-oriented', 'export-oriented' or 'technology-advanced' firms. In order to take advantage of this, foreign firms must be aware of these requirements. With respect to the Chinese government's use of taxation to determine the retained earnings available for dividend distribution, such taxation is very much on an 'accrual' basis. Income tax expense is treated as a distribution of retained earnings, not as a reduction of profit. There is a mandatory provision for staff bonuses and welfare at 17.5 per cent of gross wages. The retained earnings are distributed as follows: first, losses due to property forfeiture, followed by previous years' losses, plant expansion at 10 per cent of the after-tax accounting value, salaried staff group bonuses and welfare and finally a payout to the shareholders in form of dividends. In addition to the tax savings at the national level, local governments can also grant various kinds of tax incentives, such as reductions in local income tax, land use fees and consolidated industrial taxes and commercial taxes. In fact, local areas and the Chinese government fiercely compete with one another to attract foreign investments on the basis of their control of and influence over local taxation.

Fiscal tax is used as one of the Chinese government's economic instruments for regulating its foreign investments. Previous evidence has shown that government subsidies to local firms' investments may invalidate the viability of using taxation as a means of industrial reform. Developing a clear understanding of the various types of tax structures is important for the Chinese government. It can also be critical to the success of a foreign firm's investment plan. Foreign firms considering an international market entry strategy have a wide array of entry modes to choose from. Each entry mode has different implications for the taxation control that the Chinese government can exercise to influence a foreign firm's investment and operations. In order to attract foreign investments in designated industries and locations, the Chinese government has offered various forms of preferential tax incentives in the past and is likely to do so again in the future.

The income tax of a foreign firm is governed by (1) 'The People's Republic of China Foreign Investment Enterprise and Foreign Enterprise Income Tax Law' and (2) 'The People's Republic of China Foreign Investment Enterprise and Foreign Enterprise Income Tax Law Implementation Rules'. In the two laws, taxable income and accounting income are closely related to each other. In order to understand income taxation, it is necessary to understand the tax policies applied to various types of foreign investment. Three types of primary tax incentives are offered to a firm engaged in production-oriented, technology-oriented and export-oriented projects in China.

Encouraging foreign investment firms

Many economists suggest that the economic liberalization undertaken has been an effective means of opening the Chinese market. Any economic analysis of national taxation needs to be extended beyond the traditional tasks of raising government funds by taking a percentage of the profit of a firm's investments and production activities. National taxation reform in China is still at a developmental stage based on the assumption that if a host country creates a favourable financial environment and a better-quality infrastructure of supporting industries, foreign firms will have increased confidence when investing both capital and non-capital resources in China. A liberal tax regime is an important determinant of FDI inflows although there is growing pressure in China to open protected sectors further. Removal of restrictions on certain industrial sectors has made the Chinese market more attractive.

The Chinese government has put a great deal of effort into legislation concerning foreign investments and the regulating their production in order to encourage foreign investment development. The major effort has involved economic liberalization of relevant tax regulations to make it easier for foreign firms to enter the local markets. It is Chinese government policy to increase the number of production, technology and export-oriented firms as much as is economically justifiable. Foreign firms often lack familiarity with the Chinese investment environment and have a high sense of uncertainty about the local taxation structure. However, foreign firms in China can control the timing, location and size of their investments and production activities, and within this context it is possible to optimize investment decisions.

Production-oriented firms

Tax incentives are granted to 'production-oriented' firms more often than to 'non-production-oriented' operations as a way of encouraging production in China. 'Production-oriented' firms are recognized by the taxation authorities under the State Council. 'Non-production' refers to service industries, including hotels, restaurants, and tourism. The Foreign Income Tax Law requires local governments and relevant tax authorities to reform any production-oriented firm that offers a guaranteed fixed asset return to the shareholders because this arrangement violates the principles of equality and mutual benefit, and the principles of profit sharing. The Foreign Income Tax Law is designed to curb the current practice of some local governments of providing income tax benefits beyond what is allowed by the central authority, and to ensure that the recipients of the preferential income tax benefits meet the substantive and procedural requirements under the relevant Chinese laws and regulations.

These practices are used to attract foreign investments to regions. Unauthorized tax benefits include local government promising to refund a portion of the central income tax paid by a foreign firm with the local government's own money as a way of providing the foreign firm with an effective tax cut. It should be noted that five-year tax exemption and reductions are granted only to production-oriented firms. If a firm is engaged in 'production' activities with a contract term of ten years or more, it is exempt from income tax in the first two years, followed by a 50 per cent reduction in the next three years commencing with the firm's first profit-making year.

Technology-oriented firms

In order to encourage technological development, the Foreign Income Tax Law gives favourable treatment to 'technology-oriented' firms. To be qualified as such, firms in China must meet the following five conditions: (1) the firm must generally be in an industry in which the state encourages foreign investment; (2) the firm must use internationally advanced technology and modern equipment in production; (3) the firm must introduce newly developed products that are more advanced in terms of quality and technical performance compared to local products; (4) the firm must have a technology transfer agreement or clause in the joint venture contract; and (5) the imported machinery and equipment must have a superior performance and higher efficiency when compared with locally produced Chinese machinery and equipment.

The Foreign Income Tax Law requires local tax authorities to strictly enforce national policies on company income tax and cease any unauthorized preferential tax policies. The net income from a firm is taxed at different rates depending on its 'technology-oriented' status where this also depends on the type of activities (manufacturing or construction). If a firm exports 70 per cent or more of its products, after the initial five-year tax exemption and reductions have expired, its income tax rate can still be reduced by 50 per cent thereafter, with no time limit, but the tax rate cannot be less than 10 per cent, and under these circumstances the enterprise need not be classified as 'technology-oriented'. Technology-oriented firms are required to help the modernization drive by introducing new technologies and management techniques.

The Chinese government believes that the effective development of technology-oriented firms will spread concepts of competition and quality marketing that will help Chinese products to find markets abroad. Much of the recent growth associated with the establishment of 'technology-oriented' firms is being driven by the dramatic economic changes. Economic growth, trade liberalization and industrial firms' privatization programmes in China have provided excellent investment opportunities for both local and foreign firms. The desire of the Chinese government to facilitate both export and technology-oriented firms is also reflected in the dramatic increase in the number of bilateral investment treaties that are designed to protect and promote investment. Removal of restrictions on certain industrial sectors has made the Chinese market more attractive to international companies.

The Chinese government has put an enormous effort into legislation that establishes and governs and the operation of technology-oriented firms in order to promote FDI in this area. The major effort has involved liberalizing foreign investment regulations to make it easier for FDI to enter Chinese markets as part of the policy has been to increase the number of technology-oriented firms as much as is economically justifiable. Foreign firms face uncertainty in their technology investments due to lack of familiarity with the Chinese business environment, and hence the host government has tried to ensure that such investments are easily facilitated when there is high local market demand.

Export-oriented firms

In order to encourage exports, tax incentives are also often given to an 'export-oriented' firm. To be qualified as such, a firm is obliged to meet the following three conditions: first, the firm must engage in the manufacturing of products for export; second, the firm must export at least 50 per cent in value of products produced in that year, (to qualify for additional tax incentives, it must export 70 per cent or more of the products produced); finally, the firm must maintain a balance of foreign exchange surplus. Firms producing products that serve as import substitution can also qualify as 'export-oriented' firms. The exports must be sufficient to balance a firm's foreign exchange expenditure with foreign exchange earnings.

The more the firm exports, the greater will be the benefits in terms of tax reductions or refunds, lower financing costs and priority of access to scarce resources, as offered by the central or local governments. This policy ensures that the Chinese government is able to generate foreign exchange reserves, import strategically vital materials and implement its export-orientation policy. Hedging exposure of an export-oriented firm's international expansion has become increasingly complex. With the current system, it should be possible for export-oriented firms to forecast exchange rates, project and track exposure, track hedging options and costs and implement exposure management policies better. If a foreign firm is engaged in export-oriented production activities, after the initial 5-year tax exemption and reductions have expired, its income tax rate can still be reduced by 50 per cent for a further three years, but will not be less than 10 per cent in total. The minimum 10 per cent taxation rule applies in all cases and not just to 'export-oriented' firms.

Detailed tax regulations on foreign investment are issued by the Chinese government in order to provide a detailed understanding of financial incentives offered to 'export-oriented' and 'import substitution' investments. Export-oriented investments tend to be more capital-based and technology-intensive. There has been a profound impact on Chinese industrial growth as a result of the policies promoting export-oriented firms, and this can be contrasted with countries that pursue policies of quota-based import substitution. There is no doubt that export-oriented firms have played an increasingly important role in technological development, export growth and in creating employment in China. Apart from aiding economic growth, export-oriented firms are an essential part of the modernization drive, spearheading the introduction of new technologies and management techniques. The Chinese government believes that effective direction of export-oriented firms can spread concepts of competition and quality marketing that will help Chinese products to find more international markets. Much of the recent growth in establishing export-oriented firms is being driven by the dramatic economic growth, trade liberalization and industrial firms' privatization programmes which have created attractive investment opportunities for businesses. The desire of other governments to facilitate export-oriented firms is also reflected in the dramatic increase in the number of bilateral investment treaties designed to protect and promote investment.

China has successfully encouraged and facilitated most production, technology and export-oriented firms through its management of the decentralization of trade. The regional targeting and industrial sector policies have together facilitated the establishment of many production, technology and export-oriented firms in China. The targeting policies use instruments such as tax breaks, foreign exchange retention privileges, government provision of cheap materials and duty-free imports. As part of China's regional targeting policy, a strategy of opening local markets by combining openness towards foreign investments with the encouragement of production, technology and export-oriented firms has proved to be particularly successful. Production, technology and export-oriented firms are encouraged in China because they encourage the use of under utilized resources, knowledge and capabilities and promote the modernization of traditional industries, while developing labour-intensive projects that are in compliance with industrial policies.

A liberal trade regime is an important determinant of foreign investment inflows and there is growing pressure in China to further open protected sectors. Detailed regulations have been issued by the Chinese government to provide financial incentives to production, technology and export-oriented firms, with export-oriented firms required to have a greater capital base and to be more technology-intensive. There has been a profound impact on economic growth in China as a result of policies promoting exports and there is no doubt that production, technology and export-led firms have played an increasingly important role in technological development, exporting growth and creating employment.

Summary

This chapter provides a comprehensive overview on national institutional development and economic changes in China. The reform of national financial systems, political institutions and national taxation has been thoroughly reviewed. The identification of a firm's optimal financial structure through the acquisition of both capital and non-capital resources must include a close examination of the national financial policies adopted by the Chinese government. The development of production, technology and export-oriented firms has played a positive role in Chinese industrial growth. Experience indicates that China's economic reform has already brought rapid changes to production, technology and export-oriented firms. The national financial system has been transformed by changes to tax assignments, monetary instruments, the government of prudence regulations and banking system. The chapter also provides strong evidence that concessionary tax rates and foreign investment incentives can be an effective way to attract more foreign firms to a particular industrial sector. In addition to the laws governing income tax, a number of important descriptions of preferential tax policies and the Chinese government's role affecting FDI are included.

4
Building Blocks for Corporate Governance

Introduction

This chapter provides an overview of the theoretical perspective on corporate governance and the options for establishing 'modern corporate governance' in an international organization. The creation of a sound institutional environment primarily requires an understanding of how a country's economic, socio-cultural and political institutions influence an organization. This is particularly true where ownership of an organization is split, such as in the case of an international strategic alliance. National corporate governance systems dominate the competitiveness of a host country's economy as they dictate how firms run their business more effectively within a given society. The construction of a national institution that facilitates the effective use of a country's overall investments and international production is an essential government mechanism if society is to function properly. This chapter offers several theoretical explanations of corporate governance mainly relating to new institutional economics in emerging business environments with China as the main example. Analyses of corporate governance are expounded that encompass both the macro institution at the national level and the micro-institutional context at the organizational level.

Theoretical perspectives on corporate governance

An essential part of corporate governance is concerned with the distribution of stakeholders' rights and power within an organization. When modern corporate governance is established within a firm, it is expected to establish appropriate authorities and control mechanisms that support its stakeholders' rights and power. Theoretical perspectives in relation to corporate governance have been substantially explained through sociological discussions where great emphasis is placed on the various institutional, legal and socio-economic dimensions. The market institutional dimensions identified by Scott (1997) include regulatory, cognitive and normative forces that influence the levels of inter- or intra-organizational dependence and the process of conformity by organizations. Regulatory institutions provide a framework for standard operating conventions, pragmatic legitimacy and political norms. Regulatory institutions comprise formal and informal rules emanating from the macro-level aspects of society, including the political environment, the judicial system and cultural norms. Regulatory institutions also incorporate political bodies, economic conventions and social norms that are exercised by organizational players for business exchanges and co-operation within the given society. Normative institutions create a conceptualized process that affects an organization's social relationships and strategic behaviour. The primary cognitive roles focus on social networks and processes of organizational change. Cognitive institutions incorporate a socially constructed system of values, beliefs, myths and rituals.

With the alignment of the interests of stakeholders including owners, managers, employees, suppliers, customers and the community, the legal aspects of corporate governance centre on the structure of the board of directors or other formalized governance bodies which exercise management supervision on behalf of the owners. The establishment of a strong legal environment is perceived to encourage a firm's confidence regarding its business investment and operation. Measures that inspire confidence include improvement of the quality of the host country's investment environment, the clarification of property rights and intellectual property rights legislation, as well as the enforcement of laws that establish stakeholder rights. Creating a competitive regulatory institution within a country is crucial for the fostering of sound corporate governance. Heightened market competition and rapidly changing technology in China may challenge corporate rights by changing the way in which a firm's business is conducted, affecting ethnic codes, the degree of market competition among firms, market entry and exit rules, government facilitation, the openness of the economy and generalized business practices.

National level corporate governance law has an enormous impact on how national incentives and political judgements affect the implementation of competitive management practices. Discussions about the effect of corporate governance on certain economic aspects at the national level concentrate chiefly on issues of who should have the ultimate rights and power to allocate a firm's resources, knowledge and capabilities; what appropriate authorities and control mechanisms are needed to support those legal rights and powers for the stakeholders; whether the appropriate authorities and normative institutions to ensure a steady stream of returns for the firm in the longer term are in place; and how the cognitive systems built into an organization affect its overall performance.

A firm's corporate governance is mainly derived from its economic activities and emphasizes the requirement for competitiveness in the achievement, assimilation and management of its scarce resources in the pursuit of resource effectiveness and efficiency. A positive and healthy investment environment requires that the firm be granted legitimate rights and power to allocate its resources, knowledge and capabilities.

The regulatory perspective of corporate governance has always been contentious in that it can be seen as interference by the government. In one sense it usurps the role of a director whose job is to protect the rights of all shareholders and who theoretically has personal rights of access to all information in the company. However, there have to be appropriate authorities and control mechanisms to support the rights and powers of other legitimate stakeholders even if they only have a minority interest. Defining the economic interests that relevant parties in a firm must satisfy is a challenge as there are various categories of stakeholders with different interests involved. For example, corporate disclosure of limited specific performance measures such as profitability may comply with the legal standards required of managers but makes it very difficult for shareholders to monitor a firm's performance independently. The dissemination of detailed information about a firm helps the judiciary to combat corruption within an organization. The power and the influence of regulatory institutions are expected to enable them to independently monitor a firm's profit distribution for business reinvestment or dividend allocation under 'the stakeholder interests' as they show special concern for shareholders, top management, regulators, auditors and other stakeholders.

Finally, key managerial aspects of corporate governance are primarily in place as ways of exercising management of and within an organization to ensure that it achieves authority and control over its long-term business development. In the Chinese case, technological transformation, socio-economic progress, political realignment, government deregulation and reduction of trade barriers have given rise to a new cognitive institution milieu within which firms must effectively manage their resources. Corporate governance is often taken into account in determining a firm's overall development needs for resources and capabilities as such requirements are closely associated with managers' capabilities to satisfy stakeholders' common interests. The key managerial aspects of a firm are there to ensure that a residual return is generated for the stakeholders. Studies of corporate governance in the context of the transitional Chinese economy may provide an interesting vehicle to extend understanding and application of corporate governance to different management contexts. Table 4.1 shows the summary on theoretical contributions to corporate governance.

Corporate governance at the national level

National institutions in a country are seen to provide various control levers for exercising national rules, regulations and procedures. An analysis of corporate governance at the national level is usefully accomplished by 'borrowing' the Porter (1980) categorization of 'the diamond of national advantage' to understand how a firm faces its governance challenges including factor conditions, demand conditions, interfaces with related and supporting industries as well as the firm's strategy, structure and rivalry (see Figure 4.1).

Factor empowerment for the legal constitution

Legal theories draw significant attention to the role of the legal constitution in a firm's corporate governance. The legal structure defines the

Figure 4.1 'New diamond' of corporate governance in an international strategic alliance

Table 4.1 Theoretical contributions to corporate governance

Corporate governance	Theoretical implications	
Governance institution at the national level	Factor empowerment for the legal constitution	Scott (1997) indicates that market institutions including regulatory, cognitive and normative forces influence the levels of inter- or intra-organizational dependence and the process of conformity by organizations (North 1990; Lazonick and O'Sullivan 2000).
	Demand condition for the market competition	Market power is primarily represented by a firm's business background, distribution networks and a host country's opportunity offering versus cost (Porter 1990; Mallin and Rong 1998).
	Related and supporting industry	Experience shows that supporting industries can play a key role in deterring insider-dealing government intervention on business (Scott 1997; Shleifer and Vishny 1997).
	Strategy, structure and rivalry	The existence of national regulations concerning market entry influence a firm's business strategies, managerial efforts and level of supervising by the board of directors (Williamson 1970, 1985, 1988; Monks and Minow 1995).
Corporate governance at the organizational level	Agency theory	Agency theory is concerned with the ability of 'principals' to ensure that their 'agents' are fulfilling their objectives (Berle and Means 1932; Fama and Jensen 1983a, 1983b; Jensen and Meckling 1976).
	Transaction cost economics	Transaction cost economics is a potential low cost method of organizing international business transactions in comparison with organizing them through markets or within integrated organizational hierarchies (Williamson 1996).
	Bargaining power theory	Bargaining power theory is concerned with the ways in which firms can take advantage of their ownership advantages by securing control and influence over other firms and the host governments (Fagre and Wells 1982; Yan and Gray 1994b).

way that regulations bear upon the options for national corporate governance in a given society. Company law has traditionally focused on the rules, procedures and principles that are used to safeguard the interests of stakeholders. In the Anglo-Saxon model the primary stakeholders are the shareholders but, in other countries (including China), employees and the state have significant legal rights. In this respect, the legal function has been aimed at establishing appropriate mechanisms whereby firms' directors and managers can be compelled to act in all of the shareholders'/stakeholders' interests. The primary mechanism of corporate governance from a legal perspective is used to protect shareholders' interests by upholding their rights to appoint, monitor and replace the most senior tier of management and to take certain other fundamental decisions. The main organizational mechanism for exercising these 'legal rights' is associated with making appointments to the board of directors. Hence, in areas of employment policy and management contracts, certain powers or rights are usually reserved for the board of directors, including approval of business plans, capital expenditure budgets and senior management appointments.

Much of the debate on the legal issues associated with corporate governance in a strategic alliance has been related to the recognition of the 'supervisory mechanisms' that can be employed to exert a controlling influence on a strategic alliance's direction and business management. In the case of unitary organizations, the traditional argument often assumes that where there are a significant number of shareholders, the dispersion of their power and their passivity has a tendency to disenfranchise them (Berle and Means 1932). In short, the legal perspective is not only primarily concerned with the power and rights of stakeholders but also with ways of facilitating firms' power and rights to direct their resources, knowledge and capabilities. Hence analysis of the functioning of a firm's corporate governance can be employed to distinguish the ways that legal institutions have shaped organizational characteristics, including the standard operating conventions, the pragmatic legitimacy and management systems established within an organization.

At the macro level, prevailing forms of corporate governance are expressed through legal regulations as well as general customs and practice. National legal features are historically embedded and thus display a high degree of path dependence. Legal development at the national level is itself a function of a country's political norms, economic development and technological progress towards regulatory modernization. The legal function has political and economic roles that can be used to moderate the 'corporatization' process through the employment of favoured national investment policies and/or tax exemptions, as well as the provision of choices amongst alternative governance contingencies. Thus the legal constitution is deeply embedded in corporate governance systems and these in turn shape the firms' management structures. The embedded national legal system is reflected in a country's national norms, organizational principles and regulations.

China is in economic transition from a central planning economy to a market economy driven by free market tenets. A country's factor conditions affecting the legal constitution include national regulations, the provision of intermediate services, the establishment of a competence base, the quality of resources and knowledge supplies; these are perceived as factors external to a firm's investments, production and performance. In China, the legal system is regarded as having a significant influence upon a firm's corporate governance as it controls many aspects of business activities. These corporate governance influences are believed to impact significantly upon the various management tiers through China's central, provincial, municipal and state agencies. For instance, when local firms compete for market access to government-controlled contracts, new contenders may offer the host government attractive alternative technologies and core resources. The competitive forces that enhance the legal rights of the various stakeholders and the ability to exert significant pressure on firms are increased. Increased market competition in a host country is perceived as a salient aspect of the emerging national institutions, and this competitive intensity may enable its government to enforce national institution requirements and establish various strategic targets for the direction of foreign firms' investments and production. Scholars therefore argue that the larger and the more attractive the host country's market is, the more a government is able to facilitate, intervene and exert influence over firms in the market.

A host country's free trade and foreign investment are usually regulated through the setting of national regulations that constrain a firm's corporate governance and that define legal frameworks within which free trade, foreign investment and international production operate. Market competition is seen to play an intermediate role that affects the conditions of a firm's corporate governance. The availability of transfer pricing, transactional costs, local regulations and relevant investment rules are considered the basic framework around which a firm is offered legal protection. These premises may affect decisions about the method of a firm's market entry. For instance, difficulties in raising loans and cash capital through a country's financial markets may lead to firms being reluctant to make further investments and expand their business in a particular country.

Free trade in a country is significantly related to the transparency of rules, procedures and laws for foreign investments and there may be a need to create an independent judicial process in order to settle disputes fairly. The establishment of a foreign firm's investment and production may require a host country to enact standard operating procedures, equal tax laws and consistent public policies. The enforcement of a free trade climate in a host country is conducive to business activity because the process requires an active continuous improvement of the local institutional environment. The host government must also play an active role by offering effective law-related administration that encourages a country to generate a positive atmosphere for 'free trade' if foreign investments are to be encouraged. At the macro level, the government must have the ability to exert significant influence on the direction of the overall flow of FDI. The encouragement of FDI is believed to be a major factor in the accomplishment of the government's economic and political goals. The selection of a firm's market entry point can also affect the relationship between the firm and the relevant law enforcement of foreign investment matters. Where a foreign firm's investment is a wholly-owned subsidiary, it may have some difficulty in establishing the right links at the micro level with the government. Foreign firms in China often take an 'apolitical stance', believing that keeping out of host country's politics will ensure there is no administrative intervention by the government; but this can reduce the opportunity to establish the right day-to-day links with government officials.

Demand condition for market competition

A major objective of foreign firms in China is to exploit the market potential in the host country before, and to a greater extent than, their competitors. Market power is primarily determined by a firm's industrial and business background, market position, distribution networks and a country's opportunity offering versus cost factors. Market competition enables firms in China to mitigate some industries' wide restrictions on input or output, increase bargaining power and offer advantages from the economies of scale or the economics of scope. A firm with strong market power often has greater bargaining power when negotiating terms for FDI with the government.

For a government to create a competitive market environment, it must establish a legal framework where intellectual property rights are respected, unfettered equity markets are increasingly expanded and corporate governance at the national level is ever more responsive and transparent. Effective market access at the national level is likely to be permitted for foreign firms when corporate governance has provided sufficient protection for the local firms. All forms of market competition are liable to be greater in an emerging economy such as China because the regulatory institution of legal regulations and provisions for the protection of intellectual property are not sufficiently and effectively implemented. Under such circumstances, an international strategic alliance in China can take place through appointment of senior managers who retain strong strategic control over their resources, knowledge and capabilities for the partner firms.

Increased government activity to protect intellectual property rights is expected to facilitate business operations positively. Enforcement of property rights is aimed at safeguarding a firm's technologies, copyrights and property rights. Foreign firms' interests in China can also be protected by building good communication with those government agencies that have the authority to resolve issues relating to technology leakage or intellectual property rights. The Chinese government has shown a positive attitude and tried to be helpful in the implementation of policies on foreign firms' investment and production. This has led to an increasing number of foreign firms being set up in the country. The opening of the Chinese economy, heightened market competition and international pressure have forced the government to establish a strong mechanism for the protection of property rights in line with international law, although consequential high transaction costs are generally perceived as a major obstacle to the improvement of economic competitiveness. Other related factors hindering the demand condition for China's market competition include the lack of a sound intellectual property rights system to deal with uncertainty in a free market environment. The government explicitly indicates its expectations concerning FDI and even puts direct pressure on foreign firms in China to help the government fulfil its objectives. The government's efforts are driven by the desire to acquire advanced technology from foreign firms, increase local content and set high export levels.

Related and supporting industries

The strengthening of the national development process by widening the scope of market competition and promoting deregulation may lead to the improvement of a host country's related and supporting industries. However, these development processes need to be buttressed with increased domestic market competition through the adoption of a sound competition policy and the establishment of an effective service agency. Of particular importance to the practice of corporate governance is the need to ensure an adequate infrastructure that monitors and enforces policies and standard operating conventions in the host country. A supporting infrastructure has therefore been built to assist foreign investments in China and it enforces information disclosure as the accountability of firms is vital to the operation of this infrastructure. Experience shows that supporting industries can play a key role in deterring insider-dealing, thus cutting down or government intervention in business and building foreign firms' confidence. Reform of the macro market institutions is needed, as foreign firms want service agencies or related supporting industries to be free from political influence as this will enable them to exercise their authority in an accountable and transparent manner. Hence, a reliable judiciary and independent legal system need to be guaranteed in order to counter any misconduct by the government and this is likely to lead to the establishment of a 'rule of law' system rather than the 'rule by law' system that is currently in place.

One reason for improving supporting industries is to achieve an efficient 'match' between the information processing requirements of a firm's governance contingencies and the improvement of those information-processing capabilities to achieve better business co-ordination. The alternative is to establish an appropriate mechanism for facilitating support industries that can help both local and foreign firms to obtain the necessary resources, knowledge and capabilities. Firms in China rely on operational efficiency to keep their production and administrative costs below prevailing industry norms. The creation of an effective support industry has encouraged many firms to invest capital to improve their products, service capabilities and the general efficiency of their business. In this regard, the implementation of improved support industry process capabilities has been facilitated by the equitable treatment of investors, demonstrating that high international standards of business disclosure are a necessary part of the support industry improvements.

Strategy, structure and rivalry

Market competition in an emerging business environment such as China exerts a significant influence on the practice of corporate governance at the national level. The existence of national regulations and policies relating to market entry influence a firm's business transactions, managerial activities and level of supervision by boards of directors. If a firm's resource arrangements enable monopolistic access to a particular market, access will be facilitated by the firm's strategy and organizational structure that enable contracts to be drafted to meet a particular market's requirements. Governmental market entry regulations are perceived as being designed to protect the 'public interest' at the national level.

Firms that are insulated from market competition generally operate at a higher cost level than may be expected under the best technical and managerial practices in free competition environments. Without market forces, there can be misallocation of a firm's resources as distorted price and inappropriate profit signals at the national level tend to lead firms to make poor investment decisions. The existence of market entry and exit rules established in relation to foreign investments may block a desired purchase, sale or dissolution even if all relevant parties agree fully upon its terms. Restrictions on foreign investment in a strategic alliance may prevent a buy-out as the law can preclude a firm from buying out its partner and taking control of the firm itself. Chinese law requires government approval of any transfer of a foreign firm's ownership and such approval may prove to be difficult or impossible to obtain. A ban on the removal of strategic assets may block a firm's dissolution as local law may require that the manufacturing equipment or product lines provided by a foreign firm to the international strategic alliance remain in the host country. Economic development in China within and between regions is dependent upon local government policy restrictions on investments, production and performance. Local institutional environments can exist where the availability of favourable local government financing structures may distort regional developments in contravention of national rules and procedures.

The ability of a host country to attract foreign investment depends on its political stability and economic growth as these will impact on foreign firms' organizational structure and performance. In the context of China, uneven regional development creates performance differences in the business investment climate for both local and foreign firms. Differentiated investment polices towards local firms in China have a definite strategic and financial influence over a region's legislative and regulatory agenda. Ultimately, market competition for regional development may provide sufficient opportunities for new business investments to compete on economic merit, rather than the ability to garner local political favours, but it will take time to change.

Corporate governance at the organizational level

A firm that adopts an equity-based investment strategy focuses mainly on the exploitation of the host country's resource endowments such as the utilization of cheap labour, raw materials and components in order to enhance its own resource capability. A firm can surmount local business development barriers by relying on corporate governance that is primarily derived from its technological expertise, knowledge and complementary resources. Agency theory, transaction cost economics and bargaining power theories can be used in combination to analyse corporate governance at the organizational level. These theories explicitly provide a logical explanation of a firm's business investments including arrangement of equity investment, management structure and performance.

Agency theory

Agency theory (AT) is concerned with the ability of 'principals' to ensure that their 'agents' are fulfilling their objectives. Agents are considered residual claimants in the sense that their returns depend upon other contractual claims being satisfied. Agency theory assumes that agents cannot necessarily be trusted and it is therefore concerned with the corporate governance and control mechanisms that limit an agent's self-serving behaviour (Berle and Means 1932). However, the agency issue also involves relations between shareholders themselves. Dominant shareholders are expected to look after the interests of the minority and managers are assumed to be able to look after the interests of both. Agency theory points out that an important consideration in designing corporate governance and management control systems is the achievement of coherence between the objectives of the agent and those of the principals. Incentive plans, the structure of the board of directors and the monitoring role of the board are three mechanisms designed to achieve this coherence.

Agency theory is concerned with the control and influence that principals can maintain over their agents. The rights and responsibilities of principals are generally derived from the equity investments in a firm. A number of studies have confirmed that most owners tend to use various forms of corporate governance and incentives to safeguard their equity investments (Eisenhardt 1989). The purpose of the principal's control is to minimize the return or benefits that go to the managers. Agency theory focuses on the governance problem of ensuring a coincidence of interests between principals and their agents It accords a monitoring and incentive function to management control. Agency problems can arise at various points in the vertical chain of relations between shareholders and managers, managers and employees. When applying agency theories to an organizational situation, a discrepancy between the ownership and control structure of a firm occurs when 'principals' appropriate the return on their investments in a way other than by relying upon equity ownership. If the dominant shareholder is able to appropriate returns through transfer pricing mechanisms, its reliance on equity participation in order to share the financial outcomes will be lower and hence its incentive to negotiate for a majority position will be reduced. Such a transfer pricing effect has been shown to be associated with the control system of a firm.

Agency theory connects to the corporate governance of an international strategic alliance in two ways. First, the identification of the legal provisions of the contract between the partner firms and the managers of a strategic alliance lies at the heart of agency theory. Each partner in the strategic alliance is a principal in respect of contracts. As a strategic alliance is assumed to have different self-interests, bounded rationales, and yet to some extent to share the same interests, the control function of the principal–agent contract should avoid one of the partners being able to secure better information about the management of the strategic alliance than the other. More specifically, the principal–agent relationship draws attention to the consequence of the fact that the contract brings a range of rights and responsibilities to the partner firms in a strategic alliance. It is absolutely vital that strategic alliance partners should create a contract which frames the principal–agent relationship. A dishonest partner can bankrupt the other partners, and there have been countless cases where this has happened.

Agency theory allows the re-examination of corporate governance in terms of organizational structure. A principal–agent relationship is most clearly established when an international strategic alliance is formed such that their managers are accountable to partner firms. Agency theory will regard the relationship between partner firms and managers in a strategic alliance as problematic. The situation becomes more complicated if and when the partner firms themselves have different strategic objectives (for example, one partner may seek profit over a longer term than the other). Most strategic alliance management teams comprise a mixture of agents such as local managers and expatriates. This can result in disagreements between partner firms that may affect the strategic alliance. The agency cost will depend on the quality of collaboration between the partner firms. Implications of agency theory can also be drawn from the strategic alliance's operation. For example, each partner becomes an agent for the provision of resources to the other partners. In order to avoid or overcome a risk that one partner becomes a 'free-rider' at the expense of the other, the contract between the partners and the parent strategic alliance should play an important role in delineating the use of resources provided to the alliance and the allocation of returns from that use. The most useful contribution from agency theory lies in the identification of control mechanisms and the conditions that bear upon the effectiveness of the parent-strategic alliance relationship.

Transaction cost economics

Transaction cost economics (TCE) is a potentially low cost method of organizing international business transactions in comparison with organizing them through markets or within integrated organizational hierarchies. Control is regarded as a cost aimed at the reduction of opportunism and other sources of risk or uncertainty in transactions under conditions of bounded rationality. The question for TCE is how to exercise this in the most economical way. Opportunism in Williamson's view refers to incomplete or distorted disclosure of information, especially when there are calculated efforts to mislead, distort, disguise or otherwise confuse (Williamson 1985:47). TCE suggests that firms will try to use contracts that minimize the risk of opportunism. In environments where contract enforcement is unreliable, an alternative option is to exercise personal supervision and tight control. This option may, however, be very costly. In order to deal with uncertainties, other options are available, including the concentration of equity or control of a firm's strategic resources.

Williamson (1975) argued that firms choose how to manage their transactions by using the criterion of minimizing the sum of production and transaction costs. Production costs may differ between firms due to the scale of operations, learning and proprietary knowledge. Transaction costs refer to the expenses incurred in searching out new suppliers or customers, together with the costs of writing, negotiating and enforcing contracts and for administering a transaction. Dunning (1989) recognized that transaction costs essentially comprise the costs of organization and the cost of strategy. Williamson (1985) identified the three key attributes of the transaction context as asset specificity, uncertainty and transactional frequency. It has been noted that the degree of market imperfection in an international context may be higher than in the domestic market because the costs of resource mobilization and managing contractual relationships are higher across national boundaries as the risks of market failure are greater (Rugman and Verbeke 1992).

Efficiency is a major criterion for assessing the appropriateness of a corporate governance structure between organizations conducting economic exchange from the perspective of transaction cost theory. Based on the logic of economizing transaction costs, a firm is more efficient when the resources furnished by the relevant parties for economic exchange are characterized as being difficult-to-trade in nature and hence entail high transaction costs if traded through market exchange. Note that only when the markets for exchanging intermediate inputs supplied by both parties are simultaneously subject to high transaction costs does the formation of a strategic alliance prove to be a necessary choice of governance structure. Otherwise, the party with marketable resources can gain by transferring these inputs simply by contracting to the other party that has non-marketable resources.

Governments may affect firms' choices by imposing policies, tariffs, quotas, sales taxes and price or production controls. These may affect the costs and types of investment by offering subsidies, tariff reductions, regulations or tax exemptions, or by raising or lowering interest rates and exchange rates through macroeconomic policies. Transaction costs, such as the costs of adhering to regulations, the costs of negotiating contracts, the cost of interacting with officials and the costs of collecting information, are also strongly influenced by governments. TCE is concerned with the cost effectiveness of organizing international economic activities.

TCE analysis has been used to address different aspects related to the relationship between ownership and control of an international strategic alliance. Decisions about strategic alliance ownership and its associated investments can be considered as an extension of hierarchies across borders, reducing the cost of international co-ordination, facilitating knowledge and technology transfer and increasing the efficiency of exchange. Gatignon and Anderson (1988) attempt to integrate the literature on market entry mode decisions using long-term efficiency criteria within a transaction cost framework. They state that the choice between full and shared ownership depends on the relative costs and benefits of the two alternative ownership structures. Hennart (1991) notes the importance of taking hierarchical costs into account in making a decision on the appropriate form of ownership.

TCE links the cost of tacit resources that owners contribute to an international strategic alliance and the cost of equity investment. Killing (1983), in his empirical studies, reports that tacit knowledge transfer is often handled better through an equity relationship, due to the greater incentive to transfer personnel and to take a more active interest in the operation. Equity relationships facilitate information sharing since the transferor receives a greater reward than the receiver of the transfer. At this stage, the transaction costs are lower and the expected value of the loss from opportunistic behaviour is also lower. Teece (1976) finds that technology transfer costs decline sharply for mature product categories as measured by the age of the technology and the number of competitors using similar or competing technology. Because the requisite knowledge is well codified and widely available for hire, the entrant does not need to supplement the control offered by the market mechanism. However, there are several limitations to the explanation concerning corporate governance of an international strategic alliance primarily by reference to TCE.

First, it ignores the strategic considerations that drive a strategic alliance's ownership decision choices (Contractor 1990). This is a major shortcoming since there may be strong driving forces behind the decisions of strategic alliances regarding ownership. Transaction cost theory looks only at the minimization of transaction costs without addressing other benefits offered by a particular form of ownership. It does not take account of organizational capability as a competitive advantage or constraint. The choice of ownership under which to form a strategic alliance may be made with reference to improving the global competitive position of the strategic alliance, even if the choice of strategic alliance may be more costly than alternative market entry modes. Competitive strategy is more concerned with the maximization of profits or revenues, rather than the benefits from a particular ownership mode. Kogut (1988) emphasizes the importance of separating a rent-maximizing competitive strategy logic from a cost-minimizing transaction cost logic.

Transaction costs incurred in an international strategic alliance include those of the cost of searching for suitable partners, monitoring the provisions and the use of capital and non-capital resources. TCE ignores disturbances to the output flow and the management of market uncertainty and therefore fails to distinguish between the efficiency of an organizational form and its effectiveness in the light of overall corporate strategy. Ghoshal (1987) indicated that co-ordination demands arising from the ownership form of a firm unit must match its co-ordination abilities. TCE is too narrow as it focuses on the production and marketing-related aspects of internalization at the expense of considering benefits from common corporate governance such as co-ordination efficiencies. In a perfect market, there would be no co-ordination costs or problems because there would be perfect information with resource allocation that is wholly responsive to clear economic signals.

Finally, TCE inadequately addresses the forms of linkage between ownership and control of a strategic alliance that may derive from a partner's cultural preferences and national institutional setting. For instance, studies of Chinese economic institutions have noted that they have their own distinct logic that is very different from market economies' institutions (Boisot and Child 1996). As a result, an international strategic alliance can be faced with contradictory forces that are rooted in the conflicts between partners' task requirements and the host country's unique institutions.

Bargaining power theory

Bargaining power theory (BPT) is concerned with the ways in which firms can maximize their ownership advantages by securing control and influence over other firms and the host governments. Gomes-Casseres (1987) stated that bargaining power accrues to those firms that enjoy ownership advantages. These are reflected in having sufficient capital, the capability to raise capital in the financial markets, access to advanced technology, highly developed management, marketing skills, strong brand names and trademarks, risk reduction abilities and a global perspective. Traditionally, the study of bargaining power is classified into three categories: equity-driven, capability-driven and resource-driven. With regard to the capability-driven perspective, firms are characterized as having a strong preference for majority ownership in their overseas subsidiaries where their perceived 'relatively strong' bargaining positions allow them to realize majority equity ownership options in most cases. Capability-driven bargaining power refers to the study of bargaining power in organizations by concentrating on the ability to affect outcomes or to get things done (Mintzberg 1983). Resource-driven bargaining power is often related to power and stems from the control of critical resources.

The contribution of tangible resources will be more likely to enhance the resource provider's bargaining power to negotiate a favourable equity position while the contribution of intangible resources will be more likely to enhance the resource provider's bargaining power with respect to a favourable control position, *ceteris paribus*. However, since the resources contributed by firms should be complementary in nature, depending upon the actual bilateral negotiations, the eventual arrangement of corporate governance may involve various trade-offs in reaching resolutions. The foreign partners in a strategic alliance that transfer intangible resources will tend to demand control rights to ensure the integrity of resource utilization and to prevent the leakage of proprietary knowledge. The construction of bargaining power due to the contribution of resources has to be balanced against the degree of relative resource dependence and not merely against the existence of such a contribution.

The evaluation of the degree of resource dependence can either be based on the alternatives available to the respective partners or on a subjective judgement of the reciprocity that has been achieved. Since bilateral bargaining is characterized by lengthy negotiations, different types of resources may exert different levels of influence in the process to gain a control position that is seen as a fair compromise.

The provision of a partner firm's tangible resources may have a greater influence on the attainment of equity position than on the attainment of control position since they tend to be easily priced and are more likely to be a one-shot transaction. Nevertheless, whether or not the contribution of intangible resources is sufficient to help the partner firm bargain for a majority equity position still depends on how the other partners value such a contribution at the negotiation stage. The resource provider is likely to be highly desirous of gaining a dominant control position over decisions that affect the utilization of these resources within the strategic alliance under the rationale previously mentioned. Resource contributions may have direct implications for relative bargaining power in negotiating equity position. The foreign firm normally serves as the provider of critical resources and may be more concerned about the ability to retain the power to decide upon the utilization of resources provided in order to ensure the best use of its contributed resources and to prevent technology leakage. Regardless of the eventual outcome of negotiations for equity share, maintaining a dominant control position in directing activities related to the use of valuable resources will be the foreign firm's top priority in subsequent negotiations.

Since an ownership concession is more likely to occur at the formation of a strategic alliance in developing countries and since maintaining resource superiority is the key to enhancing the foreign firm's bargaining power, gaining a dominant control position in decision-making on critical activities will seem to be more important for the foreign partner. The bargaining power perspective points out that a sense of fair dealing is an important guideline for formulating and implementing a co-operative inter-organizational relationship and that this is different from the viewpoint that the achievement of efficiency is the critical criterion for effective economic exchange. The essence of fair dealing lies with the degree of reciprocity as judged by all the transacting parties, and their decision behaviours are highly influenced by their respective cultural and institutionalized norms. In order to achieve fair dealing in the governance structure of the transacting partners, repeated bilateral bargaining processes containing an element of mutual learning and adjustment are necessary. The eventual outcome of repeated bargaining processes may reflect some kind of trade-off arrangement between equity ownership and operational control that is based on a mutual appreciation of the respective partners' bargaining power and thus a fair rate of exchange between costs and benefits as judged by the respective partners may precipitate a resolution of the repeated bilateral bargaining processes.

The most significant contribution provided by bargaining power theory to the corporate governance of a strategic alliance is the linkage between a firm's ownership of competitive advantages and its relations to partners and host governments. Blodgett (1991) identifies four elements in the bargaining that takes place between foreign partners and the host governments: technology, knowledge of the local environment, local marketing skills and government persuasion. These are perceived as having a direct influence on the bargaining power of each of the strategic alliance partners (Blodgett 1991). Foreign firms' bargaining power *vis-à-vis* host governments erodes over time as the foreign firms invest critical resources into the strategic alliance and effectively become hostages.

The bargaining power of the local firm in developing countries has depended on knowledge of the local business environment, supply of labour and raw materials, and connections with host governmental authorities and local financing institutions (Reynolds 1984). Local firms are more likely to get their way when they possess assets that are needed by foreign firms. Lecraw (1984) has attempted to articulate the relationship between the bargaining power of the partners and the level of control they exercise. He finds that the three aspects of bargaining power are determinants of firm-specific advantages in technical leadership, advertising intensity and export capability. The bargaining power of a host developing country's government derives from its control of the environment in which the international strategic alliance operates, especially its control of scarce domestic resources and access to the domestic market.

Vachani (1995:159) reports that bargaining success is affected by three moderating forces: the political climate in the host country, the host government's perception of value to the country inherent in the multinational's operations, and the multinational's ownership preferences. Yan and Gray (1996) develop a model of a strategic alliance based on bargaining power that incorporates context-based and resource-based components. Context-based bargaining power can be derived from having alternative partners as substitutes. The components of resource-based bargaining power are based upon the resources and capabilities committed by the partners to a strategic alliance. Bargaining power theory overlooks the situation where a strategic alliance partner may only wish to have a minority interest, and is content to leave control to another partner. It safeguards its right to a return via its shareholding. The bargaining power perspective offers several contributions to the analysis of relationships between ownership and control of a strategic alliance.

When a firm possesses ownership advantages in technology, production, marketing, finance and management, it will tend to have greater bargaining power. Once the firm possesses a certain level of bargaining power, it will be able to exercise some control and influence over those particular areas. Firms may use proprietary technology and management expertise valued as equity to increase the bargaining position of a firm over the host government, particularly if other firms cannot supply technology of the same type or at the same level of development. However, once the firms have committed their assets to a strategic alliance, the cost of protecting those assets will be significant.

A firm will gain bargaining power if the resources it can provide to a strategic alliance are aligned with the needs of the other partners. Bargaining power may be reflected in, and measured, by how much the strategic alliance contract that is negotiated accords with the local or foreign partner's objectives when such objectives are in conflict: for example, if capital is a scarce resource that can best be provided by one firm, its bargaining power and its level of equity participation may increase with the size of the investment and the investment's capital intensity. This means that much of the bargaining power available to prospective partners is likely to arise from their command of significant resources. The foreign firm's access to export markets may become a significant source of bargaining power if the host country is following a development strategy based on export-led growth.

Finally, equity ownership is seen as an outcome of a negotiation that represents the relative bargaining power of participating interests. It needs to be emphasized that the relationship cannot be a win/lose game; the individual partners must expect to have some mutually desired win/win outcomes from the partnership. On the whole bargaining influence tends to be measured by the percentage equity split. It may be argued that partner firms which only have minority equity but which have effective control through technology transfer and other connections also ought to be given greater consideration in the discussion of bargaining power as it may be inappropriate to resolve their differing goals based upon the proportion of equity each partner holds. When strategic alliance partners' interests coincide or are complementary, ownership will not be an important factor in exercising influence over the strategic alliance.

Summary

This chapter indicates that macro corporate governance at the national level includes factor conditions for the legal constitution, demand conditions for market competition, related supporting industries and strategy, structure and rivalry to market entry and exit rules. By placing emphasis on micro corporate governance at the organizational level, this analysis has employed the three theoretical explanations of agency theory, transactional cost economics and bargaining power theory to give insights into the processes of 'corporate governance' in a strategic alliance. Building blocks for corporate governance analysis should distinguish between macro corporate governance at the national level and micro corporate governance at the organizational level since they both influence management tradition in China.

5
Research Undertaken into Foreign Investment and Corporate Governance

Introduction

This chapter describes research undertaken into the relationship between foreign investment and corporate governance, a subject that has attracted significant attention from academics and business practitioners in international business studies. The methodological issues in the specific context of the foreign investments and corporate governance are outlined. In particular, a range of different research areas will be used to present a key framework for conceptualizing foreign investments and corporate governance in international strategic alliances. This chapter also provides an overview of the research design and methodology that was employed for the author's analysis. The key stages in developing the research methodology for this study are: construction of research models, construction of measures, design of a sample, choices of fieldwork methods, gathering the data, coding and analysis of the data and, finally, the drawing of conclusions.

The formation model

The 'formation model' assumes that partner firms' objectives for an international strategic alliance influence the preferred equity level contributed by the partner firms in China. It is recognized that a wide variety of strategic objectives are likely to be present at the initiation of an international strategic alliance. The ownership resources contributed by each partner firm are likely to vary widely. An examination of the effects of the inter-relationships between partner firms' strategic objectives and the ownership resources that they commit to an international strategic alliance is important because these relationships may explain organizational behaviours which cannot be captured by conventional project analysis. Strategic objectives can be defined as the partner firms' motivation to fulfil certain objectives at the organizational level for the purpose of achieving overall maximization of organizational efficiency. A justification for the objectives set when forming a strategic alliance can be underpinned by two main theories of strategic management theory: the theory of strategic positioning and the theory of institutional economics for the minimization of transaction costs.

The formation model is used to examine the extent to which a firm's long-term objectives are reflected by their range of ownership investments in a strategic alliance. Justifications for the use of the strategic alliance vehicle stem from theories of how the strategic behaviour of each partner influences the competitive positioning of the strategic alliance. A business strategy approach forces the focus of attention towards market competition and corporate development needs. Mariti and Smiley (1983), in an empirical study, identify multiple core objectives that are used to justify the formation of an international strategic alliance. Porter and Fuller (1986) stress the strategic benefits to be gained from an international strategic alliance in the context of the globalization of industries. Contractor and Lorange (1988), in addressing the conditions necessary to enter into a co-operative relationship, take the viewpoint of one partner and examine the contribution it makes to a given strategic alliance's strategy.

Strategic management theory focuses on the strategic alliance as an additional means to realize opportunities in the global business environment. It considers the choice of a strategic alliance's ownership structure in relation to perceived opportunities available for partner firms' resources, knowledge and competencies, as well as the desired integration of strategic alliance operations with its partner firms. Strategic management theory advocates that partner firms' resource commitments when forming a strategic alliance will be influenced by their 'ownership advantages' in relation to global and local sector conditions. The strategic positioning approach leads to appreciation of the fact that partner firms may be driven by strategic objectives. Kogut (1988) summarizes the strategic management approach as focusing on competitive positioning and the impact of such market positioning on profitability. The main arguments of transaction cost economics are driven by cost-minimization considerations. Institutional economics postulates that the greater range of choices available to partner firms in such an alliance allows firms more flexibility than other modes of co-operation. The mapping of an overall theoretical perspective on to a firm's actual objectives is not straightforward as the theoretical approaches hardly ever map directly on to a firm's strategic objectives.

The ownership investment model

The 'ownership' model identifies the extent to which strategic alliance partners bring distinctive resources, knowledge and competencies to the partnership, and explores how the provision of these resources enable the strategic alliance partner to exercise control. The range of a partner firm's ownership resources made available to the alliance influences the alliance's control over strategic topics and operational matters. It is likely that a partner firm will possess the necessary financial resources to enable it to consider full ownership of its operations (Ting 1988) so that when the owning firm possesses the necessary technology, capital and managerial skills, taking a majority equity stake may be more efficient. A firm entering a product area which is new to it using a strategic alliance vehicle may find that the necessary product-specific capability such as technology, manufacturing know-how and distribution, and so on can be dominated by its partner firms. Under such conditions, a firm will be more likely to have a minority equity share in the strategic alliance.

The 'ownership' model considers the implications of the partner firms' ownership resources being combined in a strategic alliance to achieve a superior performance. Ownership configurations in an international strategic alliance can be factored into equity, contractual and non-contractual investments with the idea of pooling partner ownership of resources of technology, expertise and other critical assets. The actualization of ownership resources to the on-going process of a strategic alliance management has received significant attention recently from more international business studies journals. The ownership resources which provide those benefits expected to accrue to the participating partner firms are continually adjusted to align with shifts in relative power and control between the partners. Equity and contractual resources approximate to the 'task-related' complementarities identified by Geringer (1991), while non-contractual resources are likely to include 'partner-related' complementarities and competencies as well as some task-related competencies.

The utility of this two-fold distinction becomes apparent when considering the contribution of each ownership component in achieving superior performance within an international strategic alliance. Ownership resources may have a contractual basis and contractual ownership in business takes two forms: equity and formalized rights to exclude control over and/or benefit from assets including technology. Examples of technology ownership include patents, intellectual property rights and contractual acknowledgement of proprietary technology. Pierce, Rubenfeld and Morgan (1991) state that the strength of this commitment should be positively associated with each of the design features of the formal ownership system. From a legal perspective, ownership and its implicit right to control creates responsibility. Critical resources committed by partner firms on a contractual basis may increase the probability of achieving a desired behaviour or outcome through the efficient utilization of its resources and effective implementation of strategies.

Ownership resources provided on a contractual basis appear to be important in the formation and operation of the international strategic alliance since the contract can limit obligation and responsibility in terms of realization of such resources. Contractual after-sales service provides a strategic mechanism whereby foreign partner firms can gain direct access to the local market. A contractual requirement for one party to provide management systems legitimizes their power and right to control local management development and technical training. These resource contributions are explicitly specified in the strategic alliance agreement's associated legal agreements. The non-contractual bases of a firm's ownership investments in business include technological know-how, 'soft' technology, managerial competencies, professional services and training. They also extend to the goodwill and cultural capital that may derive from the provision of such resources. Madhok (1995) reported how the trust-centred approach provides additional insights that enrich current understanding of a firm's ownership preferences and increase tolerance of the foibles of the other partner when forming an international strategic alliance. Non-contractual ownership resources in an international strategic alliance context demonstrate a commitment through the visible actions and values of key decision-makers to the continuation of the joint goals and values of the partnership.

The corporate governance model

The 'corporate governance' model employed by an international strategic alliance tends to be influenced by the board of directors and the senior management team of the strategic alliance. The equity position held by a partner firm appears to be important as it determines the mix of skills, resources, operating policies, procedures and overall competitive viability of a strategic alliance. The greater the share of equity held by a parent firm, the greater will be its overall hold over corporate governance in a strategic alliance. Schaan (1983, 1988) finds that nominations of members of a joint venture's board of directors and appointment of the general manager are important control mechanisms. Yan and Gray (1994a) find in a sample of Sino–US joint ventures that the general manager has always been a board member and serves as the executive officer of the joint venture. The general manager makes all the important operating decisions for the joint venture. They find that the ownership split is consistent only with the dimension of control of board membership and no consistent relationship is observed with other dimensions. Their findings provide additional evidence that equity structure is not equivalent to management control but rather, as a type of resource committed by the partners, equity investment constitutes a primary source of bargaining power which in turn contributes to management control. Once the equity structure is agreed on, it delineates the relative positions of the partners and sets a solid underpinning for the successive foundation of control.

Yan and Gray (1994b) suggest that equity structure is not equivalent to management control although many researchers have suggested that equity carries with it a legal right to influence strategic decision-taking within a strategic alliance. They note that a majority equity share generally provides a number of formal means which facilitate an owning firm's participation in the day-to-day management of the operation of the alliance. Geringer (1991) indicates that the ownership resources committed by partner firms can be both tangible and intangible in nature. Valuation of a firm's non-capital investment as an equity share can easily lead to a dispute among partner firms, particularly if one side intends to undermine the exclusivity of the 'proprietary technology' that leads to the other partner having a greater equity share. Technologies as equity investments in an international strategic alliance are strongly associated with values, core competencies and value-creating disciplines which are precisely the kinds of firm-specific assets that are needed if it is to prosper.

The board of directors of a strategic alliance is likely to exercise overall control. There is normally a correspondence between membership of the board and the percentage of equity share-holding, although the chairman of the board and the appointment of the general manager and senior management team are not necessarily dependent on distribution of equity share. In the context of managing a strategic alliance's operations, a board of directors serves many specific purposes in deciding its long-term strategic vision, profit allocation and re-investment policy. The board of directors may also provide certain strategic indicators to the partner firms which can lead to revisions in their control policies. A partner firm may be able to influence the relative allocation of control over a strategic alliance by influencing staffing control of the strategic alliance's top management positions.

The corporate culture model

The 'corporate culture' model postulates that the more consistent is the configuration of a firm's ownership and management control, the better the corporate culture that will be established in the firm. In other words, the performance of a strategic alliance is seen to be an outcome of the 'corporate culture'. Corporate culture can be attributed to the market positioning of the strategic alliance and is very much involved with the local environment within which the strategic alliance operates. Prior study suggests that strategic alliance partners with distinctive corporate cultures that they then implement in different operational areas may experience significant difficulties in implementing potential complementarities due to business integration and national culture differences. It is generally believed that a strategic alliance's success, or the extent to which partner firms' expectations for the strategic alliance are met, is a function of the 'corporate culture'. The three success variables are: the parent's criteria for success, the activities or decisions it controls, and the organizational principles that are established and utilized. Strategic alliances achieved with a high level of shared 'corporate culture' will enjoy better performance.

Janger (1980) suggests that strategic alliance success will be enhanced when the corporate culture fits its partner firms' management style. The corporate culture perspective assumes that it is possible to identify certain cultural factors such as organizational principles, social norms and business beliefs that will determine in combination the level of a firm's performance. Deficiencies in these dependent factors are likely to stimulate the strategic alliance partners to make adjustments in their management culture. Deficiencies in corporate culture are measured by the gaps between what the market desires and what is currently established as a corporate culture in a strategic alliance. Corporate culture problems can be based on the fact that both local and foreign partners in a strategic alliance may have different conceptual frames of reference emanating from their different cultural backgrounds.

The organizational learning model

Accepting and learning foreign business practices, and experience in a strategic alliance by local managers, can reduce the totality of the cost of doing business in a host country. The concept of first-order learning can challenge status quo thinking in the strategic alliance's management or change the basic way in which co-operation between partners evolves. Second-order learning contains ideas for increasing productivity by changing the way in which departments or functions perform their tasks and/or by redesigning a product or manufacturing process. Under a traditional behavioural approach to organizational learning in a strategic alliance, second-order learning requires radical changes in existing organizational structures at the business level. Under the third-order learning perspective, cognitive values are represented by designing overall organizational change of a strategic alliance and its interactions with the external market at a strategic level. The three primary models for the technical, system and strategic learning identified explore the concept of whether a strategic alliance's investment and its corporate governance will operate at an improved level if they are anchored in organizational learning. The potential role of organizational learning in a strategic alliance is perceived as using strategic resources appropriately to achieve effective management.

Research measure construction

Yin (1994) suggests three conditions for choosing a research strategy: the type of research questions, the control an investigator has over actual behavioural events, and the focus on contemporary versus historical phenomena. This research can, to a large extent, be identified as an interview and a 'survey' type of study where the writer chooses to use interviews in the research. The advantages of interviews include the generally higher response rate, flexibility, an improved chance of assessing the validity of responses, the ability to observe verbal behaviour, control over the investigative environment and control over question order, as well as the ability to explore by follow-up probing and so forth. Among the disadvantages of interviews are travel cost, time consumed and interview bias. For this reason, the interviewer also needs to improve the validity of recorded information through the use of tandem interviewing (two interviewers). This type of study is normally conducted as part of a wider team project.

The advantages of undertaking research in an interview and a survey mode are that the data are collected at a single point in time; there is a fixed set of checklists; and responses are systematically classified in such a way that quantitative comparisons can be tested. An interview approach involves the construction of a relatively comprehensive view from a large number of cases. The methodologies used for interviews enable the use of standard statistical methods to justify results. There are pros and cons to the use of the interview method as the amount of data that can be collected is limited and the flexibility of using a variety of questioning techniques depends upon the interviewer. An interview strategy tends to favour describing the prevalence or frequency of a phenomenon. There are a number of inherent advantages including a substantial saving of time and money, greater assurance of anonymity, lack of interview bias, standardized wording and accessibility. This contrasts with a questionnaire survey where there is likely to be a low response rate, the information gathered will only concern reported behaviour, there is a lack of control over the research setting and the order in which questions are answered does not allow the researcher to repeat or clarify the question when necessary.

The research design and method of fieldwork used in the study is primarily based on the comparative interview. The study is undertaken using a relatively quantitative approach with a comparatively large sample. Interviews are chosen as the principal method for data collection since interviews allow for the development of a better understanding of an international strategic alliance. Interviews also provide an opportunity to identify cultural preconceptions that may not be possible with other methods. Interviews are of two types: initial in-depth interviews and follow-up interviews. The in-depth interviews serve as the data foundation for the study.

The interview is the most practical research method available to measure awareness. It allows the interviewer to delve much deeper into a topic, provides the opportunity to ask many long sequenced open-ended questions using screening questions and gives the ability to probe answers. This is particularly the case for topics such as the financial situation, strategies, organizational behaviour and politics, which are sensitive subjects in most strategic alliances in China. A face-to-face interview arouses initial interest and increases the rate of participation. It also enables the interviewer to ask complex questions that may require explanation or mechanical aids. Of course, the interview method allows the interviewer to clarify answers. It is usually preferred when a large amount of in-depth information is needed from respondents. Interviewers must be properly trained. It is essential to set aside resources and time to train those who do interviewing. The reliability and the validity of the results will be increased by minimizing the inconsistency relating to the interviewers' understanding of the questionnaire, their skills and their instructions. In-depth interviewing entails asking questions, listening to and recording the answers and then posing additional questions to clarify or expand on a particular issue. Questions are open-ended and respondents are encouraged to express their own perceptions in their own words. In-depth interviews are aimed at understanding the beneficiaries' view of the research, their terminology and judgements.

There are three basic approaches to in-depth interviewing that differ mainly in the extent to which the interview questions are determined and standardized beforehand: the informal conversational interview, the semi-structured interview and the standardized open-ended interview. Each research approach serves a different purpose and has different preparation and instrumentation requirements. First, the informal conversational interview relies primarily on the spontaneous generation of questions in the natural flow of an interaction. This type of interviewing is appropriate when the interviewer wants to maintain maximum flexibility to be able to pursue questioning in whatever direction appears to be appropriate. It depends on the information that emerges from observing a particular setting. The interviewer may talk to one or more individuals in that organizational setting. The strength of this approach is that the interviewer is flexible and highly responsive to individual differences, situational changes and emerging new information.

Second, semi-structured interviews involve the preparation of an interview checklist that contains a pre-determined set of questions or issues to be explored during an interview. This guide serves as a questionnaire during the interview and ensures basically that the same information is obtained from a number of people. The order and the actual working of the questions are not determined in advance. The advantage of adopting a semi-structured interview is that it makes interviewing a number of different people more systematic and comprehensive by limiting the issues to be taken up in the interview.

Finally, the open-ended interview consists of a set of open-ended questions carefully worded and arranged in advance. The interviewer asks the same questions with each respondent, using essentially the same words and in the same sequence. This type of interview may be particularly appropriate when there are several interviewers and the researcher wants to minimize the variation in the questions they pose. It is also useful when it is desirable to have the same information from each interviewee at several points in time or when there are time constraints for data collection and analysis. Standardized open-ended interviews allow the interviewer to collect detailed data systematically and facilitate comparability among all respondents.

Experience indicates that the semi-structured interview is the most effective way to conduct research in the Chinese international strategic alliance environment. The key concepts of formation, ownership, governance, corporate culture and organizational learning can be defined and operationalized. It is possible to apply such concepts across a research framework of foreign investments and corporate governance. There is evidence of the likelihood of resistance by managers to intensive studies as these take up a lot of their individual time. The semi-structured interview is carried out within a comparative design and involves a structured checklist. Some of the questions on the checklist are closed and lend themselves readily to a quantitative analysis, while others are open-ended and more 'exploratory' in nature (Yin 1994). Personal visits to each research site provide further insights of a qualitative nature and are believed to be extremely useful in assisting with the interpretation of results.

Primary data-gathering for the research described in this book was undertaken in China in late 2000. Follow-up interviews were conducted on subsequent trips to China over the following two years. These interviews allowed clarification of unclear issues that emerged during data analysis, and also allowed the researchers to investigate issues that were not originally included, but which became important during data collection and data analysis. Follow-up interviews allowed the researcher to determine if the attitudes and organizational behaviours of these strategic alliances are changing over time.

Pilot study

International strategic alliances (including equity joint ventures and co-operative ventures) were chosen to test the appropriateness of the topics of exploring foreign investments and corporate governance which one developed in this study. A basic checklist was constructed to gain insight into strategic alliance management. The resulting notes were examined and analysed for relevant insights in relation to the building of a research framework. These were based upon the data collected and, as a consequence, led to a redefinition of subject areas to make them more applicable to the business reality of an international strategic alliance in China. The pilot studies indicated that if the writer could conduct a sufficient number of strategic alliance interviews, then data relevant to the research framework on foreign investment and corporate governance could be obtained using a quantitative method supplemented by qualitative insights. As the primary study involved data collection in China, five pilot studies were conducted in which responses to the organizational items were solicited from managers in international strategic alliances.

Interview procedure

Observational fieldwork and interviewing have been supplemented by the gathering and analysis of documentary material generated by the research projects on subjects such as regulations, contracts, correspondence, memoranda and routine records on samples. These kinds of company documents are a useful source of information from which to understand each international strategic alliance's business activities and its development processes in China. In addition, these documents provide valuable information that may not be accessible by other means. A major advantage of the access to a firm's documentation is the information that is generated contemporaneously with the events they refer to. Hence, a firm's introduction brochure is less likely to be subject to information distortion in comparison with data obtained only from an interview.

Published company brochures are also consulted. Economic data of a secondary nature is collected from local commercial bureaus and libraries. This is used to identify the context for the research. Particular attention is paid to relevant regulations and provisions on international strategic alliances. Some secondary data is also collected from the *China Statistical Year Book*, the Ministry of Foreign Economic Relations and Trade, the *Foreign Investment Journal*, the *People's Daily*, the *Economic Daily* and the *Beijing Review*. To identify those strategic alliances within the population chosen, a list of strategic alliances within the chosen sectors was generated by reference to telephone directories, newspapers, journals, the 40,000 International Joint Ventures Directory published by the Chinese Ministry of Foreign Economic Relations and Trade, and publications from chambers of commerce, embassies and government departments in China.

An international strategic alliance in China that operates in a specific industrial sector may have some special features. Each interview requires adaptation of the methodology to the needs and environment of each manager working in a strategic alliance, as there are significant differences in the regional or industrial context of these strategic alliances in China. It was important to identify research locations or industrial sectors in which strategic alliances are most prevalent, although managers in most strategic alliances located in the north and south of China did not react differently in terms of access and interview. With regard to access, an approach to local managers is commonly facilitated by their management styles. Most local managers tend to answer the telephone themselves instead of using a secretary, so the easiest way to get access is by telephoning local managers directly. Foreign managers prefer to be approached on a more formal basis and generally take a more rigid view of the time they will put aside for an interview.

Confidentiality is a particularly sensitive issue in most strategic alliances in China. Difficulties concerning data access in the research project arise mainly in performance areas in terms of operational records providing statistics on strategic alliance performance and the perceptions that local and foreign managers hold of one another. Information on the strategic alliances' operational performance record is not easy to obtain. Senior managers in a strategic alliance tend to feel that the release of confidential information might put them at a competitive disadvantage. Their willingness to assess strategic alliance performance along scales and to articulate perceptions of the managers in the strategic alliance can be influenced by how open and assured their personalities are. A few respondents felt that the information would be used against them and thought that this part of the interview was not legitimate. Personal visits to each strategic alliance are necessary in order to obtain valid information on variables which are otherwise difficult to assess, such as strategies, ownership and control. Mandarin Chinese is the language of interviews with local respondents, while English is generally used with foreign respondents.

Relatively factual information on strategic alliance formation and ownership provision was obtained from interviews with strategic alliance general managers, deputy general managers and functional heads. Information on each issue was checked with at least two respondents. Partner firm objectives for each international strategic alliance and their attainments were assessed separately by most of the senior local and foreign managers interviewed. Although interviews were not conducted with managers located in the partner firms, all of the respondents who assessed partners' strategic objectives were seconded by the relevant partner firms. All the Chinese respondents for partner firm objectives have been with the strategic alliances from the start of operations, as have 15 per cent of the expatriate managers. Their secondment from the partner firms, plus regular involvement in reporting and communication with the partner, is deemed to provide a reasonable basis for them to assess partner firm objectives. Interviews were normally conducted either with a colleague from the local consulting firm, People's Republic China, or from the City University of Hong Kong.

The interview started with a fifteen-minute brief on the research and gives a three-page introductory statement about the project together with a one-page covering letter that touched on concerns about anonymity. The letter, written in two versions (English and Chinese), was prepared and authorized by the City University of Hong Kong. More sensitive questions were asked at the end of the interview after all other questions had been answered and rapport had been built up. Most senior local managers tend to be less cautious about the strategic alliance's performance data than their foreign partners. In some cases, the interviewer became aware that some managers preferred to focus on a particular market-related topic such as procurement, investment decisions, product pricing or marketing. A positive attitude was encouraged towards the interview by indicating the benefits of previous international strategic alliance research, in addition to the feedback report that the participating firms will receive.

The difference between local and foreign managers may have an effect on the quality of the data received. In order to be able to present an overall perspective for each strategic alliance, the subject matter concerning the relative influence of partners is in many cases reported separately by local and foreign managers in each firm. This permits a check to be made for national bias. This research on the subjects of 'foreign investment and corporate governance' is perceived as a 'hot topic' in China. Some interviewees know what an investigator wants to hear as they have had dealings with different investigators at various times. There is thus a risk of bias, because respondents are likely to say what they think the interviewers want to hear rather than provide their own opinions, and therefore it is always important to try to double-check information with other interviewees. There was no experience of respondents who said they could not answer because the question was too general and vague, or because they had never thought about the topic.

Specific probing questions were asked to guide the answers, as some respondents were afraid that their replies would reveal their lack of knowledge about their firms. In such situations, it was important to emphasize that there were no right and wrong answers to the particular questions. Monitoring the respondent's commitment through the interview was sometimes difficult to manage. Some respondents suggested that their time was too valuable to waste on the study or that the study was not applicable to them. It was found to be important to emphasize the number of cases that had been completed and the potential importance of improving understanding about the management of an international strategic alliance in China. To gain an insight into the mutual perceptions of local and foreign managers, some open-ended questions were asked that often contributed to an overrun of the interview beyond the previously-agreed length.

With this possibility in mind, open-ended questions were asked in the last section of the interview. Given the scope of the questions on objectives, ownership, corporate governance, corporate culture and organizational learning, interpretation of the subjects by different managers tended to vary depending upon their management positions. Several respondents from one strategic alliance were therefore interviewed, as this was likely to strengthen the validity of the information provided. It was also important to get both the local and foreign perspective, especially on foreign investment and corporate governance.

Sampling

The strategic alliances in the sample vary in term of their size. Most international strategic alliances considered were set up after 1990. A population of interest was first defined and then the criteria for selection required that the international strategic alliance had had a minimum of three years' operation and that at least one expatriate manager should be working in the strategic alliance. Strategic alliances that appeared to meet the criteria were approached to seek some details that would ascertain their suitability for inclusion in the sample, but some proved impossible to contact either because they had been taken over and restructured or had gone out of business altogether. In addition, some strategic alliances had moved location and could not be traced. In some cases, although the Chinese parent firm could be contacted, there was no longer anyone in employment with sufficient knowledge to provide the depth of answers that the study required.

Some strategic alliances established as equity joint ventures or co-operative ventures did not have real foreign parties involved at all. Some foreign firms have established several international strategic alliances located in China, often with different local partners. In exploring the sampling frame, it was important to avoid the replication of foreign firms. The most effective way of reaching the target of 980 international strategic alliances spread over locations across China was to contact the strategic alliances directly. To increase the rate of success of access, it proved helpful to have some background knowledge of the strategic alliance before making the initial approach. Gaining access to the expatriate managers required telephoning him or her in English and then agreeing to send an information sheet on the study, together with a covering letter.

Choices of industrial sectors

Most firms chosen were located in the advanced electronics, fast moving consumer industries and manufacturing sectors. The relevant industries in this study include electronics, telecommunications, garments, fibre products, food processing, beverages, leather, plastic products, chemical products, medical equipment, pharmaceuticals, electric equipment, machinery and hotels. The choice of these sectors takes into account the following considerations.

The pattern of strategic alliance investment in China is influenced by the local economic and political climate. Chinese policy has shifted from emphasizing heavy industry to the development of hi-tech industries in the electronic and electric sectors, as well as service industries such as the hotel sector. The choice of these sectors reflected the emphasis of government policy and these sectors contained large populations of foreign firms operating in China. This ensured a reasonable population from which to select the sample. The contrasting primary business needs of the sectors were expected to generate different ownership configuration patterns and control priorities: for example, technology transfer and its management in the hi-tech sectors are a key factor, with product design being a focus of technological competence in the advanced electronic sector. The choice was more likely to show distinctive characteristics derived from the foreign investment and the local business environments.

The dispersion of the sample across sectors, foreign parent nationality and regional location in China tested the extent to which general conclusions could be drawn about the findings from the sample taken as a whole. Although the sample was not constructed with the intention of building in a systematic local regional variation within China, it happens that the sample was located in three main areas of Chinese industrial development: Beijing–Tianjin, Shanghai–Hangzhou, and Guangzhou–Shenzhen. These are open cities or special economic zones, where the great majority of foreign firms are to be found. The employment in each firm ranged between 20 and 4,107 people, with an average of 480. Given the size and historical internal differentiation of

China, regional location may be expected to impact on strategic alliance management. The areas visited are believed to have a strong industrial development base as they were the first to be opened to the outside world after the implementation of the 'open door policy'.

Most major foreign investment strategies (including the encouragement of the manufacture of competitive products and the adoption of Western managerial practices) were introduced and established in these regions to spur local economic growth, and these regions have been subjected to foreign technology and management practices longer than most other areas of China. The major countries of origin of foreign firms investing in strategic alliances include the USA, Japan, Germany, France, the UK, Italy, Australia, Canada, Singapore, Taiwan, Hong Kong and South Korea. The subject of foreign investment and corporate governance in a strategic alliance made it possible to find extraneous variations in multiple industries and locations. The industries identified in this study have had to face greater technological changes and competitive market pressures because of substantial foreign investment and market competition, and have generated a rich pool of multiple sector information for comparative examination.

Data collection

The questionnaire survey gathered both quantitative and qualitative data and the interviews gathered qualitative data. A questionnaire survey was produced in both Chinese and English. The Chinese version was used with the local general manager or deputy general manager of the strategic alliance and the English version for the foreign deputy managers or general manager of the strategic alliance. Information was gathered from both local and foreign senior managers of the international strategic alliance. Data was collected in Chinese and English. To make sure of compatibility between the two versions, a Chinese–English bilingual translator translated the original English instrument into Chinese and two more bilingual translators translated it back. Discrepancies between language versions were then corrected and back-translated once again.

A total of 4,500 surveys were separately sent out in five waves and the extrapolation method was used to check for response bias arising from the fact that only respondents who were interested in the topic of a survey would respond. Of the 3,000 returned, around 820 surveys were excluded due to incomplete responses or sampling error and this yielded a final sample of 2,180 interviews. The relatively high response may be due to the fact that the designated respondents were the strategic alliance managers and that senior government institutes in China supported the surveys. During the data collection process, a total of 2,180 managers were interviewed, 1,500 from the manufacturing sector and 680 from the service sector. In terms of size distribution, 43 per cent of responding firms had fewer than 100 employees, 42 per cent had fewer than 300 employees and the rest of 15 per cent had more than 300 employees. The final questionnaire was bilingual and had three sections. The first section was fully structured, using rating scales in order to provide numerical data on all of the key variables, including performance assessments. The target interviewee in each firm was the senior manager responsible for the business in China. The response was generally good in the sense that most firms contacted expressed a willingness to co-operate, but pressure of work and frequent travel to China meant that in a substantial number of cases arranging an actual interview proved impossible within the time frame.

The senior managers from each side were interviewed, together with the heads of two or three functions: typically operations, human resources management (HRM) and technology or marketing depending on the sector. Interviews with general managers and deputy general managers were normally expected to last two hours or more, while those with other managers usually took one hour to one and half hours. The interviews were conducted with local and foreign managers separately. Both quantitative and qualitative data were collected. Results reported in this book are primarily quantitative in nature. In collecting them, interviewees were either asked directly for figures, to be verified where necessary from documents (such as percentage shares of equity held by partner firms) or they were asked to complete perceptual scales for which pre-printed cards were used to assist the process. Following the interviews, all data were transcribed on to separate schedules from the original notes and tapes. The full checklists used in the research comprised five pages of questions and covered the interviewee's details in terms of position, contact address, length of interview and previous working experience.

The checklist as a whole was divided into five parts. The first part was used to establish the strategic objectives of a strategic alliance. This included how the local and the foreign partners were brought together and their previous international business experience. The second part was to record specific ownership resources supplied from partner firms to a strategic alliance. The third part was designed to create an understanding of the parameters of corporate governance. The fourth part was concerned with the corporate culture in an international strategic alliance. The final part was to examine a strategic alliance's organizational learning. It was important to manage the interviews to ensure that all the questions were answered in the time allocated for the interview. Obviously, the time allocated also varied depending on senior managers' situation on the day, but in a fall-back situation it was essential to make sure all the questions were covered within the agreed time-frame.

Whenever acceptable, the interviews were tape-recorded and about 20 per cent of interviews were recorded. Those conducted in Chinese were fully translated and all interviews were subsequently transcribed on to schedules. It was beneficial to record interviews, but this was particularly necessary when the interviews were conducted in English. The prospect of tape recording seemed to horrify some ethnic Chinese managers. They did not like to have their voice recorded in case they subsequently had to take personal responsibility for what they said. It was very important to write full notes as soon as the interviewee left the office. Impressions were recorded of what the interviewees had said before the details had left the interviewer's memory. The presence of a second interviewer was extremely helpful in cases where only hand-written notes could be taken and where recall of further detail after the interview was required. Telephone contact with a strategic alliance revealed a preference for making arrangements at short notice. Confirmation of interviews was not necessary and it could sometimes give the firms an opportunity to cancel the appointment. Generally speaking, faxes and telephones from Hong Kong to most strategic alliances in China were helpful, as international communication carried some weight in indicating the importance of the interviews.

Coding

Some existing scales for measuring the research framework were modified and others were newly constructed. The measures used were not bound to a 'Western approach' and they were modified to suit a strategic alliance in China as much as possible. The pilot studies were of considerable assistance in this respect. A preliminary version of the checklist was reviewed by a small group of colleagues after the pilot study, who are experts in the understanding of international strategic alliances. Figure 5.1 investigates key factors for the success at the strategic alliance formation and compares perceptions of local and foreign managers from a strategic alliance based on foreign investments and corporate governance.

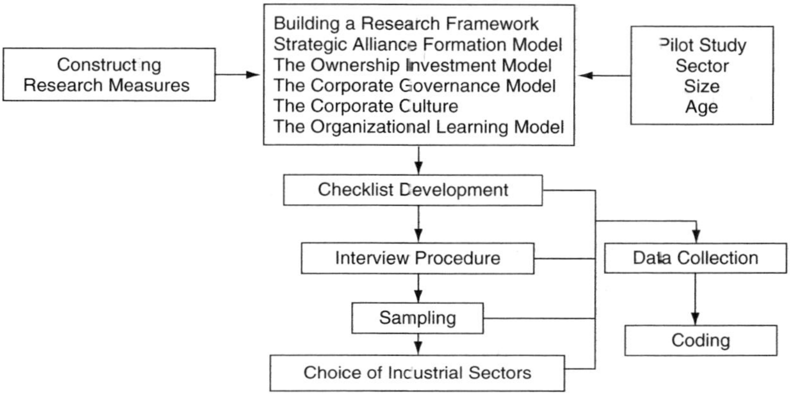

Figure 5.1 Research undertaken for foreign investment and corporate governance

Strategic alliance formation

The financial and strategic objective priorities of both local and foreign firms were chosen and then the top five were order ranked from longer lists. After collecting descriptive information about the history of the firm, each respondent was asked a number of closed questions on strategic objectives for forming an international strategic alliance formation. The questions were related to obtaining adequate information about potential partners, selecting a suitable partner, and identifying a partner's objectives.

Ownership resources

Ownership resources that partner firms have provided to the international strategic alliance on a non-contractual basis were recorded covering the same items as contractual resources. Ownership included the percentage of strategic alliance equity held by each partner firm as well as the ownership resources which the partner firms provided to the international strategic alliance valued as equity share, or provided on a contractual and non-contractual basis. Composite measures were constructed for contractual resources, based on the binary scores that indicated their provision or not by either the local or foreign partner firms. The provision of non-capital resources by the local and foreign parents was assessed through ten binary indicators with reference to product design, production technology, management systems, management services and training, provided respectively on a contractual or non-contractual basis.

Corporate governance

The data reported were the answers given by the most senior manager in each international strategic alliance. The *Board ratio* was the ratio of directors appointed by the foreign partner firm(s) to those appointed by the local partner firm(s). The percentage of local and foreign directors of the board in each strategic alliance was calculated for each strategic alliance's management structure and its board of directors. Respondents from both sides also indicated their perceptions of the degree of local and foreign influence in the areas of strategic alliance management.

Corporate culture

Identification of levels of corporate culture established in each strategic alliance provided an understanding of the potential symbolic meanings of a strategic alliance's corporate culture. Conducting culture-based analyses in this study indicated heterogeneity in international management practices, cultural practices and management values in a strategic alliance.

Organizational learning

This study has investigated factors within the strategic alliance that encourage organizational learning activities. A strategic alliance in China is more likely to engage in learning activities integral to the development of partners' knowledge and competence. The conditions for building partnering competence are found in the strategic alliance's organizational system in the form of learning intent, receptivity and transparency.

Summary

This chapter provides an indication of the research subjects identified by foreign investments and corporate governance. For the data collection, the local and foreign managers of a strategic alliance were located and interviewed. This chapter provides an overview of the research design and the methodology employed. Although the process of conducting business research in an international strategic alliance is often difficult, it can be very illuminating in terms of exploring an area of investigation that is at an early stage of development. This chapter presents a classification of the research methods and provides general guidelines for the application of the methods as well as a structured approach to the formulation, estimation and interpretation of the research result. Most of the data on foreign investments and corporate governance was secured from 980 international strategic alliances. This chapter illustrates application of the various research techniques by a discussion of the data collection methods utilized.

Part III

Managing an International Strategic Alliance

6

Forming an International Strategic Alliance

Introduction

International strategic alliances are used as effective vehicles to enter a host country's market when the host government places some restrictions on other forms of market entry. This chapter assumes that forming an international strategic alliance in China is normally associated with bringing together different combinations of participating firms' resources, knowledge and capabilities. Foreign firms may provide resources regarding advanced technology, management and financial capital, while the local partner may provide resources regarding the host country's markets, infrastructure and political framework. By pooling these resources, it is possible to increase their long-term business presence *vis-à-vis* competitors. An international strategic alliance's resources, knowledge and capabilities exchange will rely on all participating firms' management being involved to achieve strategic, cultural and operational fit in the operation of the strategic alliance. Three associated theories are perceived to provide primary insights into a partner firm's endowments of ownership investments: they are resource-based theory, resource dependence theory and ownership, localization and internalization theory.

Ownership determinants: resource-based theory

The resource-based view of firms argues that determinants of a firm's ownership resources will contain certain distinctive market characteristics. A firm's ownership resources that are scarce, valuable and difficult to imitate or substitute are critical to its competitive advantage. These ownership assets may be tangible resources such as patents, licences, brand names, or intangible capabilities such as technological skills or managerial expertise. The resource-based view of a firm offers an insight into the types of resource available such as capital, products and services that support performance. Leveraging ownership resources for application to new markets represents one of the key reasons for a firm to pursue any type of international strategy for its business expansion. Ownership resources provide a means by which a partner firm can make a distinctive resource contribution to the competitive advantage of an international strategic alliance. Although the resource-based view of the firm has contributed substantially to understanding the devices that maintain and enhance its competitive advantage, the underlying conceptual framework allows a more comprehensive interpretation of heterogeneity in a firm's ownership determinants, resources, organizational behaviour and outcomes.

The resource-based view provides insights into a firm's ownership determinants together with the deployment of these ownership resources to take advantage of market opportunities. A firm's ownership resources, knowledge and capabilities are commonly thought of as a technological system, including product designs, materials, operating systems, labour inputs and maintenance procedures. The advantages accruing from employing proprietary technologies allow a firm to provide certain types of technology and these in turn provide the leverage for the acquisition of rights based on the product or service usages. When a firm has appropriately provisioned its proprietary technologies, it needs to register them with the local government as this should safeguard the firm from the abuse of its intellectual property rights. A firm's new product developments or services tend to be strongly associated with the proprietary technologies it possesses and these are usually related to its core business.

The resource-based view of a firm considers which differential endowments of ownership are important determinants of its economic performance. These differential endowments not only produce innovative solutions to problems but also facilitate new products (Ciborra 1991). The effects of a firm's ownership investments are perceived as an integral part of its long-term success in achieving high levels of competitiveness. The resource-based view of the firm focuses on differences in performance that are based on a complex bundle of a firm's resources, knowledge and capabilities. The efficiency of a firm's ownership investments mainly depends on this bundle of knowledge. It can be reasoned that a firm which is able to establish the necessary resources and competence is more effective in achieving its strategic objectives.

Ciborra (1991) suggests that a firm's resource-based advantages must encompass a complex bundle of resources, knowledge and capabilities, many of which are embodied in a wide range of different artefacts, people, product specifications, component properties, operating procedures and organizational arrangements. In theory, when product know-how and marketing are highly integrated, an improvement in a firm's ownership investments is believed to generate competitive advantages that are expected to enhance the firm's strategic development. Thus it is theorized that those firms willing and able to develop their investments should perform better than others that are not.

Ownership leverage: resource dependence theory

Pfeffer and Salancik (1978) identify the command of critical resources as the basis for exercising power within and between organizations. Dependence on key ownership resources gives rise to control of the focus of the organization by the external resource providers. External control over an organization can arise from the power of external parties to command resources that are vital for the successful operation of the organization. Internal control over or access to resources gives some organizational members more control or power over the organization than others (Donaldson 1995). Resource dependence analysis concentrates on resource scarcity and as such provides answers to the basic question about why the resources provided by certain organizational members are more important than the resources provided by other members. The argument is that organizations are externally constrained and are not internally self-sufficient because they require resources from the environment. In consequence, organizations become inter-dependent with those elements of the environment with which they interact.

Pfeffer (1981) indicates that dependence is seen to be a function of the importance of what one actor gets from the other and an inverse function of the availability of this outcome or performance in other places. Harrigan (1985) suggests that an international strategic alliance can be a resource-aggregating and resource-sharing mechanism, which allows a partner firm to concentrate resources in those areas where it possesses the greatest respective strengths. Technology, management, distribution networks and other assets provided by the partner firms of an international strategic alliance can be used to cope with uncertainties and to build competitive positions because a strategic alliance can offer a means of leveraging synergy between the skills and resources of participating partner firms. Resource dependence analysis has been used to account for the linkage between resource provision and control within an international strategic alliance.

The resource dependence perspective implies that a partner which contributes a resource necessary for a strategic alliance's success, and which the other partner cannot provide, will gain power relative to the other partner and shift the balance of control and power over the strategic alliance. The resource dependence view leads to an expectation that the ability of a partner firm to exert control over a strategic alliance will be a function of the extent to which that strategic alliance depends on the partner for critical resources, knowledge and capability and whether it depends for the resources on that partner more than on the other.

Applying a resource dependence view, Lorange and Roos (1992) suggest that the vertical distribution of power within the parent managerial network will depend on the density of the strategic alliance's transactional and information network within its own organization set. Where this density provides the strategic alliance with the ability to secure resources independently from its parents, the hierarchical power of the parent firm will be restricted. Conversely, the greater the density of the network between the international strategic alliance and its partner firms, the more restricted will be the autonomy of the international strategic alliance and also the power of an individual partner firm. It is recognized in the resource dependence literature that there are important competitive advantages which may be derived from resource synergy such as that found in an international strategic alliance. An important advantage offered by a strategic alliance lies in the potential synergistic effects of combining the complementary assets of local and foreign partners. Foreign firms in China usually provide their specific knowledge of technology, management and capital. The local partner provides location-specific knowledge regarding the host country's market, infrastructure supplies and institutional matters.

Irreversible assets are those that are rare and difficult to imitate or substitute. Core resources, knowledge and capabilities are generally defined as the irreversible assets that a firm owns. Resource-based theory can be used to illustrate how partner firms can lever such assets to provide control in an international strategic alliance. Resource dependence theory provides a theoretical explanation for defining the relationship between a firm's ownership resource advantages and control priorities. The significance of controlling specific types of resources can be well illustrated by resource dependence theory. Resources acquired by a local partner firm from the market where its strategic alliance operates tend to be facilitated locally by the nature and type of resource requirements, market competition, technology standards and local operating infrastructure. Resource dependence requires a firm to adjust continuously to new markets, new organizational processes and management systems. A strategic alliance can build on possession of a partner firm's unique core knowledge and competence to achieve superior performance.

Ownership, localization and internalization theory

A comprehensive framework proposed by Dunning (1977) stipulated that the choice of a market entry mode is influenced by three types of factors: the concept of ownership-specific advantages (O) of firms is perceived to take explicit account of the costs and benefits derived from inter-firm relationships. The concept of locational advantages (L) of countries is perceived to give more weight to the factors of geographical areas, changing economic activities and influence of national and regional authorities. The concept holds that a firm can internalize (I) intermediate markets, allowing it to reduce the transaction costs of using such markets. The patterns of investment are determined by the configuration of these three sets of advantages as perceived by firms.

The OLI model has broadened understanding of the relationship between partner firms' investments and their corporate governance in two main respects. It identifies and evaluates the significance of the factors that influence both the initial act of ownership contribution by the partner firms and their respective resource leverage on the growth of such investments. The relevance of each factor in determining the ownership advantage of firms will vary according to the initial ownership contributions to a strategic alliance. It is in the best interests of participating firms that possess ownership-specific advantages to transfer them across national boundaries as this can provide them with advantages within an international strategic alliance.

The growth of ownership investment can be constrained by the attractiveness of a market as characterized by its market potential and investment risk. Buckley (1988) suggests that the assessment of internalization advantage is based on the relative costs or risks of sharing the assets and skills with a host country's firm versus integrating them within the firm. Three main kinds of market failure are identified by Dunning (1988:3) as:

> (1) those that arise from risk and uncertainty; (2) those that stem from the ability of firms to exploit the economics of large-scale production, but only in an imperfect market situation; (3) those that occur where the transaction of particular products or services yield costs and benefits external to that transaction.

Dunning and Rugman (1985) make a distinction between structural and transactional market imperfections. They define structural market imperfections as those arising from some kind of government intervention that encourages or discourages a particular investment, whereas transactional market imperfections are identified as country-specific and embedded in location factors.

The OLI analysis perspective on partner firms' investments and their corporate governance as applied to an international strategic alliance has received mixed support. Agarwal and Ramaswami (1992) provide broad support for the hypothesized effects of the interrelationships among ownership, localization and internalization advantages. The results of their study suggest that the long-term success of any foreign investment requires significant managerial and financial resources even in markets that do not have high risks. The contribution which OLI analysis can make lies in an understanding of how the three core theoretical factors of ownership, localization and internalization provide a link between the foreign and local partners. The partners' ownership advantages, derived from the initial investment and the growth of ownership investment, and constrained by market attractiveness, are particularly significant contributions to the modification of the relationship between ownership and control of a strategic alliance. Location-related resources may include distribution channels, local brands, political influence, human resource management skills, or any other capabilities that are idiosyncratic to a specific locality.

When a host country, where firms may not be allowed an equal chance to access the market, controls local resources an international strategic alliance may offer an effective means for a foreign firm to expand into a new market area. The capacity within a host country for local firms to supply resources to a strategic alliance is one of the basic reasons for the existence of any form of international strategy as without contributions of local resources a strategy of this type cannot be expected to offer advantages over foreign trade or bring about significant economic change. Traditional notions of comparative advantage may help to explain why foreign firms pursue a position in a given host country. The ability of a local firm to supply the necessary complementary resources may be critical if a foreign firm is to exploit the advantages of supplying its irreversible assets.

Forming an international strategic alliance facilitates various types of resource transfers from partner firms to the strategic alliance that may affect its performance. However, if resource dependence is limited to local partner firms only, ownership resources may represent an inefficient solution to the strategic alliance's needs and reduce its overall performance. Establishment of a strategic alliance's investments including resource commitments, management systems and decision making can be expected to exert a critical impact on its strategic presence *vis-à-vis* competitors in the foreign market. Successful formation of an international strategic alliance in China may enable the achievement of a synergistic benefit from the investment, because such investment is perceived by the host government as a way to obtain a good return from both the participating partners and associated supply network. The objective of forming a strategic alliance to dominate or share strategic control of the relevant parties may provide the opportunity to access a new supply chain in other parts of the world. Table 6.1 provides the summary on ownership advantages for strategic alliances.

Table 6.1 Ownership advantages for forming an international strategic alliance

Theories	Primary theoretical perspectives
Ownership determinants for resource-based theory	(1) The resource-based view of the firm argues that determinants of a firm's ownership resources may contain certain distinctive market characteristics. (2) The resource-based view considers that a firm's differential endowments of ownership are important determinants of its economic performance
Ownership leverage for resource dependence theory	(1) Dependence on key ownership resources gives rise to control of the organizational focus by external resource providers. (2) Resource dependence analysis concentrates on resource scarcity. It illustrates a basic question as to why the resources provided by certain organizational members are more important than the resources provided by other members.
Ownership, localization and internalization	(1) The concept of ownership-specific advantages of firms is perceived to take explicit account of the costs and benefits derived from inter-firm relationships. (2) The concept of locational advantages of countries is perceived to give more weight to the following factors: geographical areas, changing economic activities and the influence of national and regional authorities. (3) The idea that firms internalize intermediate markets, primarily to reduce the transaction costs of using them.

Developing a checklist for forming a strategic alliance

A foreign firm may experience significant problems in carrying out certain types of negotiation with local firms in an emerging business environment. These negotiations are strongly related to high switching costs once an international strategic alliance is formed as the foreign firm must necessarily have invested in an ability to manage its resources, knowledge and competence in a new way in order to fit into its new institutional environment. The investments and production of a strategic alliance between partners can be used as a 'platform' that will result in continued evolution of the goals of the partners, and these will overcome the cultural differences which invariably occur in an international strategic alliance. The success of negotiations to establish an international strategic alliance in China will primarily be reliant on the host country's environment and on the negotiating partners' ability to provide complimentary ownership resources that facilitate the quality exchange of these partner firms' investments. Once a foreign firm has committed to a particular market entry strategy, five items need to be determined before forming an international strategic alliance in China:

1 The objective of forming a strategic alliance in China and the scope of the investment project need to be identified. The scope defines the investment activities to be performed and the resources to be consumed as well as covering the investment baseline in terms of a new international strategic alliance's technical expertise, investment, schedule, financing cost and product design.
2 The legal form of the international strategic alliance must be established in a way that specifies the nature of the contracts and agreements between the negotiating parties. Reaching agreement between parties on the legal form of a strategic alliance will benefit its overall development.
3 The financial arrangements for forming an international strategic alliance in China will involve consideration of the level of each participating partner's ownership contributions, the sharing of profits, tax and accounting procedures.
4 The formation of an appropriate management structure and organization for the ownership investment of an international strategic alliance will specify the need for control and decision reporting procedures to inform each participating party of the status of the international strategic alliance and establish how the strategic alliance objectives will be met.

5 The expected life span of a strategic alliance will determine the length of the partners' relationship and set the conditions established by the partners to dissolve it.

Negotiations concerning the foreign firm's market entry should be 'co-operative' in nature rather than 'competitive', and the relevant parties should seek common ground that accommodates a win/win solution for each partner. If negotiations are characterized by hard bargaining, they are candidates for failure because the purpose of such negotiations is to benefit all participating parties. The formation of an international strategic alliance is based upon the view that the new international strategic alliance is not a zero-sum game but rather one in which there are synergistic solutions benefiting all participating parties. This includes business norms, underlying motivations, attitudes, expectations and assumptions. The negotiating culture must move all participating partners to positions where benefits to all parties are enhanced rather than resulting in an effort to maximize a partner's concessions. It must be recognized that this will be difficult for the local Chinese manager as the culture of negotiating in China is more likely to be a win/lose approach. The cultural background and the corresponding contractual resource environment, including the stage of local economic development, the levels of bureaucracy exercised by the relevant partners and local government policies, are believed to exert critical influences on participating partners' business norms.

On the whole, cultural complications encompass the interpretation of behaviour, language and target expectations from forming an international strategic alliance. When firms negotiate a strategic alliance project, relevant negotiating parties may commit to various exchanges of their resources, knowledge and expertise. These exchange activities lead to different decisions and consequences for the participating firms. This is especially true where the firms have differing levels of technology, cultures and economic systems. The objectives that each partner will set for the international strategic alliance will initially be based upon the knowledge and resources that each party possesses and the organizational system within which they normally operate. Over time, the resources will grow through various exchange activities facilitated by ownership, corporate governance and information exchange. The negotiation process has to establish a level of synergy between the competing objectives of all the participating parties.

The Chinese negotiation team will tend to seek a gradual solution and refine its strategic goals as the negotiations progress since most

Chinese negotiators believe their strategic goals and scope for establishing a strategic alliance's investment can be prepared in a deterministic way. The process of information exchange establishes what each firm's ownership inputs might be and increases the level of knowledge of all the parties about what is possible. Micro information exchange between participating parties relates to the particular details of the market entry, the management and operating structure, the technologies, expertise of the parties, the local legal framework and so on. The combination of these elements is unique to the parties involved in the negotiations, and thus building a picture of what resources might be available to a strategic alliance in China is different in each negotiation. There is a heavy burden placed on the negotiating teams to optimize resources and the objectives set for the strategic alliance. The cultural background of the relevant parties heavily influences the way that the information is exchanged. Experience indicates that for discussions about critical resources and knowledge, participating parties may have to meet face to face, although it is possible to exchange certain minor information details by telephone, fax and e-mail.

The outcome of an international strategic alliance may be very different from what would happen if each company were to set up a wholly-owned subsidiary. At the initial stage, each party strives to put the other in a position where what they offer is valued highly and what they need is ascribed a low value. The Chinese party needs technology and capital from foreign firms. The foreign firm wants to get into the Chinese market or to expand its business activity. Each side will try to obtain concessions from the other in order to further their own perceived strategic targets. This process of negotiation can last throughout the strategic alliance formation with positions sometimes reversed because of contextual changes (such as market shifts) or if significant changes in laws, rules and regulations occur. There are many objectives or hidden agendas held by the negotiating parties that are likely to appear entirely incompatible or unacceptable to the other. For example, the foreign partners may seek to impose their own technical norms on the whole industrial sector as this will help them to exploit their existing global distribution channels so that at the end of the joint venture term they can set up a wholly-owned subsidiary with the market knowledge they have gained from operating the joint venture. Such objectives would be unacceptable in principle to the local Chinese side. The negotiated outcome is usually a collective reflection that best meets the original objectives of the individual partner firms. Few Chinese managers wish to take responsibility alone for making a decision that may have important consequences for the international strategic alliance at its formation and will always need to refer any decisions back for consideration by all of the senior managers in the local company.

Strategic motives

A successful strategic alliance must be based on compatible strategic objectives. The ultimate objective for a firm is to maximize profits through improving its competitive position *vis-à-vis* its rivals. Foreign firms elect to form international strategic alliances in China in the hope that this will enable them to gain a competitive advantage. All partners should get to know each other and evaluate their common interests and objectives at strategic alliance formation as the extent of trust and understanding between partners can determine the degree of success of the venture. Experience has shown that successful international strategic alliances must have loyal, efficient and experienced local partners who are willing and able to deal with complex bureaucratic institutions. The local partner may be able to help resolve issues of labour, capital, raw materials and taxation experienced by the strategic alliance in an effective manner.

A key element of a strategic alliance partner's objectives is to achieve a good understanding of their partner's needs. Technology or resource transfer is often the major strategic motive for local Chinese firms to engage in an international strategic alliance. It is important to understand how both the local and the foreign partner benefit from technology transfer by asking 'why' and 'what' benefits the partner wants, and how much it is willing to forgo or contribute to the strategic alliance in China in order to get them. The local partner's strategic motives for forming an international strategic alliance (such as greater market coverage, more channels of distribution, and increased market share) must be assessed against worries as to whether a foreign partner can deliver on their expectations in those areas. An assessment of a partner's abilities may help a firm to anticipate their corresponding potential contributions and requirements. An evaluation of a partner's potential revenue, expense, profit and investment requirements will lead other partners to build a realistic view of their actual resource abilities to deliver on financial commitments. The sharing of technology and product know-how within the strategic alliance and the contribution of production process knowledge and other trade secrets are often required if the strategic alliance is going to compete effectively.

However, there are potential contributions from partner firms that relate to seconding experienced managers and technical experts to the strategic alliance. Partner firms' expectations and requirements play a crucial role in balancing costs and benefits associated with the various types of international strategic alliances established. Looking at Table 6.2, a ranking of partners' strategic motives suggests that most foreign partners' strategic motives for entering into the Chinese market are related to the reduction of production, labour and raw materials costs, including incentives from China's foreign investment programmes. Those raw materials available in the local Chinese market can either be used to meet production needs or be sold into third markets. Such activities will help foreign firms in their competitive position or simply in the reduction of competition from other firms operating in markets in the same geographical area. The relatively low operating costs in China involving labour, raw materials and other production inputs have attracted foreign firms from most industrial countries. The actual cost

Table 6.2 Ranking partners' strategic motives

Chinese manager	Ranking	Foreign manager	Ranking
Technology transfer	1	Create a strategic position	1
Benefit from tax incentives	2	Opportunity for good long-term profit	2
Obtain foreign cash investment	3	Attraction of the Chinese market	3
Help upgrade suppliers' technology	4	Establish strong business presence	4
Learning management expertise	5	Low labour cost	5
Develop export opportunities	6	Facilitate international expansion	6
Help expand in China market	7	Learning how to do business	7
Opportunity to train Chinese staff	8	Benefit from tax incentives	8
Establish strong business presence	9	Low cost sourcing	9
Assistant diversification of products	10	Opportunity for quick profit	10
Opportunity for good long-term profit	11	Advantageous transfer pricing	11
Ability to import superior components	12	Diversification of products	12
Gain a strategic position	13		
Import substitution	14		
Employment creation	15		

of labour in China is much higher than many companies expect but still remains well below that of most major industrial countries. The availability of local factory facilities and a stable labour force provide an additional incentive for relatively labour-intensive operations.

The feasibility study

Foreign firms need to become acquainted with the Chinese industrial scene and tend to stick to their core lines of business until they have gained significant experience in the Chinese environment. They tend to focus on those few local firms that they assess to have the potential to be an investment partner based on an in-depth study of information from different market sources as well as from international agents. Research indicates that the three types of information that are particularly important relate to the partner firms' ownership, information about the partner firms' potential contributions and information about the potential project.

Information on partner firms' ownership

The four information types perceived as of critical importance to evaluate potential partner firms' investment suitability include contract specifications, capital investment and royalties, goal congruence and potential investment in kind. Contract specifications usually come into force only after the relevant parties sign a written agreement. For example, the formation of an international strategic alliance such as an IJV requires that the relevant negotiators specify in a written contract or a written agreement terms that include the contract validity, interpretation, execution and settlement of disputes in ways that are consistent with the relevant laws of the host country. Any dispute may be submitted for arbitration to an impartial arbitration institution, as agreed upon by the relevant parties in the initial contracts. The date on which the contract becomes effective should be clearly stated in the written contract.

The Chinese parties' equity contribution for any form of investment will be in the form of Land Use Rights. It is important to realize that the Chinese government will have approved the rights to the specific investment ownership, and thus the Chinese partner will hold title to the land only for the period specified in the Land Use Right Certificate. Negotiations about the amount of capital investment and the royalties to be paid need to ensure that both participating partners' investments really are worth the amount of money stated. Patents and trademarks should be properly registered in China. It takes significant commitment by a skilful project team following established guidelines to make a detailed evaluation of the viability of any strategic alliance project.

Goal congruence between partner firms is important because consistent objectives for a strategic alliance usually translate into an ability to work together to achieve common goals. When the investment is in a highly regulated industry, the scope of business is subject to restrictions, and the IJV contract should specify the intended scope of the business in accordance with these regulations and policies. The final production scale for the anticipated capacity must also be stipulated. The total amount of investment contributed by all parties in China, termed 'contractual capital', is often different from the 'registered capital'.

Participating partner firms may contribute various kinds of strategic assets as their equity investment. These include, but are not limited to, cash, machinery and equipment, technology, land, factories, patents, trademarks, proprietary knowledge, skills, and industrial and intellectual property rights. The contract should state explicitly *what* particular equity or non-equity forms will be contributed and *when* they will be delivered to the international strategic alliance. When contributing industrial or intellectual property rights, participating partner firms usually include a separate contract clarifying the nature of the ownership investments attached to the main contract.

Information about the partners' potential contributions

It is crucially important to have a long-term commitment to any international strategic alliance formed in China. During the strategic alliance formation process, foreign firms must identify appropriate criteria for local partner selection as well as the relative importance of each criterion. Broadly, the criteria can be categorized into partner-related resources and non-partner-related resources. These categories are associated with partner strategic attributes that include marketing competence, relationship building, market position, industrial experience, strategic orientation and corporate image. Partner-related resources often mirror operational attributes such as organizational leadership, organizational rank, ownership investments, learning ability, international experience and human resource skills. A partner's strategic traits influence the operational skills and resources needed for the international strategic alliance's competitive success. Non-partner-related resources may be obtained from various sources such as government agencies in China, banks that have business relations with China, trade associations, advertising agencies, directories and chambers of commerce.

(1) Partner-related resources and capabilities

Assessment of a partner-specific influence is used to identify the ability and the worth of a partner within the organization by ascribing values to the necessary technological skill, management expertise and international business experience brought to the strategic alliance by that partner. Partner-related influence stresses the monitoring and co-ordination responsibilities of management that are based upon differentiated provision. Technology and management are culturally embedded within partner firms. Making the necessary operational adjustments to partner-specific influence can play a particularly important role in the way that such technology inputs, knowledge transformation and resource utilization are incorporated into the management process of a strategic alliance. The provision of proprietary resources may be dependent upon a partner's beliefs or opinions as to how work should be completed, how resources and tasks are distributed, and where priorities should lie. It appears that the greater the partner-specific influence accruing from the possession of technology, management and marketing expertise, the easier it may be for the resource provider to exercise its influence over a strategic alliance's management practices.

Partner-specific influence is leveraged from the relative endowment of resources, skills and competencies of the parent firm. The sources of bargaining power of an individual partner can be established through the internalization of key value-added competencies, as knowledge flow, sharing and transfer can play an important role in supporting human resource practices throughout the international strategic alliance's development. Partner-specific influences can also be effective when they communicate internally consistent expectations in ways that are congruent with the partners' behaviour requirements.

Its distribution channels, promotional skills and understanding of local business practices can measure a partner's marketing competencies. Building relationships with major buyers, wholesalers and relevant governmental authorities is fundamentally important for foreign firms seeking market position in China. Because Chinese society is built around a complex social and business web, the costs of establishing independent distribution channels or business networks by foreign businesses are likely to outweigh the potential benefits. Moreover, the establishment of such a network can be such a long process that foreign firms may be unable to seize market opportunities or align to contextual changes in a timely fashion. A local partner's established history and strong background in the industry infrastructure often results in a good reputation or high credibility in the marketplace. Long-term industrial/ market experience signifies that the local firm has built an extensive marketing and distribution network. As firms face the challenges of change and growth, past successes and experiences can be built upon in the development of new generations of management and leadership. The type of expertise that each partner firm contributes may affect the amount of equity that it owns. Increasingly, local or foreign firms seek influential local partners for a strategic alliance to enable them to stay ahead of the competition in today's global economy.

(2) Non-partner-related resources and capabilities

A strategic alliance's investment profile is regarded as pervasive when its organization uses the partner firm's images to project its own management systems, quality and prestige to its market and supply chains. This pervasive power can be established in many forms and is typically used when the strategic alliance's business is characterized by decision-making urgency. The influence of a firm's non-partner-related resources is used to manage invested resources in order to achieve quality, productivity and efficiency and it is culturally independent in nature. A partner's investment of capital, technology and marketing expertise can affect the long-term strategic development of an international strategic alliance and is particularly important when the requirements to be met are related to a global operation. The influence of such investments on a strategic alliance's operation requires that the provisioning firm provide a consistent and clear structure that defines the conduct of a strategic alliance's management in the handling of the resource, knowledge and capability inputs. Task-oriented influence pertaining to international business experience and management involvement is part of the non-partner-related resources, knowledge and capabilities provided at the formation of a strategic alliance in China.

When international partner firms' structural or functional specializations complement each other and they share similar structural or organizational characteristics, these can be built upon to create solid asset bases that the strategic alliance can use to enter new markets. Organizational flexibility must be achieved for task-related influences to become effective and dominant. The contextual factors of non-partner-related resources and capabilities include market conditions, business strategies, technology, and management expertise which generate new economic value to a strategic alliance by enabling its organizational human capital to be more productive and adaptable. Economic literature indicates that human capital, technology, skills, experience and knowledge can play an important role in establishing preferences for the adoption of particular management practices within the organization. Assessment of complementary tasks should include an analysis of the nature of the importance of the task-related influence to the partner, the type of knowledge involved and the nature of the partner's reward and control system.

Firms need to ascertain how effectively they can manage their strategic alliances in China. Co-operative cultural and management styles influence a firm's management participation, which in turn affects the firm's success. Symmetry must exist at the top level of management. Peer relationships among the senior managers of a strategic alliance should be established. It is difficult in a strategic alliance to balance partners' costs and benefits with their management participation. The key to managing the cost-benefit balance effectively is to manage the partner's expectations of the strategic alliance. A strategic alliance's management should put considerable efforts into understanding the strategic objectives and the operational areas in which partner firms have vital interests, concerns and fears.

Information about the prospective project

Equity ownership is seen as an outcome of negotiation and a representation of the relative power of participating firms. Partners in a strategic alliance may gain power from their commitment of various resources including technology, marketing expertise, worldwide sales, access to financial markets, geographical experience and industrial expertise. Technology is defined as expertise pertaining specifically to the product of the international strategic alliance. This definition is particularly well suited to high-technology products, but 'technology' can also be interpreted broadly to include brand names and the processing of commodities. Generally, a partner is deemed to contribute technology when its product is sold to a strategic alliance. Local knowledge is considered to mean a general familiarity with economic and political conditions in the host country and the provision of a distribution network. Information about any prospective project includes an analysis of 'strategic fit', 'cultural fit' and 'operational fit', which are perceived as being of critical importance when setting up a successful investment project in China.

(1) The strategic fit

Most foreign firms investing in China for the first time tend to be motivated above all by the desire to establish market share and gain a foothold in the local market. The emphasis that foreign firms place on market opportunities must be tempered by conclusions about the political and economic risks. The strategic fit should be defined in terms of the long-term co-operative arrangements between two or more independent firms that engage in business activities for mutual economic gain and a resource synergy. There have been various attempts to classify international strategic alliances, including the level of technology as a measure of strategic fit. The proportion of tacit knowledge in a technology is related to its age and level of sophistication. When compared with newly developed cutting-edge technology, mature technology has been much more widely used in strategic alliances in China.

An alternative way to measure strategic fit in an alliance is to measure the extent to which partners engage jointly in planning and goal setting. The need to ensure good strategic fit in an international strategic alliance context should be emphasized when specifying increased roles, responsibilities and expectations. Joint planning allows each partner firm's mutual expectations to be established and co-operative efforts to be specified. Economic rents are created when the business, organizational and technological process of a strategic alliance are enhanced by and interwoven with intellectual property such as brands or patents. Examples of improvements in partner firms' strategic fit include design for manufacturing, time to market, patents, intellectual property, low cost manufacturing, quality management and technology in general. Achievement of strategic fit in a strategic alliance in China may also need to take account of the development of talent and leadership in the process of innovation and product renewal, the leveraging of global capabilities, partnering skills, hiring and developing international managers, structuring for optimal global performance, the nurturing of global management talent, the transfer of best practices, the stimulation of critical capabilities, international negotiating ability, contractual skill development and relationship cultivation.

(2) The cultural fit

The cultural environment of the host country is a crucial factor influencing investment in, and performance of, an international strategic alliance. Previous literature has frequently mentioned that there are differing managerial styles, structures, business norms, business values and corporate cultures between developing and developed countries that can lead to serious conflicts, instability and even the eventual failure of an international strategic alliance. The foreign partner firm should adopt a flexible attitude in doing business overseas and learn to understand the value base of different cultures. Any apparent asymmetry in capacity, willingness and needs will exacerbate poor relations and cross-cultural experiential learning will be curtailed. The two main aspects of 'cultural fit' in a strategic alliance that may be of greatest significance are the differences between local and foreign partners with respect to levels of socio-cultural distance and power uncertainty avoidance. Partner mission statements are statements about what the firm wishes to become in the long run. They should reflect senior management's vision of the future, and form the basis of the strategic alliance's strategy. Cultural fit is important because it determines how decisions are made and what supporting structures are required for a strategic alliance to function in line with its business philosophy. Senior management should regularly review how major decisions have been made, who the participants were in the decision process and how decisions were modified by cultural influences.

People from nations with different cultural backgrounds, career goals, compensation systems and other human resource baggage often have to begin working together with little advance preparation. The cultural fit of strategic alliance management is key to the goal accomplishment of partner firms. This culture-oriented influence is reflected not only in the blending of cultures and management styles, but also in job design, recruitment and staffing, strategic orientation, training, performance appraisal, compensation policies, career development and labour–management relations. Among such cultural influences, the ability to surpass cultural barriers, recruit qualified employees, and establish effective incentive structures are particularly important in strategic alliances. A strategic alliance's technology, marketing and management are all open to culture-oriented influence and this factor, with its emphasis on social and inter-personal skills, is the least amenable to transfer as a packaged, transacted commodity. Management skills have to be learned through intensive inter-personal contact and require attitudinal, cognitive and behavioural change.

The success of a strategic alliance's operations will largely depend upon its local partner's international business skills, and its ability to acquire, assimilate, integrate and exploit knowledge. The strategic alliance's ability to process, integrate and deploy new knowledge and skills are closely related to the 'cultural fit' already established. During the process of product diversification, relationships can influence the strategic alliance's economies of scale and scope. A local partner can help the international strategic alliance improve its relationship with the government, gain access to scarce production factors, increase administrative efficiency and reduce financial and operational risks in both related and unrelated diversification. A local partner's market experience, international business experience and accumulated industrial knowledge are of great value for the realization of the alliance's strategic goals. A local partner's track record, business experience and market background can often be translated into benefits for the strategic alliance in terms of reputation and credibility in the industry. From the cultural fit perspective, a strategic alliance is an aggregate of complex organizational routines and business experience that allow it to compete in the marketplace.

(3) The operational fit

Physical resources and human resources categorize operational fit in a strategic alliance. Physical resources include tangible assets such as land, plant, equipment, finished and semi-finished goods, together with intangible assets such as brand names, copyrights and patents. Human resources include the education, training, experience, relationships, skills and intelligence of individual staff in the strategic alliance. The choice of product to be manufactured is a key consideration for a partner firm when setting up a new strategic alliance in China. Partners must be committed to the success of the alliance and this is reflected in their willingness to exert effort to ensure a high level of operational fit. Successful strategic alliance partnerships are marked by co-ordinated actions directed at mutual objectives that are consistent across organizations. Operational fit in a strategic alliance involves both the introduction of technology embodied in new products and/or new plants through major investment projects and the incremental adaptation of existing production capacity that brings operational efficiency and effectiveness. The operational fit in a strategic alliance involves incorporation of new technology in relatively large lumps through investments in new production facilities. The achievement of operational fit in a strategic alliance also involves the incorporation of strands of new technology into existing facilities through incremental changes. On the whole, operational fit in strategic alliances is a resource needed for the generation and management of technological and managerial change. Both Table 6.3 and Table 6.4 show application procedures and a checklist for the establishment of international strategic alliances in China.

Summary

This chapter provides an overview of international strategic alliance formation. Foreign firms rank the gain of strategic position *vis-à-vis*

Table 6.3 Application for the establishment of an international strategic alliance

Step 1:	*Application for Establishment* Upon reaching a negotiated agreement by the relevant parties to an equity or contractual alliance, the Chinese party should submit the project proposal to the local development planning commission or economic and trade commission. Project proposal approved by the competent Chinese authorities; preliminary feasibility study report; letter of intent or agreement signed by the parties to the joint venture; and credit report on the foreign party.
Step 2:	*Submission of Feasibility Studies for Approval* After the project proposal is approved, parties to the international strategic alliance should work together to compile a feasibility study report for submission to the local development planning commission for getting its final approval. Application letter to the competent Chinese authorities; feasibility study report duly signed by all parties to the international strategic alliance; agreement or draft contract; proof of the Chinese party's source of funds; and credit report on the foreign party prepared by the bank.
Step 3:	*Submission of Contract and Articles of Association for Approval* After the feasibility study reports are approved, parties to the international strategic alliance should sign the contract, articles of association and other relevant legal documents necessary to establish the international strategic alliance. The Chinese party should then submit the documents to the local foreign trade and economic co-operation department where the joint venture is located for examination and approval. Application letter to the competent Chinese authorities; feasibility study report and approval documents for the project; application for registration of the name of the enterprise approved by the provincial or municipal administration for industry and commerce; written comments on the project by various government departments such as environmental protection, fire services, health and land administration; business licences of the parties concerned and certificates of their legal representatives; contract and articles of association duly signed by the legal representatives of the joint venture parties; and list of the board of directors.
Step 4:	*Application for Approval Certificate* After the contract and articles of association are approved, the Chinese party should apply to the provincial or municipal foreign trade and economic co-operation department for an approval certificate. Ratification documents (on project proposal, feasibility study report, contract and articles of association) from the relevant authorities; project proposal, feasibility study report, contract, articles of association and list of directors duly approved by the competent authorities.
Step 5:	*Registration* Upon collection of the approval certification issued by the relevant authority, an application for a business licence should be filed with the provincial or municipal administration for industry and commerce within 30 days. Subsequently, the joint venture should complete such procedures as applying for an official seal and enterprise code, opening a bank account, and registering for tax payment and customs declaration with the local public security, technical supervision, taxation, customs, finance, foreign exchange administration, banking, insurance and commodity inspection departments.

Source: Adapted from HKTDC Research Department (2003: Table 1.1).

Table 6.4 A checklist for the feasibility study: searching out relevant information for an international strategic alliance

The partner firm's ownership	The partners' potential contribution	The prospective projects
• Line of business • Scope of current operations • International business activities • Objectives in the local market (Khanna, Gulati and Nohria 1998) • Current and future market • Sales estimate by sector • Foreign and domestic distribution • Local industry conditions • Past product imports • Anticipated competition in the host country (Kogut and Zander 1996) • Approximate input requirements for all materials • Present sources of supply • Availability of utilities • Transport routes planned • Communication system for accessing sector information (Khanna 1998) • Environmental protection plan (Larsson *et al.*, 1998).	*Partner-related resources* (Nelson and Winter 1982, March 1991, Nonaka 1994, Pinto 2000, Macher 2001) • Choice of product range • Line of business • Resource commitment • Size and scope of current business operations • Location • Financial performance • Marketing experience • Compatibility of partners' management • The control of majority capital ownership • Management participation • International activities • A long-term commitment to the partner obligations, distribution of profits and technological improvement • Technical expertise • Operational experience *Non-partner-related resources* (Oxley 1997, Powcll 1998, Phillips, Lawrence and Hardy 2000, Mowery, Oxley and Silverman 2001). • Task-related influence • Culture-oriented influence • Management participation	*Strategic fit* (Lyles 1988, Furnham 1990, Hall 1995). • Description of technology and equipment to be used • Scope of production • Products • Market segment • Financing requirements • Technology transfers • Land-use arrangement *Cultural fit* (Allport, Vernon and Lindzey 1970, England 1975, Cherington 1980, Hofstede 1980, Ring and van de Yen 1992, Brown and Starkey 1994). • Infrastructure improvements required • Production/operations plan • Cost estimate including technology transfer fees, royalty rate • Layout of proposed equipment and costs *Operational fit* (Prencipe 1997, Shapiro and Varian 1999, Simonin 1999, Rothaermel 2001, Schilling and Steensma 2001). • Organization overhead costs • Organization structure • Estimated manpower requirements • Estimated annual output/turnover • Transport and local storage requirements • Estimated total investment cost (working capital) • Proposed capital structure • Quality of product/service

competitors as the most important and commonly stated objective. The three theories of ownership advantages used to explain strategic alliance behaviour are resource-based theory, resource dependence theory and ownership, localization and internalization theory, all three are vital in understanding how an international strategic alliance can achieve long-term competitive advantage. A firm's resources, knowledge and capabilities have to be bundled effectively to form an international strategic alliance investment. At the time of the formation of an international strategic alliance in China, one of the critical success factors is the gathering and analysis of information on all partner firms' investments, a partner's potential investment and the potential project.

7
Ownership Investments and International Technology Transfer

Introduction

A partner firm with a majority of the equity shares in an international strategic alliance usually has more rights and powers to appoint its members to the board of directors and more rights to appoint senior managers within the joint venture. A firm with greater equity investment thus has superior resource leverage and this in turn increases control over corporate governance. Ownership determinants are identified as major factors in explaining the extent to which an investing firm has control over the style of an international strategic alliance's corporate governance. Technology brought in by the foreign partner is commonly treated as a critical part of firm-specific resources, knowledge and capabilities and will be valued as equity for part of the investment. It plays a disproportionate role in specifying explicitly its power and control rights. From a research perspective, it becomes important to measure the effect that the various investment contributions make to the ownership, management and control of an international strategic alliance.

Ownership configuration

The right of individual property ownership is deemed important because it ensures that citizen independence can be protected from centralized authority. In formal terms, ownership is the legal possession of assets. It is normally defined in terms of three fundamental rights which are [1] the right to possess an asset and/or its financial value; [2] the right to exercise influence over the use of the asset; [3] the right to information about the status of what is owned (Pierce, Rubenfeld and Morgan 1991:125). Other ownership rights include the right to transfer assets and the right to receive an income or return from them. The three categories of ownership rights are commonly illustrated in corporate governance literature. User rights are defined in terms of the potential uses of an asset and include the right to transform or destroy an asset. The ownership right to earn income from an asset may be specified in a contract where the terms also specify the parallel rights of other individuals. The ownership rights to transfer an asset permanently to another party are dependent upon the rights over an asset and the rights to sell an asset. Ownership is a combination of rights and responsibilities with respect to a specific asset. In some cases, those rights and responsibilities are more clearly defined than in others.

Renner (1904) defines the institution of property as the set of legal imperatives relating to the power of possession of social objects. Scott (1979) states that ownership has a dual character including both a legal relationship and a social relationship. The legal relationship of ownership comprises an owner's all-embracing legal power over a social object. The social relationship of ownership refers to the actual effective power of possession and this may diverge from the legal relation of ownership. Renner argues that effective possession can be structured in a way that does not correspond to prevailing legal forms and that, in such a situation, rights over objects become relations of social power. The argument can be extended to the study of an international strategic alliance. For example, the parent firms are legal owners of the means of generating an international strategic alliance, but the actual power to determine the use of these means is derived from the strategic alliance's board of directors and these individuals may act with some degree of independence. The partners provide resources, knowledge and competencies, but these can be dissociated from the partners' ownership rights to safeguard the providers' respective interests and establish the social relationships within the international strategic alliance.

Berle and Means (1932) argue that the traditional logic of property involves (1) the right to determine the use of the asset as one sees fit; (2) the right to alter, modify or destroy one's property; (3) the right to use the property and entitlement to enjoy and employ the right to benefit from its use. They further clarify that because the 'when' and 'how' of these aspects of property can be dissociated, it is possible to distinguish 'nominal ownership'. The right to receive revenue as a return for risking one's wealth by investing in a firm is separated from 'effective ownership' which is the ability to control the corporate assets, and thus it is necessary to go beyond mere legal forms to the 'economic and social background of law' to determine rights (Berle and Means 1932:339).

Berle and Means (1932) contend that efficient capital markets render the issue of separation of ownership and control largely irrelevant. The application of their views to an international strategic alliance suggests that managers of the strategic alliance can act in their own interests to the detriment of parent firms. If this happens, the market processes as established through corporate governance will punish managers who do not act in the best interests of parent firms, or who do not adapt to the changing strategic requirements of enacting business in a particular context. The fundamental basis of the right to control through corporate governance is based on property rights theory. In a more generalized form, Berle and Means (1932) suggest that managerial behaviour at the expense of shareholders is constrained by competitive forces in multiple domains. Given the differing objectives of partner firms in a strategic alliance, they argue that the most salient cost of ownership investments is that arising from parent firms failing to undertake their responsibilities. It is implicitly assumed that one of the tasks of all partner firms is to monitor the managers of the strategic alliance and to ensure that they perform their functions in accordance with the interests of the partner firms.

Equity investment

Equity investment, especially a majority equity share, confers certain legal rights to determine the overall direction of a strategic alliance. Equity investment in a firm may serve as a threshold to gain the right to manage its business. A firm can gain effective organizational control by investing sufficiently to obtain a majority of the equity. Equity investment in an international strategic alliance is used as a critical indicator of who exercises organizational control within the firm. However, Scott (1985) suggests that the link between legal ownership and the locus of effective possession is no longer direct or straightforward. Legal ownership of company stock provides for 'economic ownership' as defined by the right to benefit from corporate activities, and this has gradually become separated from 'technical ownership' as defined by the actual rights to use the means of production. The separation of ownership and control in the large modern corporation is recognized by Bottomore and Rubel (1956), who note that the separation of management functions from ownership occurred as early as the mid-nineteenth century in British stock firms. Later writers have expressed special concern that the owners of business assets may lose control over their use to executive managers and suggest that the minimum amount of stock required to prevent this loss of control is 20 per cent. Scott and Hughes (1976) suggest that in a highly dispersed shareholding in a unified firm, it is possible to exert control by owning 5 per cent or even less.

The relationship between ownership and control focuses on the dichotomy of interests between shareholders and managers where these may have diverged in terms of a firm's strategic objectives. Owners may seek growth of their investment while managers may favour growth of the organization (Marris 1964), and thus an owning firm may face the problem of protecting the use and integrity of its investments. The way it seeks to protect itself is through a certain level of control imposed through legal rights and social relations. When property rights and social relations are not dissociated, it is possible to distinguish the range of ownership resources that provide the rights which allow the owning firm to impose its strategic priorities. This contrasts with the traditional logic of 'nominal ownership', which focuses on the rights to receive revenue as a return for risking wealth by investing in a firm. The legal rights and the social responsibilities of equity in an international strategic alliance have additional dimensions due to the different forms of ownership resources invested by the partner firms in the alliance. The legal form of ownership in an international strategic alliance provides the general framework within which ownership resources (such as capital and non-capital resources) are committed by the partners and where 'social relations' can be established through the provision of partners' contractual and non-contractual resources, knowledge and capabilities.

Capital resources

The value of a firm's equity rights depends on the cost of enforcing those legal rights. Exercising its strategic choices may utilize the capital provision of a firm's equity. The availability of capital resources can influence a firm's options for corporate investments. Williamson (1985) defines the specific conditions under which a firm may exercise more or less control over its capital resources as they allow a firm to exercise control over risks. There is a wide range of ownership resources that each parent firm may contribute to a strategic alliance. Barney (1991) suggests that ownership resources include all assets, capabilities, organizational processes, attributes, information and knowledge controlled by a firm that enable it to conceive of and implement strategies which improve its efficiency and effectiveness. With regard to an international joint venture, Yan and Gray (1994a) regard equity as the provision of a 'capital resource' to a strategic alliance by its partner firms, typically in finance and sometimes in land and buildings. Once the capital resource of an international strategic alliance is agreed on, it delineates the relative positions of the partners and sets the tone for the successive negotiations on the alliance's corporate governance.

Capital resource-based power is primarily derived from a contribution of financial resources or their equivalence in physical resources or proprietary technology properties. Renner (1904:53, 73–4) states that 'the legal institution of the right of ownership is the set of legal imperatives which regulate the 'detention', or access to, social objects and that a particularly important part of the law of property concerns the detention of objects involved in the production of goods and services. The essential feature of ownership rights in an international strategic alliance is the set of laws and regulations that are enacted by the government of the locality where these international strategic alliances are sited. These laws may cover ownership rights such as the total capital resources permitted, the proportion of the equity that can be held by partners and the constitution of a strategic alliance's board of directors.

Non-capital resources

The provision of non-capital resources is a powerful lever for the exercise of an investing firm's investment policy and the setting of strategic priorities. Yan and Gray (1994a) categorize non-capital resources as technology, management expertise, local knowledge, raw material procurement channels, product distribution and marketing channels and global service support. This distinction between capital and non-capital resources is important because assets such as technology, market channels and management expertise have become increasingly recognized as ownership determinants in an international strategic alliance, where ownership determinants associated with the complementary assets of partner firms take on a significantly greater importance than pure financial contributions. Although the allocation of the dividend, re-investment, net income and operation appear to be managed by the strategic alliance partners, government agencies can still play an important role in enforcing ownership rights through the application of laws and regulations that act as guarantees and enforcement agencies for formal ownership rights.

Williamson (1988) claims that traditional financial theories ignore the role of the characteristics of assets in financing firms when they assume that these firms' capital investment is a composite resource. From his point of view, non-capital resources can be considered as a way of providing alternative governance structures over a firm's assets. Following Williamson's argument, perfect financial markets make a major and possibly unjustifiable assumption in stating that every asset price contains all the relevant information necessary for a firm to make rational investments. The importance of non-capital resources owned by firms includes proprietary knowledge in product development, brand names and marketing skills. Many international business studies emphasize the important role of an international firm's non-capital resource investments in providing entrepreneurial, managerial and international marketing skills, plus technical know-how which can be transferred to foreign countries.

Most foreign firms' investments in a strategic alliance are well equipped to exploit developments of their products and process technologies to gain further access to international markets. Non-capital resources of foreign firms include the introduction of not just the core technology for 'new hardware' to the Chinese market, but also the necessary 'software' for associated supply technologies, together with the managerial skills to operate it. Non-capital resources have a direct effect on the corporate governance structure of a strategic alliance in addition to the indirect effect of the senior appointments made to manage the resource. The effective transfer of management expertise from one parent firm to an international strategic alliance normally requires an accompanying transfer of its own managerial personnel and technicians. This is particularly true in a developing or transitional country environment where there is a shortage of local personnel with the technological expertise and managerial experience required to manage the sophisticated and complex organizations that exist in a strategic alliance. Non-capital resources can be used as a foundation to justify the partner firm's location of its own personnel in key alliance managerial positions, and this strengthens its corporate governance over the strategic alliance's operations.

When non-capital resources are provided as part of a contract arrangement, the ownership rights for the use and management of such ownership resources can be specified in writing. When non-capital resources are provided on a non-contractual basis, they may still confer influence and power on the providing firm because the capital resources intrinsically create an internal dependency on the associated expertise and will generate moral authority derived from the way they demonstrate commitment. Local Chinese firms may take advantage of these foreign non-capital resources, knowledge and capacities to strengthen their competitive position in the world marketplace. The local partner firms may be able to avoid the time and expense involved in developing new technologies themselves; the acquisition of foreign technology and managerial expertise definitely benefits local partners in the promotion of their non-capital resources. On the whole, acquisition of non-capital resources in an international strategic alliance is perceived as a way of providing cost-effective solutions as it promotes technological innovation, international investment and production for local firms.

Contractual versus non-contractual resources

Alliance partners can provide resources to an international strategic alliance, including management systems, management services and training, and technological know-how on the basis of formal contracts; these are termed 'contractual resources'. The structure of a strategic alliance contract depends on the legal system, social customs and the technical attributes of the assets involved in the exchange by partners. The more detailed the legal framework, the more specific will be the written contracts. The extent to which a strategic alliance's contract stipulates the various investment dimensions depends on marginal costs and benefits at the time the rights to an asset by the partners is exchanged. Rugman (1982) notes that the negotiation of a contractual agreement for a non-standardized product can be a very difficult task, but nevertheless finds that 'these contractual arrangements are of increasing importance in international production and marketing' despite the costs incurred in specifying these contractual resources.

Dunning and McQueen (1981) find that the provision of contractual resources by the local partner can reduce costs as the local investors probably have an absolute advantage in regard to knowledge of local conditions. This leaves foreign firms free to meet their own objectives through contract-based investment, but it must be remembered that the high external environmental uncertainty associated with international alliance operations tends to make the writing and enforcement of equity contracts more expensive (Anderson and Weitz 1986). Citing the case of a strategic alliance in the airline industry, Hall and Eppink (1992) indicate that airlines combine through commitment of contractual resources to optimize the utilization of available capacity. If two carriers agree to merge their coverage to target a broader customer base, the blocked-space agreement enables them to remain as competitors when marketing but the agreement provides them with market coverage.

The distinction of ownership-provision on a contractual basis has important theoretical implications for the basis on which the resource providing partner may exercise more control within international strategic alliances. Typical contracts convey formalized rights to exclusive control over the use of, and/or benefit from, assets including technology and brands. Guo and Akroyd (1996) suggest that a technological property contract will include patents and licensing agreements. These are particularly important in the case of an international strategic alliance. Such rights derive from the provision of resources to a strategic alliance by its owners and hence they may be termed 'contractual resources'. The provision of non-capital resources may provide other sources of control. When such resources are provided through contracts, the contract will typically specify user rights and may specify legal terms and controls over the management of these resources. A partner firm may, for example, use contracts to prevent the leakage of its proprietary technology through the strategic alliance to other partner firms and may specify who shall use and manage the proprietary resources. Similarly, the resource provision of an internationally established brand name by a partner firm may be accompanied by a formal agreement restricting the use of that brand and specifying the conditions under which it can be used. The provision of contractual resources gives the resource-providing partner in a strategic alliance the legal authority to control contributed resources.

Strategic alliance partners can provide 'non-capital resources' to an international strategic alliance outside any formal contracts. These typically include technological know-how, management systems, management services and training, and may be termed 'non-contractual resources'. With the development of strategic alliances, non-contractual ownership resources in general have assumed increasing importance as the key to success. It is 'social relationships' such as knowledge and skill of managing complex interdependencies within and across a strategic alliance's boundaries that provide the ability to manage multicultural units (Nonaka and Takeuchi 1995). The provision of non-contractual resources normally reflects a high level of commitment to a strategic alliance on the part of the partner firm (Cullen, Johnson and Sakano 1995) and these resources are likely to give rise to de facto ownership rights through claims to expertise and goodwill in addition to the cultural capital that they generate. The partner firms that are able to accrue trust, goodwill and loyalty within a strategic alliance may add significant intangible value to their original equity. In addition, a strategic alliance's organizational capability, if it is mainly based upon a partner's non-contractual resources, can be enhanced by the replication of knowledge on an experiential basis with the partner. The strategic alliance's organizational capabilities can be effectively enhanced via a process of learning-by-doing and the resources, knowledge and skills that are transferred happen not so much at the top management level, but as the result of daily interaction among employees at the operational level (Hamel, Doz and Prahalad 1989).

Partners in a strategic alliance can extend the scope of operations by building up trust and learning, and also through the provision of non-contractual resources to a strategic alliance at its formation. Strategic alliances provide the structural mechanisms for the sharing of partners' knowledge and for ensuring the alignment of partners' incentives through greater integration. The provision of non-contractual resources to a strategic alliance is one way to build up a partner's motivation and commitment because they appear in the form of informal goodwill. Still, the most important corporate governance gained from 'equity influence' in an international strategic alliance is associated with the 'three governance rights': the right to appoint the general manager, the right to determine organizational structure and the right to appoint personnel to critical functional areas.

Generally speaking, a firm's ownership provision is perceived as a lever to exercise control over its contractual and non-contractual resource investments. The balance of a firm's equity between its contractual and non-contractual resources can be used as leverage to implement its form of corporate governance for the control of its business investment. For example, technology is generally defined as critical knowledge about how to produce a cheaper or better product at given input prices. A partner that makes contractual inputs such as technological knowledge into a strategic alliance will find that this involves close interaction between the staff of the transferor and the transferee firm where the rights to the intellectual property transferred is commonly covered by industrial property rights clauses in the contract. The contractual provision of technical services and the sharing of product know-how are primarily provided in the form of technical drawings, technical data and management specifications. Any decision of a partner firm to adopt a contractual investment mode rather than provide them on a non-contractual basis may affect the quality of its ownership inputs. Theoretical contributions to the ownership configuration of strategic alliances are explained in Table 7.1.

International technology

The nature of the technology transferred to an international strategic alliance needs to be viewed from a strategic context to determine whether it is appropriate for an investing firm to adopt a contractual or non-contractual basis to govern the transfer. There may be restrictions placed on how technologies invested by foreign firms in a strategic alliance in China are used, and this may require formal registration to get the host

Table 7.1 Theoretical contributions to the ownership configuration of an international strategic alliance

Ownership configuration	Theoretical perspectives
Equity	Equity share and especially a majority equity share, confers certain legal rights to determine the overall direction of a strategic alliance. Equity investment in a firm may serve as a threshold to gain the right to manage its business (Hennart 1988; Demsetz 1991; Eisenhardt and Schoonhoven 1996).
Capital resources	Capital provision of a firm's equity can be employed to exercise its strategic intents. The choice of capital resources can influence a firm's option for corporate investments (Dodgson 1992; Hagedoorn 1993; Das and Teng 2000; Hagedoorn, Link and Vonortes 2000).
Non-capital resources	The provision of non-capital resources is a powerful lever for controlling a firm's investment policy and setting strategic priorities (Busoni, Prencipe and Pavitt 2001).
Contractual resources	Its owners, on the basis of formal contracts including technological know-how, management systems, management services and training, can provide contractual resources to an international strategic alliance. These are termed 'contractual resources' (Galunic and Rodan 1998).
Non-contractual resources	Its owners outside any formal contracts can provide 'non-contractual resources' to an international strategic alliance. These are termed 'non-contractual resources' and typically include technological know-how, management systems, management services and training (Gulati 1995, 1999; Busoni and Prencipe 2001).

country's government approval. If a foreign firm wishes to continue to receive technology royalties after initiating a new technology contract subsequent to an initial investment in a strategic alliance in China, it can do so but the new contract on international technology transfer must be formally executed. The technology-transferring firm is allowed to add new restrictions as to how its technology may be used that include the establishment of requirements on market sales and distribution channels or the specification of locations. Most strategic alliances in China require substantial capital investments from which the foreign partner expects foreign currency returns, and thus export-oriented projects are encouraged by the Chinese government because the export of a large portion of local high-technology products to third markets will generate foreign exchange surpluses that will pay for foreign exchange expenditure incurred in that local operation and by royalties or dividends.

Technology literature states that explicit knowledge is embodied in a firm's product designs, operational specifications and technical drawings while tacit technology commonly involves personal knowledge. Owing to the value of technology possessed by each partner firm in a strategic alliance, tacit knowledge is difficult to transfer in codified form alone and close human interaction between partners or parent–subsidiary linkage is normally required. The proportion of tacit know-how embodied in a technology is closely related to its level of sophistication. For example, engineering drawings and operating procedures can be constantly altered as an explicit type of knowledge that is easy to learn and use. However, tacit technology cannot be codified in full even if it is mature. Technological inputs from foreign firms into an international strategic alliance often take the form of patented design, product know-how or new service offerings. The value of the technology possessed by a foreign firm's organizational network but used in a strategic alliance must be analysed to establish the different organizational levels involved. Technology literature has examined in depth how the determinants of a firm's technology can be effectively transacted via each technology transfer through the involvement of the various organizational hierarchies.

Where the technology transfer is critical, strategic alliances will find it relatively easier to induce the partner firms providing the technology to work closely with them in order to ensure specified technological requirements are met. The value of a partner firm's technology can also be measured in the same way that any materials, components and services are measured through the improvement of a strategic alliance's economic efficiency. Hence technology includes not only the 'hard technologies' but also patentable aspects of production processes. The

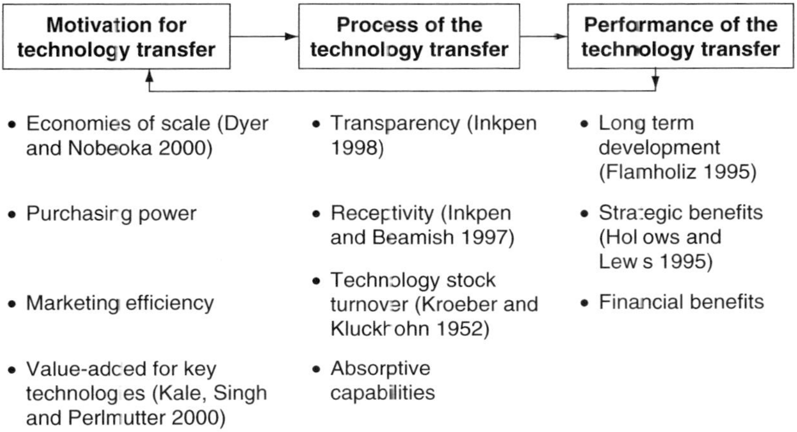

Figure 7.1 International technology transfer in an international strategic alliance

value of a firm's technology will also be included in the technological specifications of products and the service details. Figure 7.1 shows the 'soft' aspects of technology transfer in a strategic alliance that will include organization know-how, marketing, managerial knowledge and relevant skills.

Motivation for technology transfer

A partner of a strategic alliance with uniquely valuable product know-how is likely to enjoy a technological monopoly. This implies that a partner firm with technology ownership can be viewed as having the product know-how that achieves comparative advantages for the international strategic alliance, and through the leverage of this know-how it acquires, develops and retains relative control and power within the alliance operation. The advantages that technology provides will enhance the motivational disposition of the technology transferor firm to share its technology with other partner firms within the strategic alliance. The transfer of cutting-edge technology from foreign firms in a developed country to a developing country such as China can be economically attractive, particularly if the end-products can be sold in the local market. During the negotiations for technology transfer deals with a local Chinese firm, foreign firms need to be aware of some of the technology leakage problems they may encounter, especially where the technology is capable of conserving scarce resources such as electricity, gas or water.

A paramount factor determining the success of any international technology transfer is the quality of technical personnel and managerial staff available in a host country. Technical and managerial personnel in a strategic alliance are a key human resource capital and they must adapt to the new technology and the managerial knowledge that facilitates the technology transfer process. China has an excess of unskilled and semi-skilled workers, but a serious shortage of professionals at management level. International strategic alliances in China have to decide upon the degree to which they will include expatriate managers and scientists in their resource allocation, strategy implementation and decision-making processes. A strategic alliance's performance in China is a mainly perceived as a function of both the uniqueness of the technology that is being transferred from a partner to the strategic alliance and the presence of a specialized technician and managerial staff who can convey the tacit aspects of the technology and management to the strategic alliance.

The major driver of technology transfer is the need for an international strategic alliance to be more effective than other organizational investment modes within the Chinese context. Technology suppliers will increase their potential power by exploiting, sharing and assimilating their technology if their technologies are unique, rare, valuable and difficult to imitate. Technology literature generally agrees with the interpretation of a firm's intangible investments or tacit knowledge as valid proxies for 'firm-specific' resources. The adoption of a resource perspective of technology-related investments reveals that investments in R&D, advertising and human resources practices can improve the capability of strategic resources including innovative capabilities, corporate reputation and human capital. If the technology involved in the production of certain products or services is not a 'firm-specific' asset, appropriate design of a firm's information or reporting structure may allow the firm to minimize the exposure of proprietary knowledge to competitors.

The implications of technology transfer in an international strategic alliance can be manifested in three forms: the relative paucity of the local firms' technology stock; incentives that increase eagerness to learn from a transferring firm's technologies; and the control exercised by the technology transferor. Transferring technology into an international strategic alliance is hardly a new challenge and the motivation for local firms to ensure the transfer of technology to China is mainly generated by the real need of local production to satisfy government authorities that it is building local capabilities while protecting the proprietary know-how of foreign firms.

Technology transfer to a strategic alliance in China is not cost-free because it involves the use of different resources that may have different levels of technological value. The greater the value of a strategic alliance's technology stock, the greater will be its competitiveness in the market where it operates and so the presence of technology stock is very important. The value of the technology transferred from a foreign firm to a strategic alliance in China is likely to be high if the foreign firm's technology stock is in the form of tacit knowledge because of the competitive advantage created. A concentration of high value, foreign partner-owned technologies will be attractive to materials, component and service suppliers in the market where it operates.

The transfer of technology from a partner firm to a strategic alliance requires the instigation of organizational conduits by which managerial know-how and techniques can be passed on. The value of a firm's technology has a strong impact on the technology development, economic efficiencies and competitive advantages from industry agglomeration that have long been at the core of academic literature. Horizontal technology linkages with external actors are often defined as co-operative bilateral relationships with suppliers, customers, competitors or other partner firms with complementary resources. The traditional way for a local Chinese firm to improve its technology is through collaboration with universities and research institutes as they provide a means of developing technological knowledge that a firm under state ownership restrictions cannot accomplish on its own. Universities and research institutes can also provide management consulting and technological assistance at the formation of a new strategic alliance project and also offer some services for continued training for professional employees.

Process of technology transfer

China still has very little capability for technological development and thus technology transfer and the implementation of packaged technology from foreign firms probably provides the best initial basis for upgrading its technology base. Most local firms understand that they must upgrade and transform their technologies and are willing to co-operate properly with foreign firms. Heightened market competition in China drives most international strategic alliances to use technology effectively, and this requires that they deal with each other in fairness, honesty and good faith if they are to meet this market competition. The proprietary technology, knowledge and capabilities possessed by a strategic alliance are an important type of firm-specialized asset that must be supported internally by the partner firms. When a strategic alliance's internally developed proprietary assets become valuable and difficult to replicate, it is more likely to improve its performance in the marketplace. The policy of deregulation through foreign investment is perceived as a significant incentive by the government, and most local firms encourage inward technology transfer from foreign firms to China with great enthusiasm. The government may support certain local firms as 'promising' cases for technology importation and provide them with R&D grants and technology support. The mapping of a foreign firm's technology investments onto the needs of Chinese businesses requires significant attention to each of the following four critical elements that are mainly associated with process of technology transfer in a strategic alliance.

Technology resources and knowledge endorsement may bolster a local firm's technological legitimacy and competitiveness. To create more value from the available foreign technology, local firms need to mobilize complementary external resources to enable them to adapt the foreign partners' resources, knowledge and capabilities for their overall business development. Foreign firms in China transfer 'hard technologies' in patentable forms to a strategic alliance, but they also create positive externalities by transferring 'soft' technologies such as managerial skills. This stimulates competition within particular and adjacent industrial sectors. The Chinese government's strategies for international technology transfer involve the creation of greater opportunities to co-operate with foreign technology exporters. Foreign firms treat international technology transfer as an attractive way to overcome the restrictions of a host country's market. Lack of in-house technology development capabilities in domestic industries explains the high percentage of technology hardware in Chinese imports.

Technology transfer involves co-operative and bilateral relationships in which firms give or take resources and maintain long-term ties through the formation of a strategic alliance. A strategic alliance's technology transfer is expected to prompt local competitors to be more efficient and acquire the equivalent technology, imitate production processes and assimilate the managerial practices necessary to compete. The technology transfer evident in most strategic alliances often requires them to hire good senior managers and staff from local Chinese firms, and the terms and conditions offered are often good enough to attract the best. The hybrid forms of corporate governance in an international strategic alliance enable continual rapid growth as their technological activities are unbundled and globally dispersed throughout the firm. The developments occurring with strategic alliances mean that technology transfer can become a two-way street between the developed countries' firms and the emerging countries' firms. Direct assessments of comparative technological advancement are generally possible for hard technology transfers. Soft technology, taken essentially as management know-how, is measured through a series of comparative items that include managerial skill requirements and the overall efficiency and effectiveness of technological advance.

Decisions about the type and level of the technology transferred to a strategic alliance will be made by a partner firm on the basis that the power accruing from the technology depends on its availability. If a local partner firm is highly dependent upon another partner's technology within a strategic alliance, then the foreign partner firm will have power over the local partner firm. Resource dependency theory proposes that technological factors are critical in determining the dependence of one partner of a strategic alliance upon another and therefore their relative power. The more important the technology controlled by one partner, the more the other partner will be dependent upon it and the greater will be the power of the transferring firm over other partners. The fewer alternative sources there are for technology controlled by a given partner, the more other partner firms will be dependent upon it for that resource and the greater will be the power of the technology-endowed partner. The greater the degree of discretion that a partner has in the deployment of the technology, the greater will be others' dependence on it and the greater will be its power.

International technology transfer can be increased by the use of technology development projects that involve suppliers or customers in active involvement in technological co-operation. International technology transfer via horizontal or vertical linkages is assessed by using a range of variables including associability in terms of those memberships of trade associations, state grants and human capital developments that are perceived to significantly impact on business competition in China. Strategic alliances in China are increasingly extending the application of their technology through business co-operation to maximize the use of those technologies. When a firm's technology is transferred internationally, technology application extension is seen increasingly as a means whereby a strategic alliance or joint technology project can globalize production operations as they allow investing firms to take advantage of market-related factors.

The quality of technology transfer is measured by the achievement of certain significant benefits from the point of view of a host country. International technology transfer is expected to influence local Chinese firms' performance not only because a technology transfer can improve local firms' technology strength, but also because the transferred technology may lead to successful commercialization in the local marketplace. Teece (1986) suggests that the level of technology, the existence of a dominant design in an industry and the presence of complementary assets are critical conditions for successful commercialization of technology. His studies suggest that a strategic alliance's capability to integrate technology into the local production and commercialization systems is critical for the commercial success of a foreign market entry. The quality of technology transfer of this type of capability is especially important when a foreign firm enters an emerging economic region in which established distribution networks, technical specifications and designs rarely exist.

Absorptive capacity and technology transfer

The competence and absorptive capacity of the local partner firm necessary to form a strategic alliance may be of great concern to the foreign firm in the context of technology transfer, as the partners' experience in mechanistic training cannot ensure the implementation of the package of technology transferred. In the case of a strategic alliance in China, there is likely to be less concern about the investment in physical assets than about the investment in advanced technology. The main objectives of technology-related investment in China are the development of the practical technical skills necessary to implement applied product and process development. Retention of 'key experts' for the whole process of a firm's technology transfer is perceived as one of the main problems. The production facilities in most strategic alliances vary from full lines to partial lines that consist of assembly/packages. A strategic alliance in China needs to obtain a technology licence before it can import a technology structure. The process of obtaining a licence requires foreign firms to submit patent applications which may then need to be reviewed by government agencies and/or by firms appointed by the authorities.

One way to expand a strategic alliance's technological activities has been through co-operation with local universities. High levels of technology importation by a strategic alliance may create the need to recruit qualified technicians and managerial staff and this requires investment in human capital development if high growth is to be achieved in prosperous business areas. Technological collaborations are perceived as one of the most elegant solutions for foreign firms wishing to access the host country's market and use a strategic alliance as a base for production and R&D activities.

Technology-based activities in a strategic alliance can be difficult to control as the dangers of duplication of work by different partners can lead to a drift in strategic focus and the possibility of proprietary technology leakage. China is actively trying to import foreign technology, and the government evidently recognizes the strategic role of technologies exercised for a host country's economic development. China's policies to encourage technology transfer have focused on incentives such as tax exemptions offered for foreign investments that are technology-oriented or that generate export-oriented projects. International technology transfer is also influenced by characteristics of the host country, including FDI policies, technology policies and demand and supply-side characteristics of the host government's economy.

Imported technology is usually acquired through local Chinese firms operating as privately-owned enterprises, collectively-owned enterprises or state-owned enterprises. The advantages from technology transfer can generate various types of linkages with local suppliers, customers and competitor firms. The Chinese eagerness to obtain foreign firms' technology arises from evidence of the positive economic consequences of earlier technology-based policies.

The decision to engage in technology transfer requires the ability to select from available technologies because an appropriate imported technology is able to introduce a degree of novelty in products or processes. Thereafter, the assimilation of another firm's technology is heavily dependent upon the development of in-house technological capabilities. Given that international technology transfer is a complex process that usually requires both material resources and product design improvement, a range of skills and technological know-how is necessary. Technology transfer to a strategic alliance involves the assimilation of a bundle of related resources, knowledge and capabilities, and to enable this to happen the existing technology base must have the ability to serve as a source of sustainable differentiated products that generate competitive advantage.

Technology literature states that an improvement in the absorptive capacity of a strategic alliance is a measure of value of the strategic alliance's technology stock, its motivational disposition to share technology and the richness of transmission channels. The primary reason for the existence of most strategic alliances in China is their ability to transfer and exploit technology more effectively and efficiently in the intra-organizational context than through external market mechanisms.

As the market continues to become more open, competitive and global, local firms need such absorptive capabilities if they are to increase their technological levels. The transferor firm's willingness to engage in technology transfer is determined by a number of factors, including the perceived need to internalize control over proprietary technological know-how, the incentive to exploit knowledge and the availability of scientifically and technically trained manpower in a strategic alliance.

Technology transfer performance

Most foreign firms engaged in transferring technology to a host country need to protect their core technology from misappropriation by local partners when attempting to strengthen their competitive advantage through the establishment of a strategic alliance. Technology transfer to a strategic alliance means that its absorption can in the longer term create new competitors unless measures and procedures are implemented that prevent leakage of product know-how, and the technology transferor firms can stay ahead in the technological race through their own technological development. Many foreign firms are international players that have to develop global production systems, and they see China as a huge potential market as well as a base for production and source of raw materials. One of the main reasons for the establishment of manufacturing, sales, service and R&D in China is to access a new source of highly motivated, technologically well-educated people that are scarce in any part of the world. As part of the process of technology transfer, a technology transferor firm may face the risks of leakage of its proprietary technology and know-how to a strategic alliance partner. To safeguard against potential inter-firm spillage, strategic alliance partners need to specify in agreements what each partner's obligatory duties regarding joint outcomes are and create incentives for both partners to work primarily towards 'common benefits' (see Table 7.2).

Incentives for both partners to work primarily towards 'common benefits' create situations in which partner firms jointly gain or lose from the performance of the strategic alliance. In emerging economic regions, local and foreign firms have quite different interests and expectations for a strategic alliance. Local partners try to access or acquire technology and may seek to use it in other products, services or geographic markets. Typically, foreign firms bring advanced technology and strategic expertise to a strategic alliance and try to appropriate maximum earnings by exploiting the transferred technology in the local marketplace. The existence of such asymmetric interests and expectations

Table 7.2 Identification of the primary technological activities that affect the performance of technology transfer

Technological activities	Typical implications for the establishment	Typical implications for the implementation
On-going existing technological activity	Identification of general technological plans only. Predictable outcomes and direction with limits.	Formulation of specific plans and tasks. Monitoring undertaken against the experience of previous activities.
New technological activity	Careful, detailed plans. Perhaps selective. Staged release of funds for the new technological activities.	Monitor the programme in depth. Use detailed progress reports. Ensure the validity of the new technological activity projections.

often promotes opportunistic behaviour by a partner, and such free riding on the alliance provides a strong incentive for the aggrieved partner to seek control over a strategic alliance's operations. Performance assessment and the economic valuation of technology transfer are difficult since actual product know-how is usually an intangible input in the production process.

Technology royalties are based on usefulness or effectiveness. However, the willingness of firms from a developed country to exchange technology with firms from developing countries often depends crucially on the existence of a legal framework for intellectual property rights that protects the interests of technology owners locally. The protection of intellectual property in the form of patents, trademarks, service marks, design registrations and copyright is now at the forefront of the globalization of markets for ideas, technology and economics. With the exception of a few areas of technology where trade secrets are adequate protection, intellectual property laws need to be strong, effective and, most importantly, enforced if the technology transfer from the host country is to be encouraged. The Chinese legal system is based on the premise that it protects the interests of the state and society as a whole. Its emphasis on harmony and self-governance has given rise to huge concerns from technologically advanced nations about technology protection.

Whether technology transfer is successful or not depends in part on the availability of supporting infrastructure. Where the effectiveness protection of a technology transfer is unknown, a firm may become more averse to the financial risks of investment. As a consequence, it is more likely to reduce its levels of technology transfer commitment and delay entry, unless there is a well-established legal method whereby it can resolve intellectual property rights uncertainties. There are many difficulties in defining and measuring the technology gap between the partners in a strategic alliance, and it is even more of a challenge to measure how the gap is diminished by inward investment because technology development cannot be limited to defined channels, it is interactive, and technology transfer is multifaceted. The transfer of specific technological components can be shown to result in the stimulation of local firms due to the transfer of products and equipment. This is particularly visible where an existing product is updated and equipment supplied as the result of technological investment leads to new products of novel design and high quality being subsequently produced from highly automated equipment to a high production standard. The main stimulus to the creation of new products by local Chinese firms comes as a consequence of their acquisition of external technology as this leads them to pay more attention to R&D activities. Technology is one form of intangible asset that can serve as a source of competitive advantage, particularly when it is valuable, non-imitable and non-substitutable, but this advantage must be sustained as existing technology diffuses into the market or competitors will start to gain market share.

Summary

This chapter summarizes how an international strategic alliance with high-technology intensity may prefer to have complete control over its proprietary product know-how in order to preserve and/or best exploit the product know-how, given imperfections in the external markets for technology development. The management of international technology transfer is complicated as it is not only a combination of technical matters, capital and personnel, but is also influenced by different cultures and social systems around the world. The ownership determinants required in a strategic alliance will define the extent to which a firm's resource advantages are perceived as highly competitive in a host country's market.

8

Exercising the Strategic Role of the Board and Management

Introduction

This chapter describes how a firm's equity investment in an international strategic alliance may allow privileges such as veto rights and how it enables management influence through representation on the board of directors. A wide range of control strategies are available to an international strategic alliance including the board of directors, an array of contractual agreements concerning the firm's non-capital investments, the appointment of key managerial personnel and formalized reporting relationships. Foreign firms' investments may adopt a particular governance strategy in China, such as concentrated ownership in a strategic alliance that enables them to leverage their superior technologies or managerial expertise as well as to protect their proprietary assets. State ownership in a strategic alliance is frequently used as a means to achieve public-policy objectives. The actual equity share of the partner firms may serve as an adequate indicator of the extent of its influence on a strategic alliance's management and the level of a partner firm's management involvement.

Strategic role of the board of directors

An international strategic alliance may require a combination of ownership resources provided by parent firms and the acquisition of locally-based resources from the market where the strategic alliance operates in order to achieve a competitive advantage. The dual imperatives of global and host country markets demand such 'resource combinations' that not only support a strategic alliance's competitive advantage internationally but also promote success in the local market where the strategic alliance is sited. Partner firms' capital and non-capital resources are used as an indicator of a partners' corporate governance over the strategic alliance management. Williamson (1985) defines corporate governance as the activities of choosing operating rules and enforcing them to maximize the organization's objectives. Corporate governance in an international strategic alliance's context is a process by which partners influence a strategic alliance to behave in ways that lead to the achievement of partner firms' objectives as well as the objectives of a strategic alliance.

Partner firms are able to exercise a proactive strategy from their business investments if they can gain control of corporate governance over the strategic alliance's management. This is particularly true when the partners have differing agendas for forming a strategic alliance in China. Effective corporate governance built into a strategic alliance can enable the right of management participation in decision-making. The direction in which the strategic alliance moves and the ways in which pooled resources are allocated and utilized will create a direct and critical impact on the performance of the strategic alliance. Figure 8.1 employs governance field analyses that several control areas such as business sector targeting, strategic development priorities, innovation policies, and staff control are recognized as areas where the driving forces of the board of directors exercises strategic control over the management of an international strategic alliance.

Regular rotation of board members from one particular partner firm creates a new kind of strategic control. Frequent rotation of board

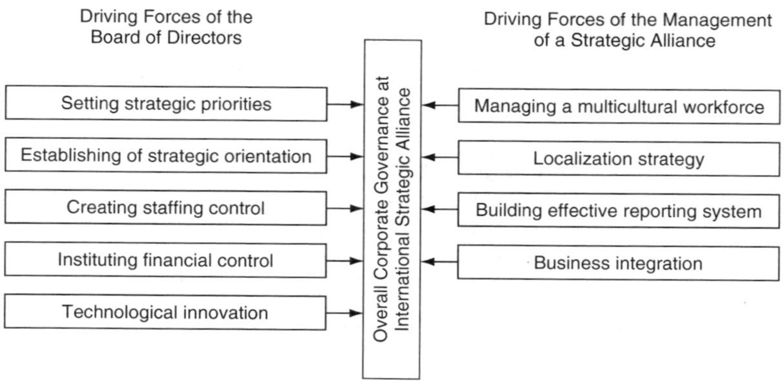

Figure 8.1 Governance field analyses of international strategic alliances

members within an international strategic alliance helps to modify or co-ordinate the strategic actions of the organization. Rotation of a strategic alliance's board members may also add new dimensions to the established corporate culture and new information networks. One of the responsibilities of a board member in a strategic alliance is to promote business contacts and enhance decentralized control of the organization, and this is almost inevitable if the board members are regularly rotated. The strategic decisions of the board of directors may impose conflicting demands on the general manager, particularly if the reporting requirements of the parent firm conflict with the needs of the strategic alliance management team. Managing the strategic role of the board and yet ensuring harmonious co-ordination with a strategic alliance management is perceived as one of the most difficult challenges that a general manager faces. In meeting such a challenge, members of the board of a strategic alliance, who often have many other responsibilities, may be limited in terms of capacity and time to attune themselves to the varied demands of the board members. The strategic decisions of the board of directors are implemented through groups at various levels in the alliance and their activities are monitored either by the board of directors itself, the management team or the steering committee. The board of directors will be made up of managers from the partner firms of a strategic alliance and outsiders recognized for their contributions in mediation.

The main strategic responsibilities of the board of directors are to provide the formal organizational link between the strategic alliance and its partner firms in order to create and direct the mission and strategies. The board of directors must be given legal authority and voting rights to define the scope of the strategic alliance's operation consistent with the strategies and business definitions of the partner firm. This includes the development of corporate governance, the establishment of fundamental organizational values and the setting of managing principles. The chairman of the board is the legal representative and responsible for overall management of the international strategic alliance. The local and foreign partners are both represented by the board of directors and they participate in the management of the strategic alliance. The board of directors has the strategic responsibility for ensuring that the appropriate levels of technology and management expertise are available to the alliance from critical resources provided by the parent firms. Furthermore, the formal strategic alliance management and organizational arrangements require a significant long-term commitment by the board of directors. The right to appoint the chairman goes to the majority partner firm and the right to appoint the vice chairman goes to the equal or minority partner. When a partner firm has a majority stake, it may have the dominant governance role as it possesses the important legal right to appoint the chairman of the board.

Some partner firms consider the right of chairman selection to be strategically important. However, other partner firms regard the chairman as a figurehead and even allow their local minority partners to have the right to appoint the 'chairman' position. The board of directors must establish control mechanisms over the strategic alliance management but these are mediated through the host country's legal institutions and the establishment of social relationships for corporate governance. The effective possession of critical resources and expertise by a strategic alliance must be constructed in a way that follows the prevailing legal forms. The achievement of high levels of control depends on how the strategic role of the board is exercised to provide the necessary guidance needed for potential market development.

The ability of the board members of a strategic alliance to provide such guidance is vital for the success of an organization as it is the board which has power over the resources and technologies that partner firms invest. In the governance of a strategic alliance, a partner firm that contributes necessary and critical resources is likely to retain more control and power over strategic matters. The ability of a partner to exercise strategic control depends on the constitution of the board of directors, as it is they who are able to exercise power and control over the strategic alliance management. Increased involvement by board members in a strategic alliance's management may pose conflicting demands on the limited time and capacity of those board members. The senior management team nominated by the board of directors is responsible for overseeing the strategic alliance's business operations, achieving its strategic plan and harnessing the inherent synergies. In addition, the proper execution of strategy defined by the board of directors provides strategic focus and motivates the strategic alliance's workforce to produce the results expected by the partner firms. The board of directors should make appointments to key management positions that are perceived as strategic control roles. The governance structure of a strategic alliance consists of the board of directors and the organizational structure it creates in order to provide effective co-ordination of the business affairs of the strategic alliance. The governance structure of a strategic alliance is intended to ensure the provision of appropriate leadership, the continuity of organizational purpose and management of the negotiated win–win agreements.

The strategic role of the board of directors is to define how a strategic alliance's investments are allocated on an on-going basis and to provide practical guidance on how the strategic alliance should be developed in order to meet market challenges. The strategic role of the board also serves to transfer a partner firm's values, objectives and 'ways of doing things' to the strategic alliance. Execution of these roles is expected to be the most effective method of meeting directors' responsibilities to the international strategic alliance. Individual members of the board of directors may also add to the management capacity by making their own existing formal and informal networks available to the international strategic alliance. The use of board meetings provides an opportunity to keep significant strategic matters under appropriate review and to keep all partner firms adequately informed. This is particularly important for strategic subjects where legalized authority has been delegated to one of the partners, but the others maintain a strong interest and have a right to know what is going on. The setting of strategic priorities, the establishment of a strategic orientation, the creation of staff control, the institution of financial control and direction of innovation may require the unanimous agreement of the board members as these strategic roles can be employed as effective weapons to control the strategic alliance management.

Setting strategic priorities

The establishment of strategic priorities for the partnership's management needs to ensure the most effective use of the ownership resources it shares with its partner firms because strategic priorities can be designed to prevent leakage of proprietary knowledge. The nature of a strategic alliance's ownership investment influences the efficiency of its governance structures. A firm's local knowledge may encompass a broad array of host country characteristics, including legal rules and the social norms for local business transactions. The combination of partner contributions in managerial skills and knowledge can affect the strategic alliance's structural configurations with respect to its strategic priorities. A strategic alliance's priorities will also be reflected in an organization's basic organizational design and management processes to co-ordinate and/or control business operations. Ownership determinants control the conditions of use of a strategic alliance's resources and will determine a partner's property rights. Where property rights are strong and environmental risks are lower, an international strategic alliance is likely to set strategic priorities locally as its ownership assets may face greater transactional opportunities and returns are highly predictable.

Board discussions of a strategic alliance's strategic priorities will include variables such as functional forms, governance system, co-ordination mechanisms and degree of autonomy.

Setting strategic priorities at the board of directors' level for the management of a strategic alliance becomes critically important when managers, who have been nominated by partner firms to work in a strategic alliance context are perceived as having differences in beliefs and values for setting financial and strategic targets. These differences can be minimized when the board of directors have decided to adopt specific performance standards, task completion targets and organizational practices. The establishment of strategic priorities in an alliance ensures the existence of economic activities that include the acquisition of low cost sourcing, the minimization of combined production and transaction costs, an increase in economic scale, the improvement of competitive position, the acquisition of knowledge through learning processes, business expansion into international markets and the addition of new skills to improve its human resource capital.

Establishing a strategic orientation

The strategic orientation defines how a strategic alliance will wish to influence the operation of the organization within the given investment profile and how this will be affected by management practices introduced by its partner firms. When an international strategic alliance is established, there is invariably considerable disparity between the management practices of the partners, and this causes difficulties in deciding which of the partner's performance standards should be adopted. Management issues are particularly significant when a partner with a strong bargaining position, derived from being able to bring advanced technology and management expertise to the strategic alliance, tries to impose specific management practices. Partner firms are likely to want to deploy their own management practices within international strategic alliances to establish fundamental strategic objectives that ensure strategic integration with their own corporate investment policies and organizational procedures.

It is key for the board members of a strategic alliance to acclimatize its workforce to the long-term strategic orientation agreed for the company if it is to establish its business presence in a foreign country. Partner firms' differences on the adoption of their own unique practices can be minimized if the long-term strategic orientation is emphasized during conflict resolution and high levels of organizational cohesion can be created. This may have profound implications for the traditional management approaches entrenched in local organizations as characterized by a tight social framework. A socially and psychologically driven business environment that maintains a high level of intolerance to business development is characteristic in China. Chinese firms normally like to establish traditional strategic orientations that ensure long-term existing business development in a way that increases their existing organizational cohesion. The development of a strategic alliance's long-term strategic orientation may need to deal with difficulties generated by the highly contextual communication, co-operation, exchange of knowledge and management commitments that are endemic in China. All of these factors are deeply rooted in most local Chinese firms and certain perceptions may be internalized in Chinese managers in the strategic alliance even though they acknowledge that managers from other partner firms will have different cultural backgrounds.

A long-term strategic orientation eventually works in the Chinese environment because most local firms are more persuaded by logical ethical evaluations than regulations. One way to improve the coherence of a strategic alliance's management is to use the concept of the 'long term' to foster internal order and co-ordination within the organization. The factors that need to be addressed at the strategic alliance board level in a 'strategic orientation' system include the objectives of the firm, the value framework, the cultivation of a collective sense, the construction of a firm's management traditions corporate image and the art of leadership. Management traditions and corporate governance can effectively enhance the establishment of long-term strategic orientation in a strategic alliance.

Creating staffing control

It is particularly important for the board of directors to exercise control of strategic alliance staff policies when technician and managerial skills are critically important to its performance. The nationalities and capabilities of managers and staff are asymmetric among the partner firms and, if the strategic alliance's general manager is appointed by the foreign partner, that person may be unable to satisfactorily evaluate a candidate's qualifications and suitability for a post. It is essential to ensure that an individual selected for a senior management position in a strategic alliance has the requisite technical and inter-personal skills and is receptive to new ideas. The senior management team in a strategic alliance must show the ability to disseminate their knowledge and a partner firm often feels the need to promote or nominate its own managerial staff in order to ensure attainment of its organizational goals.

Foreign engineers and technicians hold production skills in most strategic alliances whereas the local Chinese, who normally have the responsibility for local human resource management, mainly manage operational activities. International business literature states that the levels of both technological and managerial skill need to be high and it appears to be difficult to transfer these skills. However, it is important that the new technology and managerial skills brought in by partner firms should be assimilated into the organization if entrepreneurship qualities are to be developed. The main methods adopted to ensure the effective transfer of resources, knowledge and capability involve the social relationship processes of recruitment, selection and formal training. The importation of foreign products and the upgrading of equipment provide the foundation for local technological improvements but they also cause technology dependency within a strategic alliance because a lack of associated inflow of product know-how may mean that the technology transfer is superficial.

The upgrading of production skills of an unskilled workforce through in-service training does not necessarily promote the development of innovative ideas. The alliance partner with rights to make senior management appointments tends to retain control over strategic matters. The management system of a strategic alliance is a coherent part of its organizational hierarchy, but the functional departments of the strategic alliance can also maintain an internal reporting relationship with their corresponding counterparts in their parental organizational hierarchies. It is rare that this parallel reporting occurs with more than one partner for any particular department because partner firms contribute substantially different types of expertise and effective knowledge management to a strategic alliance. The board of directors plays a functionally distinct and separate role in the strategic alliance's management by exercising control over staff recruitment as a strategic matter, which is also true of senior manager appointments. The partner firms' expertise utilization and the need for protection from opportunism is such that the foreign firm tends to take senior managerial positions in functional areas such as product development, engineering, manufacturing and quality control, whereas the local partner is likely to hold positions in marketing, sales, human resources and public relations.

The right to appoint the general manager is a very important control mechanism. This is because the general manager is in charge of the daily operations and is responsible for implementing the strategic decisions of the board, and is also given the authority to appoint personnel to other key functional positions. The key responsibilities for the general manager are to maintain relationships with each of the partner firms and to drive the strategic alliance management. The general manager must have the support of the board of directors in areas such as senior managers' nominations as this represents an important opportunity to establish a cohesive management team to run the strategic alliance's operations.

The strategic alliance's general manager must have the personality, strategic vision and leadership skills necessary to inspire confidence and to motivate employees drawn from different business cultures. Recruitment and control of a strategic alliance's top management positions may represent a crucial control mechanism for the board of directors, as it must build a team that covers the various knowledge requirements and can solve problems in all circumstances. The importance of controlling the appointment of a chairman is less important as the position may carry no special powers such as a veto or an extra vote in China. Parent firms have different approaches to the use of voting rights to appoint the general manager of a strategic alliance. There are many challenges that face expatriates who work in a strategic alliance, including dual parenting demands, complexity and multiplicity of organizational goals, geographic differences and multiple cultural differences. Management recruitment and staff control may be an effective tool to help ensure that the expatriate managers who are selected will work effectively within, and cope with, the demands and pressures of the strategic alliance environment. An expatriate manager appointment is an important vehicle for the establishment and maintenance of a partner firm's organizational integration and control over international expansion activities.

This can be accomplished by hiring host country nationals with no allegiance to local partner firms, training them in a regional office or at the home base and then nominating them to key managerial positions in the strategic alliance. This will of course manipulate the ratio of the host country nationals in the top management team. Expatriate manager appointments are associated with a strategic alliance's bureaucracy, corporate culture, control, systems risks and overseas operations. Staff control is also influenced by the bureaucratic control of the host country's managers but can be used to ensure that candidates are selected who have the required technical skills. Local recruitment practices tend to favour those candidates who will accept traditional Chinese organizational authority and who can learn to perform in accordance with the strategic alliance's rules and regulations, and may avoid those with entrepreneurial characteristics who may make good change agents. Key functional managers must exercise influence over recruitment policies across the complete value chain of a strategic alliance including R&D staff, production personnel, engineers, financial controllers and legal and administrative staff (Yan and Child 2000).

Instituting financial control

The effective allocation of a strategic alliance's resources is normally based upon accounting logic as a firm's business financial control system always influences its operational process and investment behaviour. The power to exercise financial control in a strategic alliance is dependent upon authority-based power arising from equity structure. However, the power to allocate dividends is often exercised through the board of directors who act in their strategic role to take decisions about reinvesting profits and establishing cost structures that will affect the probability of a strategic alliance achieving an excellent long-term performance. Financial control is typically concerned with establishment of organizational targets or a set of financial goals that will be used to direct the application of a strategic alliance's explicit and tacit resources. Financial control is used to maximize the value that the organization can extract from its resources, knowledge and capabilities and guides the use of technological resources towards markets in which the strategic alliance's managers can most effectively apply them. Instituting financial control can help explain the strategic alliance's performance in terms of the attainment of its financial goals. Williamson (1985) suggests that effective financial control requires managers to identity the different development stages at which a strategic alliance's scarce assets will need to be employed over a period of time.

Technological innovation

A strategic alliance's corporate governance, as set by the board, plays an important role in determining its ability to be technologically innovative as it influences the organization's ability to monitor, co-ordinate and integrate its business operations activities. Successful technological innovation requires that strategic alliances manage their operations at a high overall efficiency under conditions of change. Attainment of a strategic alliance's long-term objectives is contingent upon its ability to implement technological activities that exploit its distinctive competences along one or several critical dimensions of corporate activities. The achievement of business success through adherence to the dictates of a strategic alliance's corporate governance requires that the board of directors ensure that an effective technological innovation policy is implemented within its organization.

Where there are significant differences in the desire of organizations to acquire new technologies, strategic alliances that are competing in the emerging business market may differ in their 'absorptive capacity'. The ability to recognize the value of new technology requires that a strategic alliance not only explore, but also apply, technology to commercial ends. There are at least two reasons why absorptive capacity for technology innovation may differ between local and foreign firms. The first is related to their previous experience of technology development and the second is concerned with the extent of the ability to utilize new technology that is transferred, and this is to some extent dependent upon the existing technology base.

The characteristics of the host country and its business environment are expected to exert a dominant influence over the technologies a firm uses. The technological innovations a strategic alliance brings to the market may vary considerably in form, and the level of local technological contributions will change over time. Foreign firms invariably have to operate within the boundaries set by the host country government. A significant level of technological innovation means the host country needs to have absorbed technology transferred from outside and this is dependent upon a number of variables including R&D expenditure, rates of capital investment, corporate investment in training, protection of property rights and the number of technical personnel per capita. The ability to explore, assimilate and to make effective use of technology is entirely dependent upon a firm's absorptive capacity.

Technological innovation is often the basis of a strategic alliance's sustainable competitive advantage, since technological capabilities comprise product patents, technological knowledge and production skills that are valuable and difficult to imitate by competitors. Technological innovation also comprises trade secrets and product know-how that is generated by R&D and other technology-specific intellectual capital. Intellectual property confers the ability to create value by allowing strategic alliances to commercialize their new products, seize market opportunities and differentiate themselves from incumbents. Technological innovation provides a strategic alliance with unique competitive advantages, but the transfer of technology developed in foreign countries to a strategic alliance brings with it the possibility of leakage of the technology and the encouragement of copy-cat market competition. Strategic alliance partner firms in China must construct their ventures in such a way that there is a strong incentive to exploit technologies only within their boundaries of their organization.

Technological innovation plays a crucial role in enhancing the competitiveness of a strategic alliance. Partner firms will encourage a greater dispersion of technology activities within the organization when they have proper control over product know-how and technology patents. The main driving forces for technology dispersion include competitive pressures that increase the need to access new knowledge, expertise and skills in whichever foreign countries the strategic alliance is located. The enhancement of a strategic alliance's technological capabilities enables a partner to disperse its R&D to geographically separate locations. A policy of technological innovation within a strategic alliance permits inputs from partner firms' technology bases, better access to universities and research centres as well as the building of additional advanced intellectual property rights. The dispersion of technological activities can have an important positive impact on technological innovation in strategic alliances as the size of a partner firm's technology base can be increased through involvement in a strategic alliance.

Figure 8.2 provides a model of resource provision, key appointments and management of an international strategic alliance. The scope for technology innovations granted to managers by the board of directors is critical to how those managers perform their duties. The advancement

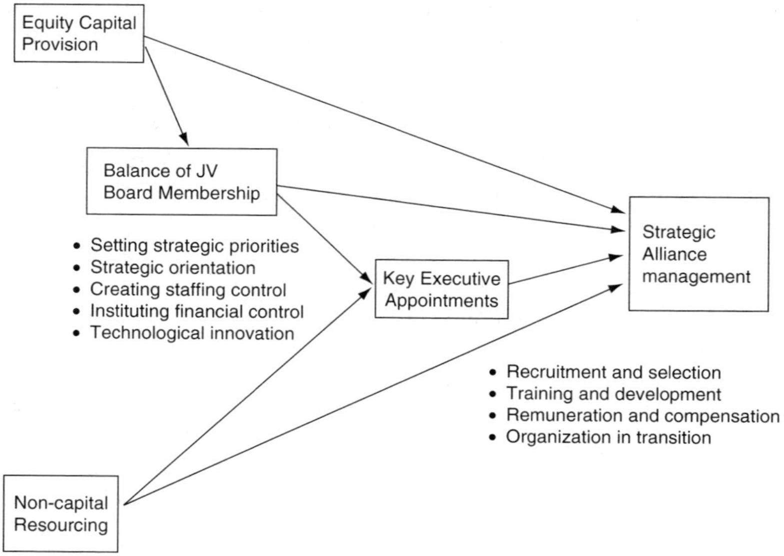

Figure 8.2 A general model of resource provision, key appointments and management of an international strategic alliance

of a firm's technology innovation capability *vis-à-vis* competitors is the most frequently mentioned objective of local partners in a strategic alliance. The acquisition of management and technology expertise are among the top two objectives mentioned by the local partners. Foreign partners in an international strategic alliance tend to commit to a range of product and production technology on equity capital provision and non-capital resource basis, but they rarely allow their brand name or trade mark to be included as part of any equity stake. Foreign partners tend to exercise control over technological developments, whereas the Chinese partners are forced to take some control in operational areas such as personnel management. In these situations, there can be a marked asymmetry in partners' relative ability to provide resources, knowledge and capabilities for further technological innovation. This asymmetry may enhance the potential for a foreign partner firm to manage technological innovation because it enhances the legitimacy of the partner that provides the technological resource, and this may facilitate technological development activities in China.

The strategic alliance's management

The management of a strategic alliance can exercise explicit control over the implementation of an alliance's strategies, as established by partner firms, and business operations. The level of partner firms' management involvement in explicit business roles is likely to be influenced by the relative equity levels within the strategic alliance. Senior management positions are normally filled first by selection from the strategic alliance's managerial pool and then recruited from the general labour market. Clearly, one of the most important criteria that senior managers of a strategic alliance must consider in making any effective business decision is to ensure that a strategic alliance's management team has the requisite skills to perform its business roles effectively. The management team of a strategic alliance normally includes talented individual managers seconded from the partner firms because of their unique management skills, technical knowledge, operational skills, experiences and qualifications. Until middle managers within a strategic alliance prove their capabilities, the senior managers from partner firms may have to undertake significant supervision of these people and will devote high levels of attention to the internal affairs of a strategic alliance.

Managing a multicultural workforce

The development of Western-style human resource management in a strategic alliance creates a major challenge to traditional cultures and indigenous local management approaches of managers and personnel seconded from the local partner companies. Managing a multicultural workforce in a strategic alliance encompasses formal legitimized legal procedures, organizational reporting relationships and authority based on rules, procedures and regulations. The management of a multicultural workforce in a strategic alliance is regarded as a complex and challenging job because issues occur primarily with respect to people's work ethics, values, attitudes and behavioural norms that would not normally be encountered in a single culture workforce. Research into cultural influences in the context of emerging economies such as China offers an opportunity to extend an understanding of the application of a strategic alliance's management activities. The pressures of operating in an international business environment can create uniformity of activity across all global business operations within a company and yet differences from the traditional culture entrenched in a strategic alliance's management are still observable. Research covering the management of a multicultural workforce in strategic alliances has so far paid scant attention to the fundamental question of how such indigenous cultural influences transform international practices at operational levels. There has, however, been research interest in the diagnosis of how business values and organizational principles affect the application of a strategic alliance's business.

The adoption of new technologies can be the driving force that leads a strategic alliance to unify its organizational behaviour in the handling of a multicultural workforce including the establishment of recruitment standards, training, increasing knowledge competence and the implementation of international business conventions. The management of a multicultural workforce involves recruitment, training, motivation and modification of ingrained organizational practices that are embedded within the strategic alliance, and this combination produces unique management practices. Differences in a strategic alliance's cultural values may account for the major operational differences in management practices, because the consequences of a strategic alliance's cultural influences, including business ethics, values and behavioural norms, may affect managerial patterns of behaviour. One should expect differences in the management of a multicultural workforce in a strategic alliance where an increase in the complexity of control is needed to mitigate the effects of personnel recruitment, management reward, organizational motivation and production.

The management of a multicultural workforce in a strategic alliance normally requires organizational linkages between parents, between parents and the strategic alliance, and co-ordination within the strategic alliance. Such linkages will also include customers, suppliers, competitors or professional and regulatory bodies. Mutual partnership dependence, obligation, reciprocation and consideration guide relationships in most strategic alliances in China. Managers can use the power and resources at their disposal to do favours and provide benefits for workers. The establishment of a trust relationship within the strategic alliance is perceived as essential if managers from partner firms are to be able to achieve the stated strategic objectives. The use in strategic alliances of managers who have received formal training offers a reliable channel for organizational learning and also ensures that adequate management of partner firms' resources, knowledge and capabilities can be secured.

The evidence suggests that it is more effective to rely on the development of a strategic alliance's own pool of managers and employees than to recruit people from local areas who may have a tendency to try to secure advantages in recruitment through the cultivation of special relationships. Equally, the implementation of formal recruitment and the use of formalized training rather than personalized procedures in a strategic alliance can be useful instruments to improve its relationships with external bodies and enhance managers' attitudes. Most managers perceive the development of a strategic alliance's trust and management practices as of paramount importance since it enables them to recognize the value of their partner firms as well as of the strategic alliance per se.

Localization strategy

Many strategic alliances in China with superior technology find that they need to be sensitive to local market needs, such as localization. Localization strategies refer to the degree of product differentiation demanded by different regional markets and the local availability of all necessary technology (Yan and Child 2002, 2004). The capability to improve 'localization' in a new local marketplace and the capability to earn profits from the commercialization of the transferred technology are highly specific. Localization strategies can increase 'local content' of specialized materials or components by the sharing of both technological knowledge and product know-how to achieve commercial ends. Specialized technology is more critical to the commercial success of an entry when the technology is highly tacit and/or its commercial application is complex and difficult to imitate.

The geographical and cultural distance between the foreign firms and the host country can be an important factor for adopting 'localization' strategies. It must be remembered however that more managerial time has to be spent to localize the content if the recipient is located in a distant country. Cultural differences further add to communication costs, and culturally sensitive staff members have to be deployed by the local partners to handle foreign firms' investment projects in order to avoid any cultural misunderstanding or conflicts. Localization policies as an organizational subject have been studied over a long period of time. Localization creates issues related to the partner firm's granting of corporate governance control to the strategic alliance management. To a large extent, localization strategies in a strategic alliance are considered as endogenous variables, subject solely to the strategic alliance's investment choice. The exercise of localization can be calibrated by measuring the quality and quantity of products or services delivered during a period of time. Localization can be secured throughout the operation of a strategic alliance by the selection of appropriate local managerial personnel, and foreign partners can exercise their technological influence over the 'local content' by the technology and management support they provide. In order to keep the foreign exchange position in balance, many strategic alliances in China are forced to source inputs such as raw materials, parts and components locally.

A serious issue for the high-tech producer is that local sourcing of the required inputs may not be possible in China. Even if inputs are available, local suppliers may not be able to deliver on time and the product quality may fail to meet the stringent standards demanded by high-tech production. Production can be disrupted by the failure of suppliers to meet delivery schedules and a large inventory may have to be kept in the firm, increasing the cost of production. Some strategic alliances in China work with local suppliers to solve quality control and other technical problems by arranging separate technology transfer agreements with them. Foreign firms often need to implement extensive training programmes for the local Chinese suppliers to make sure that the quality of supplies is assured. A market support service system should be included in the technology transfer package.

Facilitation of a strategic alliance's local supply becomes more focused with the increase of management competence. A strategic alliance's management becomes progressively more critical of the efficiency and quality of local suppliers as it becomes embedded in complex social organizational interactions and teamwork within a strategic alliance. Emphasis on a strategic alliance's relationship with suppliers, customers and competitors can be extended to promote managers' shared values, principles, beliefs, norms, aspirations and distinctive management competences. The management of a strategic alliance's provision of technology and relevant service skills to the supply chain requires the strengthening of decision processes used in the facilitation of a firm's recruitment, motivation, training and promotion of individuals.

Building effective reporting systems

The establishment of a strategic alliance's reporting system provides a stimulus for appropriate business ethnics, managerial values, social norms and organizational behaviours to be learned. An effective reporting system for a strategic alliance requires that personnel recruitment, management rewards and training are tailored to make sure that the operation of the reporting system can be understood in the context of an examination of a strategic alliance's managerial vision, organizational structure, career management, remuneration and motivation strategy. A well designed reporting structure allows a strategic alliance to harmonize the local management practices of partner firms and creates a high level of organizational cohesion. This has profound implications where a strategic alliance's management uses traditional Chinese organization structures and methods that are characterized by a tight social framework in which obedience, conformity, autocratic decision-making, close supervision, strong fulfilment and happiness is crucial to the harmony of the group.

A socially and psychologically driven business environment that maintains a high level of intolerance to organizational change and creates emotional barriers to the application of modern management practices characterizes China. Local firms may have limited incentive to increase organizational cohesion, and the establishment of a free exchange of information between departments through both horizontal and vertical flows within an organization can help. The effective development of a strategic alliance's reporting system needs to deal with its highly contextual communication, co-operation, explicit exchange of knowledge and management commitments, because these factors are deeply rooted in an organization and are constrained by the different cultural backgrounds of individuals.

Information sharing in a strategic alliance ensures that people with different cultures can exchange information despite the long-standing cultural patterns of traditional Chinese hierarchical management. The requirement to build an efficient communication structure within a strategic alliance demands an intermediate level of culture-brokers, including local and foreign practitioners, to facilitate organizational development. To be effective in this integrative role, managers must receive support, both internally from management and externally in the form of professional associations where practitioners can learn from others' experiences. It is important to engage people with the ability to develop into culture-brokers during the development of an effective reporting system within a strategic alliance. Building an effective reporting system into a strategic alliance is a challenge to management and, ultimately, to the strategic alliance and its partner firms.

The form of a strategic alliance's reporting activities across cultural barriers can be dependent upon whether or not the partner firms are interested in creating an efficient reporting system. The establishment of an appropriate reporting system will affect strategic values that regulate a strategic alliance's business behaviour. The Chinese management philosophy that knowledge is power gives rise to attitudes of information hoarding or information manipulation. Information can often only be obtained from a complex network that has to be developed and nurtured. Information sharing in a strategic alliance allows the managers an opportunity to anticipate problems. While the cultural values of harmony, hierarchy and attention to protocol probably render disagreement unlikely, the act of verbal acquiescence makes co-operation more probable. Effective reporting structures in strategic alliances involve the co-ordination of human effort and material resources towards the achievement of organizational objectives. The basic objectives of industrial organizations are economic in nature and ultimately reflect the desires of society for useful products and services. Clear reporting structures capture the utility of the information exchanged and are deemed to be a key indicant of the partnership's vitality. Three aspects of organizational behaviour are important in strategic alliance management and involve information quality, the extent of information sharing between partners, and participation in planning and goal setting.

The use of management reporting as an organizational control mechanism may take several forms. In a strategic alliance, partner firms that want to maintain control over the allegiance of a strategic alliance's personnel sometimes attempt to do so by keeping the strategic alliance's general manager or other key employees on the partner firms' own payroll. The major issue associated with this approach is that these employees may become merely a subset of the parent firm's operations and are not regarded as representing a distinct operating entity, as they may be biased towards the pursuit of the partner firms' objectives. This tends to produce an unstable situation where conflict and related performance problems are likely to result, especially if parameters generated from the reporting system are used to tie managers' bonuses, and possibly their career path within the partner firms' international operations, to the attainment of the strategic alliance's long-term objectives.

Business integration

Business integration in the current competitive environment demands great creativity in the crafting of solutions acceptable to a strategic alliance in China. Demonstrations of this creativity may be central to any increase in the influence of managers of a strategic alliance when forming new business strategies. With increased foreign investment in China, an understanding of business integration from the perspective of tactics for marketing mix, technology transformation and knowledge developments is essential. Indeed, the opening of the Chinese market has ushered in not only foreign investments of technology and management expertise, but also foreign cultures that challenge the traditional thinking processes and behavioural patterns of the local people. Many international strategic alliances find that integration should be regarded as a key factor in the avoidance of clashes between the corporate cultures of parent firms as the increased exposure of one culture to another in the context of business globalization is bound to lead to cultural clashes.

People cannot be expected to completely accept a foreign culture at the expense of their own. Business integration involves human organization that is cognitive, or 'of the mind', and has network characteristics that are as important as the business dealings themselves. Traditional local Chinese management practice is based on the importance of rituals and ceremonies. Social values and history have shaped the economic development and the current environment of business in China. The implicit and explicit rules that are embedded in Chinese society may have a significant impact on the development of businesses and the local economy in general. Business integration, including hiring and training, are extremely important to the success of a strategic alliance's operation in China. In order to meet such challenges, the selection of local people who have the potential to succeed and the provision of the training and learning experiences they need for development is the most effective way for a strategic alliance to retain the best managers.

Business integration can be an inflexible process that makes it difficult to acquire and utilize knowledge. It can also be used to facilitate rules, procedures and regulations adhered to in strategic alliances. In the strategic planning context, business integration enables a vast organizational memory of best practices that makes knowledge use more efficient. Business integration includes methods to build standards for the organization, its reporting strategies, its decision-making structure and its business practices. Some studies confirm that the most important advantages of business integration relate to officially established rules, regulations and procedures that help a firm search systematically for information that has emerged within the organization (Becker and Huselid 1998). When a strategic alliance applies integration to its operating system, the rules, regulations and procedures established become very important as the strategic alliance can then use a standard reporting structure to facilitate information flows and exploit its rent-seeking opportunities.

Chinese managers may find it difficult to hire people with the conscientious, proactive and creative approach to work that is valued in the West. In Chinese business practice, when problems are finally addressed the local managers' solutions are based on precedent and usually involve a reference to authority. Chinese managers value employees who anticipate and respond quickly to problems, and they also value employees who rely exclusively on experience or hierarchical authority because continuous improvement is important. Learning more about cultural factors that increase identification of national and corporate culture can be useful. The management of a strategic alliance plays a key operational role in investing, controlling and managing an organization, and an examination of the senior managers' role suggests that business integration involves activities to manage the linkage between a firm and its external environment, (i.e., the facilitation of government, legal and other public relations activities). The management of a strategic alliance's decision-taking activities is needed to guide the managerial values and behavioural norms that distinguish many operational attributes of its performance.

Establishment of a strategic alliance's management provides new stimuli within which appropriate business ethnics, managerial values, social norms and organizational behaviours can be learned. A fundamental assumption in studying a strategic alliance's decision-making activities is that personnel recruitment, management rewards, training and control mechanisms map onto the specific organizational properties of corporate culture. The application of decision-making can then be better understood in the context of an examination of the strategic alliance's managerial vision, organizational structure, career management, remuneration, motivation and recruitment strategy.

The ability to continuously improve a strategic alliance's management capabilities in a multicultural environment is associated with trust, relationship building, motivation, incentives, skills and entrepreneurial leadership. Deshpande and Webster (1989) find that trust and relationship building is positively related to customer satisfaction, as a participatory approach increases management effectiveness and enhances a firm's image in the eyes of its clients. A strategic alliance's trust-building mechanisms can be tracked through consideration of the need for local management practices and local knowledge. The management of a strategic alliance's decision-making activities should be implemented on the basis of best organizational practices, recruitment and training programmes as these are pre-eminent methods that achieve continuous quality improvements as measured in performance evaluations. Managers face huge challenges when they change to a new style of decision-making within well-established strategic alliances in China. Table 8.1

Table 8.1 Influence exercised over different areas and management issues by local and foreign parent firms

	Mean scores		Paired samples *t*-test	
Areas/issues	**Foreign parent(s) or representative**	**Chinese parent(s) or representative**	**Value of *t***	**Two-tail probability**
Board of Directors				
Setting strategic priorities	3.54	2.70	3.81	0.000
Establishing strategic orientation	3.70	2.61	4.23	0.000
Creating staffing control	3.45	2.67	2.84	0.006
Instituting financial control	3.94	2.21	6.09	0.000
Technological innovation	3.57	2.69	3.49	0.001
Strategic Alliance Management				
Managing a multicultural workforce	3.63	2.57	3.32	0.001
Localization strategy	3.78	2.42	4.62	0.000
Building effective reporting systems	3.97	2.37	5.99	0.000
Business integration	3.52	2.67	2.77	0.007
	3.57	2.69	3.02	0.004
Average of nine items above	3.66	2.58	4.75	0.000

Note: Influence is scaled from 1 = very little, to 5 = considerable.

shows influence exercised over different areas and issues of management by the board of directors, as well as by local and foreign parent firms in China.

Summary

This chapter provides an overview of the strategic role of the board and the strategic alliance management. The greatest influences on strategic alliance management concern the areas of managing a multicultural workforce, localization strategy, the building of an effective reporting system, decision-making, business integration, organization integration and building quality assurance systems with local suppliers. There is a marked asymmetry in local and foreign partners' relative ability to provide valuable resources. Such asymmetries may enhance the potential for one partner to gain control of corporate governance matters that deal with strategic alliance management, and this in turn can reduce the likelihood of disputes between the partners.

9
Corporate Culture and an International Strategic Alliance in Transition

Introduction

This chapter provides insights into cultural studies, including national culture, corporate culture and culture specific to a strategic alliance's management. It is believed that the exploration of the development of indigenous approaches is essential to the understanding of national culture and thus to the cultural influence on the management of an international strategic alliance. Management practices in a strategic alliance are embedded in partners' management traditions that influence their organizational behaviour at an international level. This chapter provides various alternative views of corporate culture and strategic alliances in transition that are directly related to differences between partner firms' national culture, legal institutions, social norms and management practices, since large cultural differences between the host country and foreign countries significantly constrain the effective application of management practices in most strategic alliances.

National cultural model

A strategic alliance's organizational principles, norms, business approach and management can be likened to the tip of an iceberg where the national cultures that facilitate its business management are equivalent to the iceberg's bulk under the surface. Behavioural aspects of culture, organizational principles and the management culture of a specific organization are the tip that floats above the surface. A strategic alliance's management practices, values, norms and managerial beliefs differ operationally in the organization from indigenous firms in China because of the alliance's multicultural nature. The enhancement of a strategic alliance's managerial values, cultural norms, organizational capabilities, competences and the ability to generate a culturally intermixed corporate culture may lead to better value-added based practices in the operational environment. National cultural analysis asserts that the country of origin may influence a strategic alliance's management practices through the mediation of a strategic alliance's strategic orientation and its corporate investment profile.

The influence of such corporate cultural practices can be highlighted for each country in terms of the strength of the institution's characteristics at the national level. National origin implies that business institutional foundations in different nations comprise the state, the legal rights, the financial and the socio-economic system. The magnitude and detail of the host country's institutional influence on the corporate culture of a strategic alliance can also be used as a foundation for country-specific predictions about the adoption of management practices. This implies that a strategic alliance will develop its own distinct characteristics from specific cultural preferences. Hofstede's model describes cultural value differences between nations in using five bipolar dimensions. These national culture dimensions are: power distance, individualism versus collectivism, masculinity versus femininity, uncertainty avoidance and Confucian dynamism. Figure 9.1 shows how the different dimensions of national culture will lead to different management approaches.

Power distance

Power distance denotes the extent to which members of a society accept the unequal distribution of power in an organization. The cultural dimension of power distance is defined as the degree of inequality among people that is accepted as the norm. In a high power distance country such as China, people accept differences in power more willingly and therefore have more hierarchical tendencies. For example, the Chinese manager in a strategic alliance is always expected to treat superiors and subordinates differently within the organizational hierarchy. The high power distance management of a Chinese firm may also be reluctant to negotiate with anyone but high-ranking members within an organization, because it assumes that those of lower rank will not have sufficient decision-making powers. Inequalities within the workplace are the expected norm in local Chinese firms. Subordinates are dependent on their more powerful superiors who are expected to protect them. Chinese social traditions dictate a rigid social hierarchy and this implies a distribution of power by ranking positions.

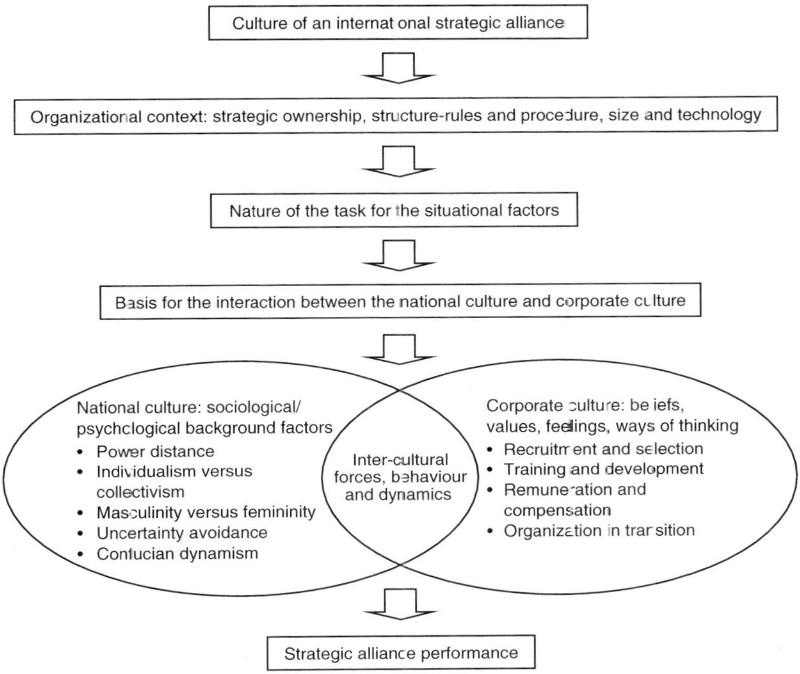

Figure 9.1 Exercising cultural attributes in an international strategic alliance

The results of power distance are often manifested by a lack of efficient vertical communication in most local Chinese firms. Blind obedience is expected in the execution of instructions from superiors, and avoidance of a direct challenge to power is typical behaviour. The top-down control approach results in general managers of many Chinese firms having inadequate operational feedback, so this type of control structure often leads to one-way communication. Open arguments with senior managers in a meeting about corporate strategies or job-related issues are rarely seen in local firms. Chinese managers in junior positions often feel unable or unwilling to voice their opinion freely in meetings when senior managers are present. Managers of a higher status are clearly being perceived as different from those of lower status within the local Chinese organization, and the managers have to be treated with great respect by junior managers and staff.

Individualism versus collectivism

Individualism implies that people are socially supposed to take care of themselves, as opposed to 'collectivist cultures' that are expected to take care of their members or reference group. Collectivism underlies egalitarianism in welfare and income distribution. This inclination towards egalitarianism driven by collectivism should be taken into consideration in managing employee relations. Collectivism usually demands strong requirements from, and commitments to, in-groups; it is defined as the degree to which people prefer to act as members of an organization and demand significant commitment from that organization. A collectivist orientation affects the social rules used to maintain the harmony of an organization. For example, a superior is responsible for maintaining an effective balance between subordinate human relationships and organizational goals.

Masculinity versus femininity

Masculinity versus femininity indicates the extent to which the dominant values of a society are gender oriented: for example, masculine values are assertive and competitive. The concepts of nurturing, intuitive 'face' or *mianzi*, are extremely important to those managers who run businesses in China. Causing someone to lose face in public or in front of his or her colleagues through criticism may result in a loss of co-operation in the near future. In China, 'face' cannot only be lost and saved: it can also be given. Doing something positively to enhance a firm's prestige and reputation are important. Actions to boost a firm's standing in a given community or society carry a great deal of weight among Chinese managers. Traditional Chinese culture is heavily dependent upon relationships, informality, internal hierarchical respect, the bond of trust, and long-term strategic orientation towards the organization.

Uncertainty avoidance

Uncertainty avoidance indicates the level of anxiety within the members of a society in the face of contingencies and unstructured or ambiguous situations. Connections, or *guanxi*, refers to situations where one's official position is used to obtain personal favours and commitments. The relevance of *guanxi* defines both the quality and importance of relationships outside an individual's immediate family. *Guanxi* ties people together according to the specific relationship between them. Chinese managers are expected to have different obligations within *guanxi* networks. People tied together by social ties are duty bound to fulfil mutual obligations even without personal relationships. Relationships are more highly valued in Chinese firms than in a Western management culture as business in China is carefully built on networks of relationships that are carefully nurtured and conducted in a spirit of reciprocity. Chinese management culture regards relationships as extremely important because they facilitate harmony and consensus around business objectives.

Confucian dynamism

Confucian dynamism can be defined as the extent to which a culture exhibits a pragmatic and long-term oriented perspective rather than a normative and short-term point of view. In China, this dimension reinforces the other Hofstede dimensions and can be explained by China's roots in the basic teaching of Confucius. There are two areas in which Confucian dynamism can be applied to cross-culture management in China. The first area focuses on long-term orientation and strategic goals, while the second area concentrates on pragmatic approaches. This degree of pragmatism may lead to difficulties in business situations: for example, where a Western manager may perceive an action as breaking the rules, a Chinese person may see the same action as bending the rules, due to Confucian values of flexibility. Confucian philosophies are so deeply ingrained in the minds of Chinese people that 'long-term strategic orientation' forms the essence of Chinese national culture. The principles of Confucian philosophies of a 'long-term strategic orientation' and a 'pragmatic approach' can be mapped effectively on to the Chinese business environment. The development of Chinese culture and the establishment of strategically-oriented approaches are consonant with indigenous thought essential to furthering the understanding of traditional Chinese culture. Table 9.1 shows the differences between strategic orientation and financial orientations as displayed by international strategic alliances in China.

Management of corporate culture

Corporate culture embodies a group of ruling ideas that includes methods of reasoning, ways of acting, common shared values, codes of behaviour and ethical standards. Corporate culture in an international strategic alliance takes account of the optimum combination of materials and production, as well as regulations and 'human resource management' (HRM) of an organization whilst functioning as a potential

Table 9.1 Long-term strategic orientation versus pragmatic business orientation on finance aspects displayed by an international strategic alliance

Application of human resource management practice	**Mean scores for a strategic alliance**		***t*-test for independent samples**	
	Chinese	**Foreign**	**Value of *t***	**Value of *p***
Long term strategic orientations				
Gain strategic position in China	2.23	3.42	1.29	0.23
Establish strong business presence in China	4.32	4.54	0.33	0.72
Opportunity for long term profit	2.56	3.69	1.24	0.21
Learning how to do business in China	2.90	3.43	0.64	0.42
Financial orientations				
Low-cost sourcing	3.72	3.93	0.32	0.73
Low labour cost	3.42	3.99	0.67	0.44
Benefit from transfer pricing	1.71	4.25	2.64	0.02
Benefit from tax incentives	3.77	3.68	0.10	0.92

Note: value of p is shown in $^{*} < 0.05$, $^{**} < 0.001$.

productivity driver for different partner firms. The critical outputs of corporate culture contribute to substantiating perception and a codified communication system. It should be noted that the corporate culture within a strategic alliance exerts significant influence on organizational structure which can be unencumbered by national contexts in different specific environments. Some studies include corporate culture as an aspect of the customs, practices, business norms, values and codifications of organizational principles. Management of corporate culture in a strategic alliance centres on embedded values, beliefs and priorities that interact with the organizational behaviour which ultimately influences performance. A strategic alliance needs to establish and successfully exercise its own corporate culture in order to improve its organizational co-ordination. A dominant organizational culture in a strategic alliance provides cohesiveness and principles that can be applied in tactical activities. This, in turn, should also improve organization effectiveness and lead to improved organizational performance (see Figure 9.2).

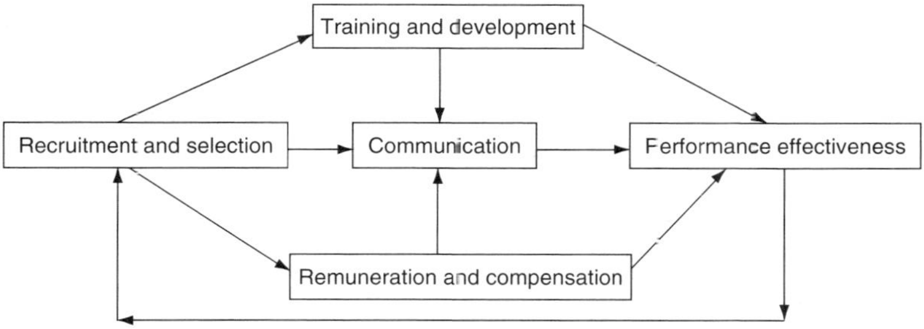

Figure 9.2 Management of corporate culture in an international strategic alliance

Recruitment and selection

The recruitment procedures and management selection process in a strategic alliance are seen as an asset that can be used to establish long-term organizational commitment to managers and employees. Recruitment has to be organized, within the constraints of government policies, to respond to labour market conditions. In recent years, the Chinese government has introduced many new human resource strategies to state-owned enterprises. Group work management, flexibility, harmonious peer evaluation and the building of subordinate relationships in management selection are typically found in most Chinese organizations. Employees in most strategic alliances are recruited freely through various external market channels. Multiple methods of recruitment are used by an international strategic alliance in China, such as referral from universities, recruitment consultants, job fairs, newspaper advertisements and labour agencies. The high-ranking factors in recruitment and management selection for most strategic alliances in China generally include: age, education, sex, marital status and training. At managerial levels, patronage in most local Chinese firms still exists. The aim of recruitment and management selection in a strategic alliance involves the identification of personnel who have the potential to succeed in senior management positions in the near future.

The recruitment of people from local state-owned enterprises, government departments or collective-owned enterprises may bring certain benefits for a strategic alliance based in China. Such recruits will enable these strategic alliances to gain access to existing business networks, and often their *guanxi* can be extremely beneficial when access to, or favourable treatment from, the government is required. It may be strategically appropriate to recruit such personnel, but in the long-term there is little chance for such recruits to move to senior management positions on the basis of merit. Most strategic alliances in China recruit mainly through the Chinese university system and have put in place various training programmes that identify and develop potential managers. Most strategic alliances in China have established excellent rapport with local educational authorities, who serve as successful and high-profile networks for Chinese graduate students. However, strategic alliances acknowledge that Chinese universities are not producing enough high-quality graduate students with the ability to meet the increasing demands that the market places on international firms in China. International strategic alliances are allowed to recruit candidates from outside the university system with or without the help of the local labour department. They are free to advertise in local newspapers, conduct interviews, and arrange written examinations and psychological tests to select the best candidates. One advantage of employing fresh university graduates is that they do not bring bad management practices into the workplace.

International strategic alliances in China benefit from the recruitment and management selection policies of Western management practice. A strategic alliance's management has to be perceived to be actively involved in the evaluation of local and expatriate managers recommended by partner firms. Recruitment and management selection policies established by a strategic alliance in China are best carried out through the establishment of an effective contract-based system where employees of a strategic alliance are required to enter into individual labour contracts, covering terms of employment, job descriptions, labour protection, working conditions, remuneration, discipline, termination and liability for contract breach.

In early international strategic alliances, foreign partners often relied on their Chinese partners to recruit employees to the venture. The overstaffed Chinese partners were keen to transfer excess employees to the international strategic alliance experience; however, too many employees from an existing Chinese partner firm would lead to inheritance of the power and social structure of the local organization. The foreign partner of a strategic alliance normally provides general managers, engineers or financial controllers for its strategic alliance. Local partners feel the need to be heavily involved in the appointment of Chinese managers as it is these managers who will provide them with accurate strategic and operational information channelled back from the strategic alliance to the Chinese parent firms.

Chinese managers commonly provided information that was a consolidation of detailed reports on items such as budgeting, product pricing and quality control. In many cases, the Chinese parent firms have greater confidence in the information that emanates from the local Chinese manager that they recruited than the original reports. This is in part due to the need for a manager who was previously employed in the local Chinese parent firm to demonstrate the ability to communicate effectively with his or her superiors in the parent firm and thus establish a solid relationship basis for the trust this creates. The Chinese economies comprise thriving local business communities with long-standing links of kinship. Foreign partners need access to the informal networking activities among ethnic Chinese employed in the strategic alliance, and this will possibly entail the recruitment of managers of Chinese origin with no ties to the local partner to take up various management appointments. The management selection of such candidates is in the control of the most senior management authorities who will use formal recruitment methods that take various criteria into consideration, ranging from age, experience and qualifications to loyalty and commitment.

Reliance on internal recruitment for management positions can be used by the local partner as effective 'selection policies' to create career advancement for its own people within the strategic alliance management team. Management of corporate culture in a strategic alliance relies on standard procedures for selection, appraisal, time-keeping, assessment of attitudes and discipline. Foreign managers typically find it quite difficult to persuade Chinese staff to accept external recruitment, especially if there are candidates for the internal management position who are local Chinese friends or colleagues in the *guanxi* tradition. In addition, there is usually resistance to the introduction of differential salaries, jobs where specific responsibilities are defined or jobs where the activities to be undertaken are defined. Chinese managers in a strategic alliance tend to be highly protective of their local employees. In Chinese culture, loyalty is generally appreciated even if the manager or staff member is totally incompetent.

Loyalty is a prerequisite quality of an effective recruitment and selection in Chinese firms. This inevitably means that there is a lack of clarity about the job responsibilities of the employee and the skills necessary to perform them effectively. It is clear that to conform to foreign recruitment standards, the introduction of job analysis to specify job definitions in a strategic alliance is essential and this facilitates the equitable distribution of workloads. Recruitment of technicians and managerial staff is usually through direct application by potential candidates who are then interviewed at monthly recruitment fairs in local *Rencai* centres. Recruitment can also be carried out by recommendations in most Chinese firms rather than through demonstrable evidence of effective job performance or competence. Although some management selection criteria are used in most strategic alliances in China, academic success counts for a great deal in the initial recruitment and management selection processes. The level of the degree held, the university attended and the subject studied are all highly significant determinants of success.

Expatriates in a strategic alliance complain that friends or relatives of the senior Chinese managers have been brought on to the international strategic alliance pay roles because they pay better than state-owned enterprises. Perceptual differences of recruitment and management selection are due to differences in the skills, job preferences, and attitudes displayed by foreign and Chinese managers in strategic alliances. Foreign managers tend to emphasize professional training, English language skills, and adaptivity, whereas local Chinese managers are inclined to put more emphases on work experience and personal relationships.

Training and development

Training and development aimed to equip people for their work is commonly provided to managers who work in an international strategic alliance and, as training and development are highly valued by Chinese employees, this is an acceptable way of introducing foreign management practices into a partnership. Training combined with job rotation can be used to develop a wide variety of skills and can be used to encourage Chinese staff to accept job responsibility as well as to eliminate traditional barriers between organizational departments. The recognition of an individual's job responsibilities, rewards for competence in performing tasks and systematic training programmes should be introduced into international strategic alliances to counter some of the less desirable aspects of traditional Chinese work culture. Chinese managers very seldom provide their personnel with feedback during and after training sessions, and formal evaluations are rarely available so few expatriates understand exactly whether the participants really have grasped the contents of the training. A widely used training solution in a strategic alliance is to send key Chinese managers overseas for formal as well as on-the-job training as this removes them from their own culture and allows a formal and objective assessment to be made. In addition, they are exposed to the partner firm's business practices and subsequently are likely to introduce some of their management training into strategic alliance operations.

Expatriates receiving training are expected to report on their learning experience and to specify how they are going to utilize this experience upon arrival at the strategic alliance. Training in a strategic alliance is used not only as an important management strategy but also as a way to persuade high-level local managers to accept certain organizational changes advocated by expatriate managers. Training abroad constitutes an important reward, and some foreign managers managing a strategic alliance in China even regard it as the single most important incentive at their disposal. The training provided to local Chinese managers, when combined with the possibility to travel abroad and receive overseas daily allowances paid in hard currency can be perceived as a major incentive.

When the training takes place in a strategic alliance, language problems arise that make it difficult to engage the participants in role-playing, discussions and employee presentations. Chinese managers may be uncomfortable with such training activities because these techniques are alien to the Chinese educational system. The aim of training in a strategic alliance is to improve the service, products and components received from suppliers, and to build good relationships with customers. Expatriate managers working in a strategic alliance are under constant performance pressure to run the operation and, as a result, they tend not to spend enough time coaching and training their Chinese colleagues. The tendency for many Chinese employees to transfer responsibility for their own development to their foreign superiors aggravates the learning and communication problems. Training is limited to just technical rather than management skills in many strategic alliances in China.

Management training includes the creation of values, education, working manners, regulations and procedures in line with new Western management styles, operational criteria, organizational objectives and quality consciousness. Training in most strategic alliances in China is mainly used to serve two goals: a 'technical' target and a 'social goal'. The strategic alliance may provide high-performing employees with an opportunity to attend technical training in China in pursuance of the technical target, although a spirit of technological training can also be cultivated through participation in the development of new products. There is ample evidence that formal and organized technical training for engineers and technicians in strategic alliances take place. 'Social goal' training, as exercised in a strategic alliance, concentrates on adaptive personality profile development together with cultural differentiation.

There is little opportunity to proceed beyond the interface of the established corporate culture until technical and managerial training have been successfully accomplished. The perception of management as a science and the preference for structured methods of training are related to the way in which managers are traditionally educated in China, expected to perform their tasks, and controlled. More and more foreign experts and specialists in different fields are invited to work in China with the expectation that they will bring new knowledge, advanced technology and special managerial skills and expertise. Many of the training courses in a strategic alliance are not controlled by expatriate managers, and the different approaches to training may prevent foreign experts in a strategic alliance from getting involved because this will create obstacles to the implementation of foreign training and development programmes in China.

The development programme for a strategic alliance can take the common bonds that corporate cultures have laid down in moral regulations through associated management practices. Such management practices and technology standards have considerable commonality with the sense of conscience in the foreign and local management cultures. Training preferences affect business practices and organizational conduct in strategic alliances. The training and development of organization members is also an important strategy in the development of strategic alliance businesses. Moreover, the focus of technical and managerial training in most strategic alliances has shifted from traditional topics such as internal selection and rewards to include concepts such as globalization, power and strategy.

Training and development in a strategic alliance have been important areas in international business studies. The adaptation of different managerial styles and structures among strategic alliances is a new area in training and development. The increased demand for managers who can work in strategic alliances in China has led to orientation training becoming particularly important in both local and overseas assignments, especially in terms of cross-cultural development programmes. Some strategic alliances now offer firm-specific quality training programmes which are designed to ensure that goals, values and policies are clearly understood and implemented. Training and development issues, functions, policies and practices may emerge from the increase in strategic alliance activities in China which will affect the quality of labour and efficiencies of the managers available. Positive training is cultivated by the encouragement of a sense of belonging to the international strategic alliance through the specific organization of teamwork activities. Increasingly, participative management styles can largely enhance effective management practices in a strategic alliance. Changes in important cultural features of a strategic alliance will also alter the management power structure.

Management development programmes concentrate on the improvement of the current or future strategic alliance business performance and anticipate changing managers' attitudes and increasing their skill level and knowledge. When implemented correctly, management development programmes can be regarded as useful control mechanisms because they can remove performance deficiencies, thereby improving a manager's ability to perform better. Development can also be used to encourage people to think and behave in ways consistent with the partners' culture, objectives and interests. In addition, management development in a strategic alliance can be used as a mechanism for the establishment and perpetuation of a unique corporate culture. The content of the development programme is of critical concern and many staff development activities are characterized as being too culture-specific or otherwise inappropriate for their intended cultural settings.

Remuneration and compensation

The subject of remuneration and compensation in a strategic alliance has received much attention, as the introduction of pay differentials for the local and foreign managers has met great obstacles. The widespread application of formal appraisal systems in a strategic alliance has been introduced with caution and very few strategic alliances in China have made explicit attempts to link performance appraisal to the local compensation system. The differences in remuneration and compensation between local and foreign employees are both sensitive and culture-bound. An important conclusion is that remuneration and compensation policies do matter if greater organizational control over the management of operations is to be implemented in a strategic alliance, but remuneration and compensation policies have a strong influence over a strategic alliance's contractual agreements and their labour protection policies.

In many international strategic alliances, the retention of managers and professionals is a significant problem, especially in large cities. Strategic alliance managers will participate in different kinds of social and professional networks in the locality, and this is an important vehicle for spreading ideas about appropriate packages for remuneration and compensation. Expatriate managers are often not in a position to control compensation policy decisions and are left out of decisions relating to compensation policies within the organization, but more often than not it is market forces that decide what has to be offered. Compensation packages in an international strategic alliance include three major components: basic salary, bonus and subsidies. Many foreign firms are attracted to China because of the low basic salaries paid to local labour. However, the total compensation package is much higher than might be imagined because the numerous bonuses and subsidies add significantly to the totals. Employees in some local Chinese firms are paid according to grade-based wages stipulated by the government and workers of the same grade are paid equally regardless of their performance, skills, knowledge, abilities and so on. Merit-based wage systems are now the norm in most strategic alliances in China.

The vast differences in compensation levels between advanced and developing countries means that expatriates enjoy a salary many times greater than that of locals even if they are occupying similar posts. This huge gap in the wage package often results in a deep sense of injustice and disgruntlement among local managers. Strategic alliances in China use various remuneration benefits and compensation assistance to attract and retain good expatriates. These employees may rely on benefits such as medical subsidies, vacations and retirement to secure their financial well-being.

The generous reward systems of most strategic alliances in China ensure the retention of quality people as the reward systems lead to high satisfaction, commitment and loyalty. The five most popular compensation components offered to employees in a strategic alliance are: basic salary, annual leave, paid sick leave, year-end bonus and maternity leave. Factors that retain employees are: basic salary, merit pay, year-end bonus, annual leave, and mortgage loans. Effective compensation policies in strategic alliances systematically co-ordinate all individual management practices and implement them so as to influence directly the management's attitude and behaviour in a way that helps the partnership in China to achieve its strategic objectives.

Employees who have benefited from effective compensation policies in a strategic alliance need to be able to pursue long-term objectives and devote proper consideration to the quality and quantity of products and services provided. Compensation policies and career development are normally emphasized by strategic alliances in China. The complete wage package in a strategic alliance commonly consists of the basic wage, bonuses and subsidies that include insurance, welfare, pension funds and housing fund payments to both the local employee and local authorities. The provision of numerous subsidies to employees is perceived as a distinct feature of the Chinese management system. Under socialist principles, in addition to meeting output quotas, state and collective-owned enterprises in China have to achieve their financial objectives as well as social objectives associated with wage packages and welfare benefits. Many international strategic alliances in China find that their ability to offer attractive housing benefits is crucial to hiring and keeping good technical personnel and managerial staff.

The introduction of a bonus system is meant to provide monetary incentives for the achievement of performance above the norm. The ideological legacy of egalitarianism is deeply ingrained in Chinese society and bonuses tend to be distributed rather evenly to all workers within a work group or production floor. This egalitarian mentality is likely to be transferred to the international strategic alliance by Chinese managers. Foreign managers who do not have the same ideological legacy, experience or expertise as their Chinese counterparts may oppose this. The remuneration and compensation systems introduced into a strategic alliance are often far removed from the 'collective norms' of Chinese tradition and the egalitarianism of socialist ideology. Although the organizational system of welfare benefits in China tends to emphasize economic equality, there are some significant changes in local management thinking in terms of a shift from egalitarianism to an emphasis on individual and team responsibility in the strategic alliance management context.

If a strategic alliance is to be successfully established in China, it must select an appropriate local partner and then formulate strategies, co-ordinate partners' activities and resolve conflicts, and so on. Although most strategic alliance contracts are for a fixed term, it is usually assumed that their intentions are to stay in China on a long-term basis. If managers do not expect to return to their firm of origin, they are likely to be faithful to the strategic alliance as the current employer and the partner will lose influence and control over them. One way to avoid conflicts of interest is to rotate the people assigned to the strategic alliance by making their assignment of short- or medium-term duration, even though the manager may not know whether he or she has to be loyal to the objectives of the strategic alliance. The external hiring of managers overcomes this dichotomy and has the advantage of being a rapid process, apart from favouring the creation of a strategic alliance's own remuneration and compensation culture.

The differences in remuneration and compensation in a strategic alliance can also affect the behaviour of the partner firms, strategic alliance management, and governance structure. When the difference in compensation packages between partners is small, local partners should have less difficulty transacting within the strategic alliance (i.e., compensation policies should have little or no influence on the ability of the local firms to achieve their goals). Compensation strategies are one of the main tools for a strategic alliance to improve and maintain the level of organizational competitiveness. Compensation issues arise every day in the course of joint operations in a strategic alliance, although their level of implementation may partly depend on the compatibility existing between the co-operating partner firms.

It appears that attractive compensation packages are necessary but not sufficient to retain good local managers, and managerial migration does take place. Continuous technical and career development for local managers now seems to be the key factor in manpower retention for a strategic alliance in China. A strategic alliance must recognize the long-term career aspirations of its local managers and satisfy their developmental and growth needs. A strategic alliance that has the reputation for development and promotion opportunities which enable local managers to enhance their career development will also be able to retain good employees. In addition to career prospects, inter-personal relationships within the strategic alliance also have a long-term impact on the retention of Chinese managers. It is very common for the Chinese managers who are recruited by the local partner of a strategic alliance to invite their best subordinates from their existing parent firms to follow them to the new strategic alliance. Equally, it is common for local employees to stay in a local Chinese firm mainly because they may have established strong personal relationships and organizational allegiance with their superiors.

The generation of fair remuneration and compensation policies promotes constructive inter-personal relationships and this has a positive effect on the commitment of managers who work in a strategic alliance. Local managers with a strong sense of security and strong links with their superiors and colleagues will commit to the strategic alliance and seek long-term career development within it. The most common way to ensure commitment is to use the strategic alliance's own staff to conduct internal training sessions. Foreigners are often impressed by the analytical skills of their Chinese employees, and stress their eagerness to learn new things. The initial training sessions for a new employee should reinforce the concept that the compensation package and bonus scheme are linked to the participant's performance in the short term and economic well-being in the long-term. The acceptance of a competitive compensation package in a strategic alliance is linked to the provision of the necessary preparatory training either internally, or through out-sourcing to local educational institutions.

Each person in China has a personal file that is controlled by the local government, and nobody can work for an organization unless their personal file is transferred to that employer. The local labour bureau's ability to assist in the transfer of a recruit depends very much on the political clout of the recruit's existing work unit. Recruitment of good personnel can be a complex process in China. An international strategic alliance in China can dismiss any employee who has become redundant as a result of changes in production and technical conditions. They can also be fired if, after training, they fail to meet new work requirements and are not suitable for transfer to other types of work. Several elements are used in strategic alliance compensation systems that can generate issues regarding pay differentials and performance rewards. Age-related and service-time wages plus basic pay are used in some strategic alliances in China, but these payments are relatively small as such a payment structure is considered to be designed only to benefit older or less skilled workers. Historically, people in China who have worked for the same length of time get almost the same pay. Every few years the state will raise the wage level of groups with the same service time and, although it is acknowledged to be anachronistic, as a compromise it is now added to basic pay. With more job openings becoming available for each qualified candidate, competition to recruit outstanding employees is intense and is probably one of the greatest challenges that both local and foreign firms are facing today in China. The results of adoption of human resource management practices in an international strategic alliance are shown in Table 9.2.

An international strategic alliance in transition

The role of management practices varies considerably depending upon the size, sector, cultural influences and type of ownership of an international strategic alliance. Foreign firms contemplating entry into China are faced with numerous management decisions regarding the financial and logistical requirements underlying their investment decisions. While investments are based upon various considerations, many foreign firms approach the Chinese market with the assumption that managerial demands will be similar to those in their domestic base or their other overseas operations. But, in reality, the attraction and retention of staff is one of the greatest challenges that these foreign firms have to face in China. The challenge includes overcoming

Table 9.2 Adoption of human resource management practices in an international strategic alliance

Application of human resource management practice	**Mean scores for a strategic alliance**		***t*-test for independent samples**	
	Chinese	**Foreign**	**Value of *t***	**Value of *p***
Formal recruitment versus relationship	5.52	3.26	1.24	0.21
Reliance on contracts	5.71	3.41	0.64	0.42
Formalization versus personalization	6.11	4.06	1.24	0.21
Emphasis on training	2.77	2.65	1.24	0.21
Integration between parent and affiliates	4.23	2.73	0.64	0.42
Reliance on formal reward system	4.80	2.98	1.24	0.21

entrenched management approaches and attitudes in the form of work ethics, intrinsic motivation, systems management, performance evaluation, personnel selection, production and quality control that are based on centuries of tradition in local firms. Such management practices and thinking are deeply rooted in the Chinese culture.

Employees who feel personally appreciated, respected, and involved by their managers in a strategic alliance are far more likely to stick with a job than those who do not. Managers must strive to show interest in, and concern for, their employees by asking about their families, and organizing and participating in their firms' outings and other social activities. This personal interest must start from the general manager and radiate down through the various levels of management. The practice of management in the local firms is generally guided by the belief that the role of managers is to implement specific rules and methods that can be learned and easily applied without the need for further development or independent critical thinking. The key factor that dominates traditional management thinking is that the rules and methods do not have to be set by the government in power but that they should not contradict the principles of the government's ideology. Foreign management techniques are accepted as long as they do not interfere with the local politics, national culture and traditional management practices.

The optimal management practices for a strategic alliance in China should place a major emphasis on explicit and detailed job descriptions that will direct the internal workforce. These will provide multiple avenues for promotion and encourage regular job rotation for employees in the strategic alliance. Good management practices emphasize training and will pay attention to internal and external pay equity. A systematic job analysis should be used to strengthen management roles and facilitate best management practice within the organizational system. All employees in most strategic alliances must sign contracts of employment with job specifications that are differentiated between first-line workers, technicians and management staff respectively in line with the social structure existing in China.

The role of the management in an international strategic alliance is different from traditional Chinese perspectives only in so far as ordinary personnel administration is much more flexible. Managers in most local firms are constrained by a pay budget that emphasizes welfare benefits, leaving limited room for manoeuvre when it comes to relating pay to individual employee performance. The most important work-related factors are attitudinal, including job satisfaction, organizational commitment and turnover. A strategic alliance may benefit from incorporating a more Western management approach that emphasizes more transparent, open and fair procedures for communicating with employees and for the allocation of material rewards. These management practices can be effective in the long run and it is possible to build up a long-term trust relationship if these management practices become the norm and the stated organizational principles are consistently applied. Many strategic alliances operating in China find it advantageous to invest in training and development programmes and in creating communication channels that subject employees' conduct to disciplinary regulations.

It is to be expected that local and foreign partners' views will differ widely across all major areas of management practice in a strategic alliance. The Chinese perspective takes into account the socio-economic and local environment, such as employment rates and government policies, whereas the foreign partner is mostly concerned with the overall management effectiveness of the strategic alliance. In the implementation of organizational regulations, rules and procedures, the Chinese partner is likely to favour rules that take into account contextual demands and mutual agreements, whereas expatriates normally favour procedures that are contractual and legalistic. Management in a strategic alliance in China is dynamic and changing rapidly due to the different management practices that most local and foreign partners adopt, causing conflict that hampers the overall management effectiveness of the international strategic alliance. In bridging this gap, it is important for both sides to discuss management practices openly right from the beginning and to negotiate a set of organizational policies that both sides can accept. The development of sound HRM practices in a strategic alliance must optimize joint interests and perceived fairness where open discussion of concerns, objectives and constraints is encouraged.

A central issue in recent debates has been concern for the overall management effectiveness of a strategic alliance in a debate that centres on the extent to which the distinctive management practices in a strategic alliance should reflect the characteristics of its originating parent firm's business systems. The pattern of management development in most strategic alliances in China has been uneven and the precise configuration of constructive management practices has been influenced by a variety of factors including past practices, rapid economic change, diversity of ownership and traditional management practices. The tenets of these local management practices are to boost organization performance through the careful selection of flexible job design, staff development, management participation and flexible rewards.

Empirical studies of Chinese management values at the organizational level are rare and differentially emphasize professional values in contrast to national cultural values. Chinese managers feel less comfortable than their foreign counterparts in dealing with uncertainties at work and emphasize more loyalty, belongingness and caring. The local Chinese managers' attitudes vary selectively with age, education, occupation and economic sector. The traditional Chinese hierarchical values that exist in local firms today emphasize power distance and the extent of resistance to acceptance of Western management values. Since China is a hierarchical and caste-based society with high power distance, Western management practices in a strategic alliance definitely create problems for the traditionalist. The power factor and its role in managerial actions are relevant in the socio-cultural milieu of hierarchical relations. However, the non-hierarchic, egalitarian sharing practices of the more competitive foreign firms are increasingly exercising their influence on strategic alliance management. The greatest challenge for an international strategic alliance in China is the need to earn public trust and credibility. They are expected to accord ethical standards higher priority than economic efficiency and legal compliance in organizational decision-making.

Effective management practices for the achievement of useful organizational purposes are theoretically more likely if the managers engage in open communication with personnel in their strategic

Table 9.3 Management of corporate culture in an international strategic alliance

	Recruitment and selection	Training and development	Remuneration and compensation	Performance effectiveness
Chinese managers' perceptions	• Recruitment is organized by employing government policies to respond to labour market conditions. • Group work management, flexibility, harmonious peer evaluation and building subordinate relationships in management selection are typically found now in most Chinese organizations.	• As training and development are eagerly sought by Chinese employees, it is an acceptable way of introducing foreign management practices in an international strategic alliance. • The training provided to the local Chinese managers with the possibility of travel abroad and the daily allowances paid overseas can be perceived as an additional incentive.	• Workers of the same grade are paid equally regardless of their performance, skills, knowledge, abilities and so on. • The merit-based wage system has been recently introduced in most strategic alliances in China. • An egalitarian mentality is likely to be brought into the international strategic alliance by Chinese managers	• Heavy support from foreign parent and active links to parent; local managers are given an active role in local networking. • Attracting or retaining employees for strategic alliances in China may prove the most challenging area. The typical challenges include work ethics, intrinsic motivation, systems management, and performance evaluation.

Table 9.3 (Continued)

	Recruitment and selection	Training and development	Remuneration and compensation	Performance effectiveness
	• Recruits will enable strategic alliances in China to use their existing business networks and often their *guanxi* can be extremely beneficial when access to, or favourable treatment from, the government is required.			
Foreign managers' perceptions	• The foreign partner of a strategic alliance normally provides general managers, engineers or financial controllers for its strategic alliance. Management of corporate culture in a strategic alliance relies on standard procedures for selection, appraisal, time-keeping, assessment of attitudes and discipline.	• When the training takes place in a strategic alliance, language problems arise that make it difficult to engage the participants in role-playing, discussions and employee presentations. • Expatriate managers working in a strategic alliance are under constant performance pressure and, as a result, they typically do not spend enough time coaching and training their Chinese colleagues.	• Foreign managers in a strategic alliance do not have the same ideological legacy, experience and expertise as their Chinese counterparts.	• Realistic and compatible goals are necessary. • Shared management based on cultivation of close relations and trust is preferable. • When goals are in conflict expectations will be unrealistic. • Conflictual relations lead to a high-blame, low trust climate.

	• Recruitment of talented, ambitious graduates straight from the local prestigious university is an important strategy for most strategic alliances in China as regards successful recruitment.		• The introduction of remuneration and compensation systems in a strategic alliance is furthest removed from the 'collective norms' of Chinese tradition and the egalitarianism of socialist ideology.	• Local parent often gives a low priority to the management of a strategic alliance.

alliances. These strategic alliances are encouraged to evaluate the effectiveness of their resources, knowledge and capability inputs, but they are also motivated to utilize management information to ensure procedural and substantive justice. The managers must display an appropriate leadership style and build an organizational ethics system that will enhance their reputation. Table 9.3 shows the management of corporate culture in an international strategic alliance.

Summary

This chapter shows how the formulation of a corporate culture is perceived as a conduit for transferring specific operational styles, types of customer-focused service, resources and capabilities in a strategic alliance. Emphasis on a strategic alliance's cultural variables can be extended to promote managers' shared values, principles, beliefs, norms, aspirations and distinctive management competences. This chapter also suggests that national culture and the corporate culture embedded in a strategic alliance's organizational system influences its organizational behaviour at an international level. In addition, the linking of partners' interest within an international strategic alliance in China should be greatly encouraged. Modern management practices in most strategic alliances have been affected by the rapid economic changes in the Chinese environment. This has dramatically led many strategic alliances not only to adopt the Western style of working and management behaviour but also to pay great attention to the utilization of local management conventions.

10
Organizational Learning

Introduction

This chapter examines how strategic alliances absorb, store and assimilate knowledge from their partner firms as well as how they update their own knowledge from the market where the strategic alliance operates. Organizational learning involves channels of knowledge acquisition through the management of an international strategic alliance. The formation of an international strategic alliance offers a novel learning experience that can provide a broad learning platform to allow access to knowledge about partner firms' resources, knowledge and capabilities. In transition economies such as China, foreign firms normally invest in those items of technology and organization know-how that are perceived as vital resources and useful knowledge for operation of an international strategic alliance. It is important to assess the learning activities that must be conducted in an international strategic alliance, as this will enable a partner firm to decide 'where' and 'how' it delivers its resources, knowledge and capabilities to maximize the benefits in foreign trade, international investment and international production that it will receive from its investment.

Learning conceptualization

The nature of an international strategic alliance shapes organizational learning, given that its partner firms have very different systems of corporate governance, political thinking and socio-cultural characteristics. The organizational linkages between partner firms may have a significant influence on the effectiveness of organizational learning in a strategic alliance through the operation of quasi-organization relationships. Current research focuses on how efficiencies achieved from organizational learning may affect the bargaining power relationships between partners and change their respective patterns of resource investments, control priorities and performance. Organizational learning is primarily treated as an organizational attribute as it contributes to the enhancement of the knowledge available to an organization and its ability to apply that knowledge effectively. The intrinsic nature of organizational learning in and between a strategic alliance and its partners requires an exploration of the strategic alliance's knowledge boundary within and between partner firms.

The full exploration of organizational learning in an international strategic alliance context involves the study of three types of transfer: (1) the transfer of knowledge by the partner firm to the strategic alliance; (2) the transfer of knowledge from one partner firm to the other via the strategic alliance; and (3) the creation of new knowledge by the strategic alliance itself. Organizational learning established in and through a strategic alliance is derived from elements that include strategic objective-setting, the abilities of the partners to understand or absorb new knowledge and the mechanisms to assimilate new knowledge in a way that increases its successful use. Organizational learning in a strategic alliance context is embedded in the partners' strategic objectives, institutional attributes and distinctive resources. The beneficial development of a strategic alliance's knowledge base relies primarily upon appropriate and effective feedback mechanisms being introduced by both local and foreign partners' management.

Technological and managerial staffs are transferred from partner firms to ensure the strategic alliance has the appropriate technology and management capability to fulfil its objectives. Strategic alliances are often established under the assumption that an injection of cash capital, advanced technology and management expertise from the foreign partner combined with local knowledge and distribution channels provided by the local Chinese firm, will deliver success more rapidly in the changing marketplace in which it operates. The success of learning can be most effectively examined by identifying the variables such as knowledge resources, skill competencies and structural attributes which have been invested in the strategic alliance to see how the associated knowledge is learned and effectively socialized between partners.

Achieving learning advantages

Organizational learning activities established within a strategic alliance involve the implementation of technology transfer, the management of partner firms' resources, and knowledge about the business environment in which the strategic alliance operates. Prior research indicates there is a gap in overall technical and managerial competency between local and foreign partners when an international strategic alliance is formed between firms from a developed country and firms from developing countries. Organizational learning mechanisms built into an international strategic alliance define the extent to which a firm can directly access a partner firm's resources, knowledge and capabilities. The strength of the learning mechanism generally describes how ambitious a strategic alliance is to learn and improve its organizational competencies. Figure 10.1 shows organizational learning in a strategic alliance is crucial in the case of a partnership where the geographical distance between the strategic alliance and the partner firms is large.

Learning in an international strategic alliance

Learning success within an international strategic alliance is often structured in such a way as to indicate the extent to which the strategic alliance has assimilated its joint partner objectives through the effective structuring and formulation of both explicit and implicit organizational routines in the market where it operates. A partner firm's organizational know-how dictates the establishment and management of new collaborations between partner firms in the form of a strategic alliance. Organizational learning in a strategic alliance is a complex, multifaceted construct as it must respond to a diversity of inputs including strategic objectives, reporting relationships and resource complementarities. Given this broad spectrum of learning issues, it is useful to conceptualize organizational learning in terms of its ability to help the strategic alliance's management to deliver the benefits sought from the market in which it is based.

The institution of learning mechanisms in a strategic alliance will enable managers to accurately assess the technological, marketing and

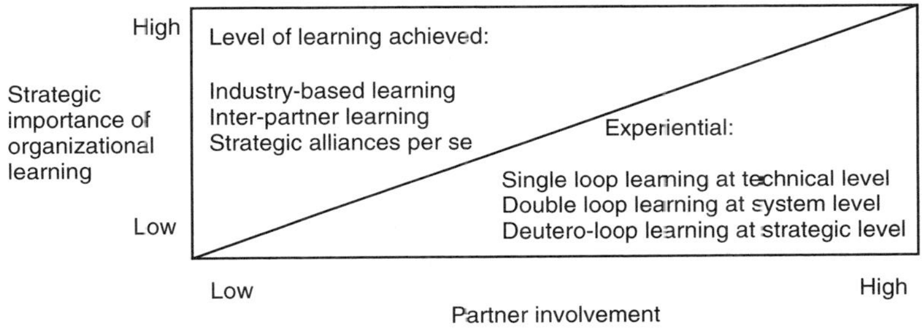

Figure 10.1 Organizational learning in an international strategic alliance

management capabilities available from its partner firms which they might have to use to respond to various organizational contingencies. The development of an international strategic alliance involves the acquisition of technological and managerial experience that can only be accomplished through learning processes and the ability to externalize new strategic assets from the market in which it operates. Organizational learning in a strategic alliance is generally limited by the context of particular partner firms, organizational configurations and local institutions, because each partner brings its own set of strategies and operating routines, which define its view on corporate governance. However, the consolidation of new resources, knowledge and capabilities into a newly formed strategic alliance provides a forum in which learning mechanisms can be used to glean new knowledge from local market sources where the strategic alliance is located. Learning how to integrate many of these novel resources and knowledge acquisitions will be difficult until the strategic alliance management has established a strategy to address its own unique business situation.

It is assumed by foreign firms that the unique organizational structure of an international strategic alliance offers an easy way to acquire resources, knowledge and capabilities from the local Chinese market as local partners will help to rapidly achieve an advantageous market position in comparison with competitors. Critical strategic alliance learning by a firm includes developing skills to identify potential collaborators including suppliers, customers and business competitors. Learning within a strategic alliance involves understanding the capabilities of pooled partner firms' resources, knowledge and experience. Negotiations about the form of a strategic alliance must involve the specification of agreements that define the means to manage and monitor business arrangements and transfer knowledge. Learning in a strategic alliance is only valuable if seconded strategic alliance managers' experience is positively internalized within the organization and their expertise can be employed to guide future actions, and part of the learning process is ensuring that the strategic alliance's management shares and transfers the required tacit organizational know-how of the parent firm within the strategic alliance. Learning success in a strategic alliance requires an appreciation of the complexities of acquiring, transferring, and integrating resources, knowledge and capabilities from the environment within which the alliance operates.

A strategic alliance may need to establish an effective resource base such as market sourcing, customer market and local institutions before it can create unique learning opportunities for its management. The actualization of a strategic alliance's learning processes can be regarded as a basis on which new resources and knowledge can be acquired from the market and overall strategies and management actions honed. To cope with heightened market competition, strategic alliance managers are often urged to improve their organizations' learning systems as the best way to leverage new knowledge into core competencies. The establishment of a learning framework in a strategic alliance will provide practical management insights into the learning processes that will constantly influence the organizational linkages between partner firms and a strategic alliance itself. As a consequence of learning, strategic alliance managers may take many more proactive and explicit steps to improve the strategic alliance's business.

Inter-partner learning

Inter-partner learning happens when the partner firm participates in the management of the international strategic alliance. Inkpen (1998) states that organizational integration for headquarter visits of a strategic alliance are perceived as an effective means for managers operating in the partner firm to learn about their strategic alliances. The horizontal sharing of information between strategic alliance partners promotes organizational learning as it offers a significant and equal opportunity for the partner firms to share the strategic alliance's tacit and explicit resources, knowledge and expertise. The product know-how and the international business experience of strategic alliance managers are perceived as primary drivers in the acquisition of new resources and knowledge from the local market. Senior managers seconded to an international strategic alliance may find it easier to understand the dynamics and complexity of the strategic alliance partnership than headquarters staff. The operating style of most foreign firms in China reflects the objectives that link their international market portfolio to the development of their strategic alliances. Most strategic objectives associated with the establishment of strategic alliances are 'market-related'.

Inter-partner learning in a strategic alliance is related to the establishment of new market presence and assimilating local marketing practices. The strategic alliance environment offers foreign partners excellent opportunities to learn by working with their local partners and they can also acquire knowledge about how to inter-connect with the local government, economic, social and cultural institutions. The partner firm that uses inter-partner learning to understand how the other partner operates will enjoy a high level of bargaining power and control in the management of a strategic alliance. A high level of involvement in strategic alliance management provides a rapid learning experience about the best way to direct a strategic alliance's strategy, control and performance to develop the most appropriate products for their new market. When a foreign firm faces a novel situation in an international market, managers will invoke various learning activities aimed at defining the situation and developing ways of dealing with it. The measurement of strategic alliance inter-partner learning success will include an examination of whether the strategic alliance has provided novel and useful management experience, especially if the knowledge has been acquired from partners. The exploitation of the inter-partner learning potential in a strategic alliance needs to be based upon clearly specified partner learning targets that have to be set for each strategic alliance manager sent to work in the organization, as inter-partner learning is perceived as an important determinant of a strategic alliance's ability to internalize new strategic assets from its partner firms.

Industry-based learning

The measurement of learning effectiveness in a strategic alliance should be carried out with reference to the extent to which the strategic alliance has increased its attractiveness and competitiveness at an industrial level. A strategic alliance can produce more products and organizational know-how as well as enjoy better performance if it establishes effective ownership investment and corporate governance strategies. Effective ownership investment may facilitate access to new resources, knowledge and capabilities developed from input from their partners and from the new markets that the strategic alliance gives them access to. Learning achievement at the industrial level involves the transfer of resources and knowledge between different partner firms in a shared market context in which different partners' corporate governance may need to become more aligned to one another. Organizational learning studies indicate that the corporate governance of a strategic alliance will be embedded in its extensive parental networks which are co-ordinated through organizational processes of knowledge transfer and resource sharing.

The strategic alliance's development in China may increase its cost-effectiveness at the industrial level through dissemination of resources, knowledge and capabilities of partner firms, and it is only achievable through organizational learning. A strategic alliance may have the autonomy to determine its organizational access to, and the amount of, resources, knowledge and capabilities from the market where it operates in order to build co-operation with suppliers, customers and business competitors. It is in this way that external business co-operation and internal resource-sharing facilitate a strategic alliance's ability to recognize and respond to new market opportunities.

The strategic alliance's market competitiveness and attractiveness depend upon relevant prior knowledge from its partner firms and it also has to achieve a good understanding of local industrial policies, development of industrial priorities, cutting-edge technology and organizational know-how concerning existing local conditions. From the organization learning point of view, a strategic alliance that is able to operate industrial-based learning successfully is likely to be able to incorporate new resources and knowledge from its partner firms to extend the overall product development cycle of its parent's existing products in a new market. Generally speaking, the competence and learning capacity of a strategic alliance is based on its ability to achieve industry-based learning and this depends on its endowments of relevant technology and management-based resources, knowledge and capabilities from the market. The establishment of a strategic alliance's organizational learning at the industrial level creates the potential for an individual strategic alliance with unique resources to share its knowledge and experience to advantage with partner firms as well as with the 'five competitive market actors' identified by Porter (1980).

The knowledge and capabilities from the partner firms that connect with a strategic alliance's management can be assimilated, further developed and then shared. The knowledge and capabilities exposure in a strategic alliance can be further developed and transmitted back to its partner firms. If the formalized corporate governance of the strategic alliance is consciously managed, the distance that often exists between partner firms and their strategic alliances can be minimized. The extension of industrial firms' connections between strategic alliances and their partner firms can be established through both formal and informal relationships based upon partners' resource contribution and relevant market factors. Table 10.1 shows that main learning experience acheived from organizational ties between strategic alliance partners also can be used as an initial base for inter-partner trust and the creation of a learning platform.

When there are significant organizational differences between the partners or gaps between the new strategic alliance and existing market rivals, the learning potential is likely to be reduced because the new knowledge may be located outside the strategic alliance's knowledge, resource and capabilities base. Many strategic alliances will become more efficient at utilizing industrially based market factors, as learning is commonly associated with the diffusion of 'ways' and 'levels' of learning

Table 10.1 Main learning experiences gained in a strategic alliance

Learning from working with counterparts	**Mean scores for a strategic alliance**		***t*-test for independent samples**	
	Chinese partner	**Foreign partner**	**Value of *t***	**Value of *p***
*Industry-based learning**				
• Competence in understanding management	4.32	4.54	0.33	0.72
• Competence in understanding marketing	2.56	3.69	1.24	0.21
• Communication within or between departments	2.90	3.43	0.64	0.42
• Dealing with information	2.56	3.69	1.24	0.21
Inter-partner learning				
• Ways of approaching the government	2.56	3.69	1.24	0.21
• Strategic decision-making	1.71	4.25	2.64	0.02
Learning in a strategic alliance				
• Company values and objectives	2.56	3.69	1.24	0.21
• Personal relationships and trust	3.42	3.99	0.67	0.44
• Language barriers	3.77	3.68	0.10	0.92

* The most senior local and foreign manager in the strategic alliance was asked to answer the questions on the management of the company's operations in terms of the items shown in the table

within the organization. A strategic alliance will move up the learning curve as it develops experience of collaborating with suppliers, customers, existing rivals or potential competitors. Substantial resource and knowledge acquisition by a strategic alliance can increase the value of the resources and knowledge contributed by industrial level market-factors. Such environmental learning should be considered as an inevitable result of a strategic alliance being active in the learning processes that enhance its competitive advantages.

Dynamic organizational learning

Learning processes at the technical, system and strategic level not only include strategies for increasing a strategic alliance's ability to acquire new external resources and knowledge but also how to apply such resources, knowledge and capabilities to commercial ends. An international strategic alliance with high knowledge competence and absorptive capacity is likely to consistently apply new knowledge to improve its operations. Partners' managerial involvement in the formulation of strategies can enhance performance as the strategic alliance can achieve benefits by learning how to use the new resources and knowledge it has absorbed. Although strategic alliances may provide important access to new resources and knowledge through parent-subsidiary organizational links, the impact of such resources on performance may depend on the extent to which an individual partner perceives the level of achievement that can be achieved.

Single-loop learning at the technical level

Single-loop learning is undertaken during the acquisition of new specific techniques, such as more advanced production scheduling or managerial techniques. Single-loop learning at the technical level is suitable for routine or repetitive tasks. Standard routines are embedded in many of the business tasks in a strategic alliance that can be perpetuated by single loop learning processes and so underpin inter-firm partnering competence. The learning platform established may involve the development of its partners' organizational desire to internalize their resources and knowledge into the strategic alliance operating routines. When one partner takes a protective and defensive approach to another partner firm's methods, the less they will want them to become established and the fewer learning activities will take place within the strategic alliance. When the interface between and across strategic alliance partners is highly integrated, the partners will want to be fully involved in competence building and will contribute to the learning of operating routines. Single-loop learning relies heavily on both partners' involvement in daily operational decisions and experimentation. Management involvement from partner firms in a strategic alliance is a typical means of emphasizing that they are learning oriented. This happens when managers in a strategic alliance are aware that their partner firms' knowledge and expertise is obsolete and that they will have to take the initiative in actively promoting learning. Ultimately, the goal of a strategic alliance's management is to encourage its managers to strengthen their operational involvement through encouragement of learning by doing. New knowledge from partners or the market assimilated into the strategic alliance operation may provide a solid foundation for new expertise that can lead to competitive success.

Single-loop learning at the technical level determines the extent to which a strategic alliance can adopt new operating routines that are provided by its partner firms. Investing in a strategic alliance's learning capacity at technical levels allows the strategic alliance to assimilate and apply internal knowledge from the partner firms for its own use. A strategic alliance's technical level learning achievements are associated with the ability to successfully apply partner firms' new knowledge, produce more service expertise and achieve better business performance. The ability to access partner firms' knowledge and to integrate it operationally is entirely dependent upon the power balance between partner firms. The proper formulation of operational strategies is critical to the successful implementation of single-loop learning in a strategic alliance and allows managers in the strategic alliance to integrate the partner firm's organizational planning, control systems and information reporting procedures. The assessment of a partner's management involvement in the operating routines provides useful information to a strategic alliance in terms of the degree of conformity and co-ordination required to perform the tasks and operations of the organization.

Double-loop learning at the system level

Double-loop learning focuses on changes in organizational systems with an emphasis on learning how to better integrate organizational activities by concentrating on the assumptions behind organizational action. Double-loop learning at the system level requires the ability to question existing systems. The strategic alliance partners' resources, knowledge and capabilities can be positively facilitated through a formalized learning system as they commonly depend on the various types of organizational knowledge invested in the existing or new markets. Specific path dependencies in the case of a strategic alliance resulting from multiple partner inputs are likely to result in unique and difficult-to-replicate knowledge.

The depth of organizational learning in a strategic alliance varies across the breadth of its learning processes and types of knowledge produced or employed. Although scholars differ in their beliefs about the veracity of organizational learning, there appears to be fairly broad agreement concerning the organizational learning process and the types of learning that can result from the technological and managerial knowledge transfer between partner firms. Double-loop learning at the system level states that learning about a strategic alliance's organizational system may become institutionalized. Learning at this stage can also be placed in a multi-period context because the co-ordination between functional areas that arises from this learning will add to and reinforce a strategic alliance's cognitions, skills and experiences. The more that a strategic alliance tends to accumulate its diverse experiences through functional co-ordination, the greater is the likelihood that a new organizational system will be able to extend the strategic alliance's boundaries. Strategic alliances in China evolve as they accumulate resources, knowledge and experience.

The concept of double-loop learning at the system level has been employed here, a strategic alliance's organizational extension of its knowledge and competence can be viewed as a lateral resource support that connects a specific function to the organization as a whole. Second-loop learning can be a complement to double-loop learning which moves the process along the 'formalization' dimension to where double-loop learning becomes possible in order to predict the desired direction for the evolution of policies, procedures, rules, and standing orders that prescribe the expected action. They are then backed up with systems that recode and document what has taken place in the way of performance improvement. There is strong evidence that 'system' involvement in double-loop learning is more likely to focus a strategic alliance's technological and managerial development to align it with new market developments.

Deutero-loop learning at the strategic level

Deutero-learning reflects on the learning processes themselves and emphasizes changes in managerial mind-sets, especially in understanding the criteria and conditions for organizational success. Deutero-loop learning at the strategic level is learning-oriented (Argyris and Schön 1975). Learning how to cope, accommodate and excel is viewed as an essential part of the strategic coupling between the strategic allaince partners. The effects of involvement in deutero-loop learning are often stimulated by exchanges between experts from different corporate culture backgrounds (Lyles 1988). Deutero-loop learning relies upon a strategic view of learning success in and through strategic alliances and its focus is aimed at the strategic alliance's sustainability through the achievement of partnership 'win–win' situations. Learning at this point may illuminate how the development of a strategic alliance benefits from the increased overall understanding of the partners' knowledge resources.

Deutero-loop learning at the strategic level can be used where the individual partner intends asymmetry in knowledge gains from the other partner. Under these circumstances learning is associated with a race or a battle between partners to learn from each other. Strategic alliances usually set up feedback mechanisms within their organizations to ensure that actual learning takes place. Deutero-loop learning at the strategic level enables the establishment of a long-term market presence through the efficient use of learning feedback at each level of the management hierarchy.

A strategic alliance tends to be treated as a static entity generated to fulfil rational strategic objectives. Transaction cost economics offers a useful tool for an analysis of a strategic alliance through cost-benefit analysis using a market/hierarchy classification. The types of strategic alliances imposed by headquarters or government organizations may limit the range of business options available to a strategic alliance manager. These managers may be fully aware of these limitations and temper the imposition of financial targets by the use of personal judgement. Deutero-loop learning at a strategic level is a complex concept that encompasses both process learning and a new organizational structure for strategic alliance development. The organization structural element provides the organization with the ability to implement behaviours suggested by the new wisdom it develops. Deutero-loop learning at a strategic level affects the strategic alliance management in terms of the partners' technology and managerial entrepreneurship.

Too much organizational learning may lead to excessive resources being spent on generating and disseminating unnecessary information as opposed to on the partners applying themselves to strategic alliance organizational activities. This may be particularly relevant in the management context, where all partners have mixed goals and organizational loyalties, and managers in the alliance can direct or shape organizational learning in tangible dimensions.

Determinants of organizational learning

Determinants of organizational learning can be regarded as major components of a strategic alliance's learning platform that indicate the strategic alliance's organizational capacity or potential to learn. A strategic alliance's attitude towards inter-partner learning depends upon its ability to absorb, assimilate and process information within an organization. When there is a positive attitude towards learning in a strategic alliance, control mechanisms are developed and allocations are made to cover learning activities. The development of inter-partnering competence requires that the strategic alliance has strong learning intent, is highly receptive and has high levels of transparency. If a strategic alliance's learning intent is coupled with receptivity, inter-partner learning will occur. This study shows how combined partner perceptions of their respective products and shared organizational know-how can be examined using three determinants of organizational learning (see Figure 10.2).

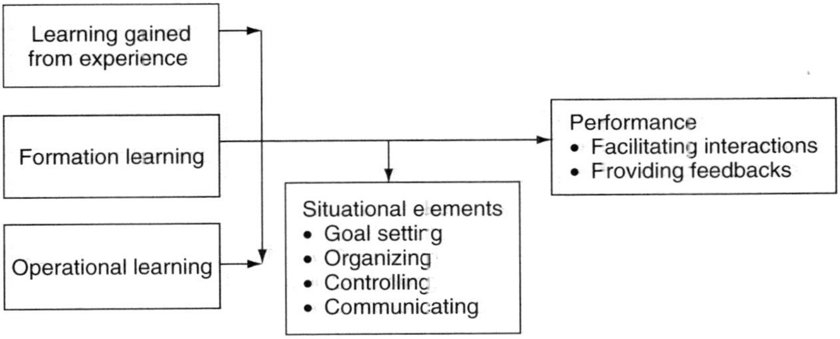

Figure 10.2 Determinants of organizational learning

Learning gained from experience

Organizational learning has been adopted by a growing number of strategic alliances striving to achieve 'learning from experience'. Learning from experience has gained strategic importance in the quest to compete in a more dynamic market for alliances. From a resource-based view, knowledge is part of the intangible resources that should represent a strategic asset upon which a partnership can be built. A strategic alliance's experience, its learning traditions and its ability to transfer knowledge more effectively and efficiently than the market are some of the main ways that it can remain competitive. Major organizational learning research studies have focused on the acquisition of learning from experience through internationalization.

Learning from experience consists of different phases that need not be sequential. These learning development phases include the identification of information and the generation of new knowledge. Learning may be facilitated by cultural clashes. In a strategic alliance, there will be multiple cross-cultural settings where partners with different culturally-bound management attitudes and behaviour patterns collide in a way that will influence their experience learning. Learning from experience is expected when managers seconded to a strategic alliance are appointed to certain key management functions by the partner which possesses the superior technology and managerial resources associated with the function. The structure of a strategic alliance should allow the diffusion of these managers' experience and knowledge throughout its management levels. The various levels of a strategic alliance will attribute value to the possession of types of knowledge that their parallel organization in the parent company already possesses and will carry with it the right to arbitrate over its value when used in the strategic alliance. The role of social differentiation and integration in knowledge transfer within and between strategic alliances can modify the balance between the benefits from acquiring knowledge from a partner and the overall costs of supplying such inputs to the strategic alliance. The role of organizational learning is vital to the process of securing experience and knowledge sources across the entire management hierarchy.

Formation learning

Formation learning is the process of learning how to use resources, formal knowledge and capabilities provided by partners at strategic alliance formation. Strategic alliances are intended by the Chinese authorities to play an important role in facilitating the acquisition of advanced management knowledge and technological expertise, and these objectives are clearly identified by the central government. The government initiatives at lower levels are geared to needs that are embedded in its economic, social and political constitution, and reflect the real problems the Chinese partners have in accessing the international market with their limited capital and marginal technological strengths. There is usually a gap between the objectives of the central government for the acquisition of advanced management knowledge and technological expertise and the investment resources of capital, technology and management inputs available from the central government through state-owned enterprises to be injected into strategic alliances.

Formation learning is important to the Chinese government in its quest to upgrade the technological base of the country's industry. The resources, knowledge and capabilities acquired from strategic alliance partners are perceived both as the basis for learning in the strategic alliance's context and as a general learning outcome for the benefit of the country. Formation learning represents a social process characterized by dynamic interaction between strategic partners as they adopt different styles of learning. The diffusion or transformation of certain types of resources, knowledge and capabilities between partners is strongly linked to the types of resources and knowledge they already possess. Explicit knowledge can be easily codified and transmitted in the form of documentation, but tacit knowledge is hard to codify and can only be transferred through experimentation, learning by doing and social communication. Tacit knowledge is tied more closely to a particular socio-cultural context such as partner-related resources and it is thus much more difficult to transfer from partner firms to the strategic alliance. Formation learning in a broad sense comprises declarative knowledge as well as general management expertise.

The societal institutions that shape the relationship between partners significantly affect formation learning. Learning attitudes and behaviours are reinforced by partners' culturally-bound norms, organizational principles and strategic objectives. One important aspect of formation learning refers to the specific content of learning achievement in the skills to be acquired or improved by partners working in a strategic alliance. An example would be the speed at which local employees or expatriate managers absorb technical and managerial skills within the strategic alliance. The transference of implicit knowledge to local employees represents a more complex process than the transfer of explicit knowledge and requires considerable personal effort from expatriates with that knowledge to teach those who need it.

Operational learning

A strategic alliance increasingly represents a new hybrid type of organization in the business environment that can differentiate itself by exploiting its operational learning potential for a strategic alliance. By bringing together different partner firms' unique skills and capabilities, a strategic alliance can create powerful learning opportunities but, without the active involvement of a strategic alliance's management, many of these operational learning opportunities will remain unexploited. The ability to realize operational learning within a strategic alliance is critically important because it provides a basis for creating competitive advantage. The management of a strategic alliance involves a dynamic process of acquisition, retention, deployment and abandonment of technologies and organization know-how over time. Managers in a strategic alliance have to consider organizational options when deciding which technologies or organizational know-how will be the most appropriate for current and future use. Operational learning provides broad repertoires of organizational responses to future contingencies.

Operational learning is a means to create an effective management system and must be treated as a strategic resource in a strategic alliance. It must be resourced properly and designed in a way that makes it valued by creating outputs that are important to customers and suppliers. Operational learning happens only with the consent of the management of a strategic alliance. The implementation of an efficient management climate requires the adoption of a paradigm focused on operational learning systems in an organization where flexibility, responsiveness, creativity and timeliness are extremely important. From this perspective, Table 10.2 provides details of a strategic alliance's valuable resources to facilitate an effective management system in that it subtly but pervasively steers

Table 10.2 T-test for the learning outcomes achieved in an international strategic alliance over operational, system and strategic levels

Learning outcomes	***T*-test for independent sample**		
	Chinese	**Foreign**	**Significance of *p*-value**
Strategic learning			
Attraction of industry characteristics	2.23	3.42	0.84
Economic conditions	4.32	4.54	0.70
Government function	2.56	3.69	0.06
Resources allocation	2.90	3.43	0.48
Technology transfer	2.23	3.42	0.61
Socio-cultural factors	4.32	4.54	0.34
System learning			
Economic scale	2.90	3.43	0.24
Corporate tax	2.23	3.42	0.48
Brand development	4.32	4.54	0.61
Information processing	2.56	3.69	0.34
Learning how to export	2.90	3.43	0.48
Learning management expertise	2.23	3.42	0.61
Upgrading Chinese suppliers' technology	4.32	4.54	0.34
Operational learning			
Organizational objectives	2.90	3.43	0.01
Division of labour and function	2.23	3.42	0.57
Required activities	4.32	4.54	0.23
Required actions	2.56	3.69	0.72
Required attitudes	2.90	3.43	0.17

organizational behaviour towards satisfying the needs of effective strategic alliance management.

Learning achieved throughout an alliance's hierarchies

An international strategic alliance will be actively involved in knowledge production and exchange systems. Organizational learning achieved by a strategic alliance can generate great value if the resulting resources and knowledge are shared within their own organization and between partner firms. Organizational learning theories provide rich perspectives on operating processes that generate and change knowledge production throughout a strategic alliance's organizational hierarchies. Learning theories describe how an organization can change its knowledge or behaviour in response to different types of learning requirements. The common integrative mechanisms in a strategic alliance involve the appointment of senior managers to positions within the organization and the creation of communication channels through the use of internal reporting systems. These mechanisms form a continuum from vertical hierarchical line systems of reporting to a matrix structure, depending upon the complexity of the business. Organizational learning in a strategic alliance context operates in an environment that must accommodate the varying strategic objectives of each partner organization. Figure 10.3 shows how the preferred means of learning attainment, the behaviour patterns required for effective performance and the rules for the maintenance of organization identity and integrity should be modified to conform to the learning requirements of all partners involved.

The element of technological knowledge transfer and the degree of management autonomy provides the focus and constraints for organizational learning between strategic alliance partners. The trade-off for undertaking such learning in a strategic alliance is that the central Chinese government or foreign company headquarters may require safeguards from the partners to protect their investments when they make valuable information available. The use of information is always selective and so strategic alliances must build learning mechanisms that ensure the information flow across organizational levels and boundaries is appropriate to the needs of the people who use that information. The resource capability of any organization has its origins in being able

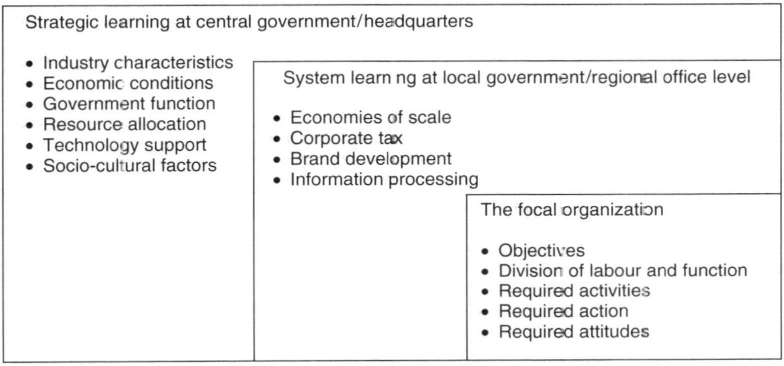

Figure 10.3 Learning successes affected by an international strategic alliance's hierarchies

to access external knowledge and direct it to the members of the organization. As strategic learning develops at central government and foreign firm headquarters the competitive learning needs of the partners may change and requirements may emerge for new complementary skills and competencies to be developed for their organization. The implementation of such changes depends on the availability of the organization's know-how and technology-based resources across the entire organizational system.

The focus of strategic learning at company headquarters and central government levels in respect of sharing knowledge is to foster the integration of knowledge contributions across different functions within the organization. Strategic learning consists of cycles of relevant activities including the incorporation of new knowledge, knowledge transformation and knowledge utilization. It is important that the top management reviews learning achievements within an organization as this will indicate to them how the inter-organizational hybrid forms of collaboration are working in terms of both trust and power. The 'trust dimension' defines the extent to which the transactions are dependent on 'social relations' such as inter-personal trust via non-hierarchical strategic partnerships. The 'power combination' indicates the extent to which the strategic decisions are made through a formalized hierarchical authority. Strategic learning at central government and company headquarters levels is geared towards ensuring control through repetitive organizational improvements within the boundaries of existing organizational knowledge. Strategic learning requires examination within a broad context, as it generally leads to behavioural outcomes such as new rules, procedures and regulations to be followed. Higher 'levels' of strategic learning achieved by the strategic alliance top management are characterized by insights that are non-routine and include the ability to learn how to change an organization as a whole.

Learning at local government/regional office level

In China, the local government and the local state-owned enterprise that acts as the local partner in the strategic alliance are so integrated that there is often little difference between the two. Any learning that happens at senior management levels in the state-owned enterprise can also be considered to have happened in local government. Information about production plans, R&D and HRM development is integral to the achievement of system learning by the local government or in the regional office of foreign partners. A strategic alliance's formation involves the movement of existing technology, knowledge or management into a strategic alliance setting, where it provides a new knowledge profile.

Generalized technical and managerial knowledge is often expressed in widely accessible international standardized forms and has relatively few boundaries between strategic alliance partners. The acquisition of such knowledge can assist people to circumvent organizational barriers and creates enhanced management behaviours. However, in adapting that knowledge to different contexts, learning about company systems may need to be established within the strategic alliance if the new knowledge requires innovative types of collaboration between people from different specialities or cultural backgrounds.

Information regarding a strategic alliance's business transactions, corporate tax variations, brand development and the marketing focus within the host country may provide a critical means of control of the strategic alliance by the foreign regional office or the local Chinese government. Such information may also be employed to resolve conflicts between financial, technological and managerial resources used by the strategic alliance. Foreign firms will often take advantage of transfer pricing policy to reduce taxable earnings and consequently corporate taxes, and thus financial reporting (along with local market data) can be an essential instrument of strategic alliance control. The process of 'corporate system learning' occurs whenever constructive integration of the different inputs offered by the strategic alliance partners takes place. System learning varies in speed and direction depending on the people and organizations involved, and multicultural aspects complicate the understanding of the system learning process between partners during the formation of a strategic alliance.

The complementarities of technological expertise, managerial practices and organizational structure can be influenced by differences in the learning speeds of the respective partners. The process of retrieving knowledge and adequate information processing may facilitate system learning. The creation of new knowledge or experiences within the context of a strategic alliance involves a process of system learning that affects the relationship between a strategic alliance and the local government, state-owned enterprise and regional office. This compromises the quality of system learning that can be achieved through the process of managing a strategic alliance. Evaluating the effectiveness of a strategic alliance involves the retrieval of knowledge that is systematically internalized in the strategic alliance.

Learning at corporate level

The organizational learning approach utilized at a corporate level usually highlights the benefits and the interests of the individual partners' organizational requirements. Foreign firms operating in China often

Table 10.3 Main features of organizational learning in an international strategic alliance

Theoretical approach	Competitive Approach	
'Single-loop' learning at the Technical level	*Chinese: highlight the individual partners' interests*	*Foreign: highlight the individual partners' interests*
The acquisition of specific new techniques, such as more advanced production scheduling or managerial techniques.	Technological, managerial and capital inputs are devoted to the integration of a strategic alliance.	Setting of realistic expectations and determining activities to ensure that they are accomplished as planned. Decisions often involve production planning and training and recruitment policy
'Double-loop' learning at the Systemic level	*Local government*	*Regional office*
Changes in organizational systems, with an emphasis on learning how to achieve better integration of organizational activities.	Establishment of links with local government where the information is concerned with local rules, procedures and tax structures.	Establishing inter- and intra-relationships between strategic alliances and organizational performance appraisal. Decisions often involve nomination of senior managers, brand development and marketing issues.
'Deutero-loop' learning at the Strategic level	*Central government*	*Corporate headquarters*
Changes in managerial mind-sets, especially in understanding the criteria and conditions for organizational success.	Policies on general foreign direct investment in China, corporate international business portfolio, import and export restriction and quality control standards.	Defining goals, establishing strategy, directing and co-ordinating all involved parties to achieve the organization's stated objectives. Decisions often involve profit allocation, re-investment policy.

face a choice between retaining exclusive control over their technology and managerial expertise and sharing their knowledge and expertise base with local Chinese partners. The choice for the local Chinese firms may be between maintaining the traditional norms of complexity of its social system, organizational structures and domestic market integrity or adopting foreign technology and management structures.

The technical learning between strategic alliance partners can be facilitated by unique working styles, management principles and organizational structure. There is a need to adjust to the new and precarious nature of technical learning at the corporate level by finding ways to deal with feelings of discontent and being locked in. A strategic alliance's resources are dependent upon the interaction and interpersonal relationships of managers where daily business communication is more direct in enforcing technical standards and carries a basis of legitimacy derived from the preservation of a partner's operational practices. Technical learning at the corporate level can be jeopardized if the disposition of critical resources is highly concentrated in the hands of a single partner. Table 10.3 shows the main features of organizational learning that can be achieved in an international strategic alliance, which include liaison with different levels of management.

Summary

This chapter suggests that the setting of a learning objective might be best understood by the identification of the influences derived from the formalized managerial hierarchies of each partner. Learning has been applied to a strategic alliance's strategic continuous renewal. This chapter also argues that examination of the organizational linkages between strategic alliance partners may develop an ability to influence the states of learning achievements in strategic alliances via quasi-organization relations. Hence learning gained from experiences, formation learning and operational learning in a strategic alliance must be related to the specific cross-cultural character of partner firms, and these three aspects must be applied in the given corporate context.

Part IV

Implications for Research and Practice

11
What We Still Need to Learn

Introduction

This chapter concludes what we have learned and explores what we still need to learn in terms of the value enhancement of foreign investments and the types of corporate governance exercised in international strategic alliances in China. Investigations of the performance of international strategic alliances suggest that the linkage between a partner firm's investment and its corporate governance is contingent upon the environmental factors that include heightened market competition, economic liberalization and local institutional support. This chapter shows a consistent picture of the factors which are important in shaping foreign investments, and their effect on the corporate governance and performance of an international strategic alliance.

Performance conceptualization

In emerging economies, the absence of modern institutional systems to direct foreign investments and the limited availability of resources may add to organizational challenges in the achievement of superior business performance that most international strategic alliances face in China. As a major host country for foreign direct investment, China has orchestrated the implementation of FDI primarily through the establishment of international strategic alliances with foreign partners. In more recent years, the economic liberalization and growth of the potential Chinese market has become a salient factor in attracting further foreign investments. However, the performance record of foreign investments and operations investing in China is still quite variable. Various explanations are offered for good or poor performance strategic alliances in the

Chinese market. Environmental factors such as increasingly tough market competition, multinationals operating pricing wars and uncertain regulatory and tax environments tend to be singled out for blame. China's legal system, governance structure and other institutional systems need to be further developed in areas such as infrastructure, quality resource supply, general technological development and managerial competence.

China is a particularly instructive location in which to examine international strategic alliance performance not only because of the large number of international strategic alliances that exist there but also because it is quite difficult for an international strategic alliance in China to achieve superior business performance. China is still perceived as a relatively complex investment environment that presents significant problems for foreign firms investing in and operating businesses there. Foreign firms investing in an international strategic alliance may have their own preferred explanation for their business performance achievements in China. Previous organizational researchers have used the three broad performance measures of 'goal', 'system' and 'contingency' models together with theories from international business studies to evaluate operations in China. These three performance measures account for the majority of variations in actual performance achievements amongst international strategic alliances.

'Goal' model of business performance

The 'goal' perspective takes as its performance criterion the extent to which the 'goals' expressed in a firm's objectives for forming an international strategic alliance are met. The goal model (Etzioni 1964) seeks a definition based upon explicit goals or goals that can be implied from the behaviour of organizational members. 'Goal performance' is therefore defined as the extent to which the objectives that a firm has in undertaking foreign business are actually realized in practice. One of the main arguments in favour of applying the 'goal' model is that foreign investment is commonly made for a variety of reasons, and it is therefore not legitimate to assess its performance by reference to a sole indicator such as profitability or in a way that prejudges other partner firms' objectives in forming an international strategic alliance. On these grounds, reliance upon the 'goal model' in international business research should be based on widespread use of 'goal attainment' measured by various partner firms' objectives for forming international strategic alliances.

'Goal performance' is thus the extent to which the strategic objectives that each partner firm has in forming an international strategic alliance are realized. This avoids the complication that partner goals for establishing a strategic alliance can conflict or may become obsolete. Partner goals can amount to straight aspirations that are not expressed in terms of ownership resources actually committed to an international strategic alliance. The objective of employing the 'goal model' is to reflect partner goals for an international strategic alliance that are best addressed through a comparison of all partner firms' goals within the same strategic alliance. On these grounds, assessments will indicate whether different partners of the same organization provide different interpretations and, if so, to what extent.

Applying the goal perspective in an international strategic alliance is not only legitimate as a way to assess its performance by reference to a sole indicator but also allows an examination of how it may prejudge partner firm objectives. Some previous studies have examined strategic alliance performance from the viewpoint of a single partner, normally using perceptual measures applied to the attainment of that partner's goals. A lesser number have included performance evaluations in terms of an assessment of all partners' goal attainment. One problem that emerges is that many strategic alliances are asymmetric in partner objectives and this means that the partner firms are unlikely to meet their objectives to the same extent. Thus a study may indicate that the strategic alliance has failed in terms of one partner's goal attainment, but this does not necessarily mean that the strategic alliance has failed to anticipate the other partner's criteria on goal achievement. Goal assessment stems from the acknowledgement of the varied portfolios of goals that partner firms bring to the establishment of a strategic alliance.

A partner firm's goal attainment is not a stable referent for identifying the predictors of a strategic alliance's performance through comparative research, because what is being measured for each strategic alliance partner does not refer to the same set of goals. The lack of consistency in the partners' goals implies that somewhat different performance perspectives will be required for different strategic alliances and even for the same strategic alliance at different points in time, thus avoiding the complication that partners' goals can be inconsistent. A partner firm's goals can amount to various aspirations that are not necessarily expressed in terms of the ownership resources actually committed to its strategic alliance.

'System' model of business performance

The 'system' perspective takes the 'health' of the international strategic alliance as the performance criterion in respect of its viability. 'System performance' is therefore defined as the extent to which an economic unit performs well as a business unit. The systems model (Yuchtman and Seashore 1967) provides a framework to assess organizational performance in terms of the key internal and external factors upon which the organization depends for survival. The system perspective suggests that a strategic alliance ultimately has to meet normal business criteria and be able to prosper under competitive market conditions. System variables, by contrast, provide a more consistent set of performance criteria by use of market share, growth rate and staff development factors that refer to organizational fundamentals for business survival.

In the development of a strategic alliance as an independent business unit 'system performance' may provide a better basis for comparison by the use of performance criteria such as economic and strategic performance as indicators. A strategic alliance is expected to operate under the same competitive market conditions as ordinary companies, and therefore an evaluation of its performance should be made on the same basis. Most studies of business performance employ a variety of system measures including profitability, growth and costs. The difficulty of quantifying these financial measures has led some researchers away from objective measures towards subjective performance measures that are based on managers' perceptions of an international strategic alliance's performance. Nevertheless, it is possible to predict a substantial proportion of a strategic alliance's performance variance when a 'system' model of performance measures is used.

'Constituency' model of business performance

The 'constituency' performance measures assume that an organization exists to benefit numerous 'community needs' or 'constituencies' that fit internally and externally with the organization and organizational performance assessment that mainly focuses on the fulfilment of its constituency needs (Thompson 1967). Market attractiveness appears to be the fundamental aspect of the business environment that influences a firm's performance. Firms vary in their ability to take advantage of the local legal system, government policies and tax credits to protect firms' business transactions in the institutional environment of a specific host country. It is difficult to predict such variations in a strategic alliance by using goal or system measures, performance, or internal variations in a partner firm's involvement with their strategic alliances' management.

The constituency model of a firm's performance measures the impact of environmental factors on a strategic alliance that cannot be wholly mitigated by the strategic action that managers take. Managers in most strategic alliances can pursue identifiable policies that have an independent impact on performance over and above that of the environment where their cross-border operations are internationally located. The 'constituency' model of business performance suggests exogenous variables of market concentration, entry barriers and product differentiation that will impact on the performance of a strategic alliance. A more recent development of industrial organization theory incorporates the conduct of business development within an industry as a performance determinant. The 'constituency' paradigm is also evident in organizational ecology linked to the industrial organization approach of performance analysis as in Porter's 'five forces' model of competitive structure. The constituency model states that a strategic alliance's operations in a highly competitive market will exhibit considerable environmental complexity for the business operation.

The constituency model of business performance focuses on the international effects of joint action that a strategic alliance undertakes in a market where it operates. The collusion between partner firms constitutes another form of 'collective action' that is quite clearly directed towards the enhancement of performance of the strategic alliance involved. The collective-action perspective implies that the performance of foreign investment in China will benefit from the formation of a strategic alliance with local firms in order to gain access to better knowledge about the local environment. Numerous researchers have argued that when the constituency model of business performance is used, the performance assessment must include broader societal environment perspectives and take local organizational dimensions into account in the performance measures. The constituency performance measure is useful in attempting to operationalize broader institutional environment issues in relation to dimensions of a strategic alliance's organizational functions. Factors such as the legacy of corporate cultures and the absence of developed organizational systems may be used as negative factors that reduce the probability of a strategic alliance achieving success.

Objective versus subjective performance measures

Prior research evidence suggests significant differences in the operationalization of an international strategic alliance's performance. No consensus on the appropriate definition and measure of this concept has yet emerged. Early studies used a variety of financial indicators typically employed in business research such as profitability, growth and cost position. Others have used objective measures of performance such as the survival of the international strategic alliance, its duration, instability or ownership. The use of subjective and objective measures is believed to be critically important in the evaluation of an international strategic alliance's performance. An international strategic alliance commonly generates financial returns through various control mechanisms other than dividends including supply contracts, management fees, technology licensing fees, royalties and transfer pricing, as well as takings at the strategic level through the establishment of long-term business presence *vis-à-vis* competitors. These figures are seldom incorporated into calculations about an international strategic alliance's financial status or strategic measures of its performance.

This approach has fallen out of favour with researchers due to its conceptual limitations in addressing performance measures as only a limited range of targets established by strategic alliance partners can be measured due to limitations of data availability, performance distortions associated with transfer pricing, and creative accounting. Researchers studying the organizational performance of a strategic alliance often have difficulty in finding objective data, and the problems of creating meaningful quantitative performance measurements for an international strategic alliance have led some researchers away from objective measures towards the use of subjective alternatives based on managers' perceptions of performance achievement.

Assessment of the performance of a strategic alliance is difficult because profitability is influenced by industry-specific factors, and performance data must be accurately measured across different business units controlled by local or foreign managers. The use of subjective performance data to supplement objective performance measurement is perceived as an ideal way to assess a strategic alliance's performance. A prior study suggests that, based on a survey of managers from a sample of strategic alliances, objective data and subjective measures of return on assets, sales growth and market share are found to be highly correlated. Subjective measures should also be useful in the assessment of broader organizational-based factors and environmental performance determinants. Financial and strategic measures of a strategic alliance's performance may fail to adequately reflect the extent to which an international strategic alliance achieves its long-term strategic objectives.

Many international strategic alliances in China operate in contexts where measures of short-term financial performance may suggest that the strategic alliance is performing poorly, but financial measures evaluate only one dimension of performance. Other factors including qualitative ones, such as technology development, quality of resource supply and managerial improvement – must also be examined in order to adequately evaluate an international strategic alliance's performance. Thus, even if the financial results are poor as the business is in liquidation or is unstable, an international strategic alliance may have been meeting or exceeding its partner firms' strategic objectives and thus be considered successful by one or all of the partner firms. Conversely, an international strategic alliance may be viewed as unsuccessful despite good financial results or continuous stability. The main advantage of subjective performance measures is their ability to provide information regarding the extent to which an international strategic alliance has achieved its overall objectives. Many research methods, such as those based on archival or other secondary data sources, do not generally permit collection of these types of data, and thus they have to rely on the use of financial performance measures.

Much of the literature on performance assessment is prescriptive in nature, seeing subjective performance appraisal as a tool that can enhance human relations within an organization. The performance assessment of a strategic alliance is generally presented as the acquisition of extensive information from managers that is used to recognize a process of rational decision-making and resource allocation by strategic alliance partners. The performance assessment at an organizational level gives information on the level of achievement of the strategic alliance partners and what these partner firms should be doing differently as well as the reasons why partner firms are reaching a particular level of achievement. It is assumed that an appropriate performance assessment will lead to an improvement in performance of a strategic alliance.

The subjective assessment for the performance of an international strategic alliance has been recognized as a central issue as the criteria used to measure each partner's performance in a strategic alliance are difficult to achieve and can be judgemental to some degree. Control and accountability over a strategic alliance's business expansion is thought to be one of the main subjective measures of performance appraisal for a strategic alliance. The political, social and organizational context will always influence the performance evaluation, as partners in an international strategic alliance have to take into consideration their strategies, ownership resources and the control dynamics between the partner firms themselves. The utilization of more objective and subjective measures is dependent upon the validity and reliability of the performance measures. The validity of any performance assessment will be increased if it is conducted at, and data are collected in, both the partner firms and in the strategic alliance.

Recent studies using subjective assessment have primarily focused on issues such as strategies, ownership and corporate governance, corporate culture and organizational learning. The application of traditional performance measures across partner firms' organizational boundaries has been attempted but much more remains to be done to improve the understanding to a level where generic subjective performance measures can be justified for general use in an international strategic alliance. One of the prime uses of subjective performance measures is the identification, selection and development of strategic alliance management. The subjective performance measures are also linked to the strategic alliance's governance structure as financial control begins with the designation of corporate goals and relevant strategies to support the achievement of the partner firms' strategic objectives. Managers of the strategic alliance may receive 'objective' goals that come from corporate levels at the partner firms. Numerous research concerns relate to subjective and objective performance assessment, including the measurement of divergent corporate cultures, legal and political factors and varying environments.

Strategic alliance formation

Foreign investments under dynamic market conditions can be better understood by understanding the types of ownership investment used for strategic alliance formation. The performance of cross-border investments such as investments in an international strategic alliance continues to be a problem for both practising managers and academic researchers. The practical challenge of performance achievement for a strategic alliance arises from the greater difficulties normally experienced in a foreign environment, where unfamiliarity and geographical distance generate high levels of uncertainty. The uncertainty arises from the fact that the legal, political, financial and other corporate governance systems affect the way that international business is done and differ significantly between territories. Such differences may add to the risk of foreign investments. The formation model raises an obvious issue related to a strategic alliance's transaction costs.

Performance measures used show the extent to which strategic alliance partners have achieved their strategic objectives from forming a strategic alliance. The use of the formation model fits well with observations of how a partner actually provides ownership resources to form a strategic alliance. The local partner will achieve its objectives if technology is up to date and advanced management techniques are learned from running a strategic alliance, and thus the local partner will be satisfied with the strategic alliance's business growth because of the continuous addition of new products. However, this objective will have been achieved only to a limited degree because the Chinese expectation of extending the business through exports to foreign countries has not necessarily been met. The overwhelming objective of the local partners in co-operating with foreign firms is to gain access to the more advanced foreign technology. Significant differences may exist in the strategic objectives of the local and the foreign partners at strategic alliance formation. Foreign firms are in China primarily to penetrate the local market and to pursue financial goals. For the foreign firms, the achievement of market share and profitability are important measures of strategic alliance performance.

The quality of resources provided by foreign firms is critical in a developing country context such as China where inward foreign investment and business operation is perceived as a necessary vehicle for the transfer of technology and management expertise. If the quality of resources is poor, the local partner will be critical of the foreign partner and will seek to compensate for this through the exercise of a higher level of control. When the quality of resources is good, advantages accrue from sharing control with the local partner who can assist in dealing with the complex local resource supplier and networking. Foreign firms that possess cutting-edge technological resources are posited to be the most valuable associates. Strategic alliances can act as endorsements as they build public confidence in the value of an organization's products and services, and thereby attract customers, suppliers and business competitors.

A central notion in the international business literature is that a realization of the potential benefits from forming an international strategic alliance depends on a business finding an appropriate partner who provides complementary resources, knowledge and capabilities that match its own and enable the alliance to meet its strategic objectives. In a developing country, there may be limited public information on the attributes of potential local partners and this makes the partner search and assessment a critical learning process for foreign firms. A strategic alliance's performance will benefit from careful partner search and assessment, since many local firms will not be very familiar with dealing with foreign firms. These considerations suggest that a longer period of partner search and investigation before forming a strategic alliance should benefit performance. One reason for firms establishing a strategic alliance in China is that they hope to remedy a resource deficiency or to take advantage of an opportunity that they cannot realize on their own.

If this is the case, a policy of dominant control may increase the contribution a partner can make but it may damage a local partner's willingness to contribute to what it regards as an unequal partnership in which its own strategic objectives are not given due weight, and thus the level of trust and quality of the relationship between the partners is likely to suffer.

Local partners can help their strategic alliances to succeed by providing country-specific knowledge, contacts with regulatory authorities, and management of the local workforce. Complementarities between local and foreign partners is less likely to be achieved in the area of tangible resources, where the foreign partner usually has a large ownership advantage, than in the management of an unfamiliar and dynamic environment which can appear hostile because its institutional and cultural features are not highly transparent. Moreover, the costs of employing expatriate managers to take charge of management in an international strategic alliance can substantially 'eat' into its profits. The ownership resources of foreign firms are found to be critical to an international strategic alliance's performance even in a complex and turbulent environment such as China, although the business press and some academic studies have understandably focused primarily on exogenous market influences.

The present investigation indicates that factors endogenous to an international strategic alliance and the way it constitutes a strategic alliance at its formation have a strong bearing on subsequent performance. Attention to strategic factors at the formation of an international strategic alliance deserves to be complemented by attention to the means whereby international business strategies and ownership resources are implemented through the alliance. This is not to deny the theoretical or practical significance of strategic factors such as market entry policy, complementarities of partners' resources and goal congruence. The viability of an international strategic alliance as separate business units also depends on the quality of the intangible and tangible assets provided by partner firms. Adopting a broad theoretical approach with respect to partners' objectives and ownership investments in strategic alliance formation can be extremely beneficial to the long-term operation of the alliance.

Ownership investments

Measurement of the performance of an international strategic alliance in China often begins with a discussion of the role of ownership investments. Foreign firms investing in China need to build ownership investments not only around products, but also upon deep knowledge of a few highly-developed core skills. This ownership dimension concerns whether the dominant influence in achieving performance is predicated by unique aspects of a firm's ownership investment. The 'resource-based view of the firm' stresses the contribution that possession of key resources and competencies can make to the performance of firms. This perspective singles out, as a source of economic rent, the strategic value of possessing distinctive resources that are costly to imitate. The deployment of such resources, knowledge and capabilities within an international strategic alliance should be based upon a competitive advantage that cannot easily be duplicated by rivals. Tangible resources include financial reserves and physical resources such as industrial units, equipment and stocks of raw materials. Intangible resources include technology, know-how and reputation. Partner-based resources from a strategic alliance include skills, expertise and motivated employees. Organizational capabilities of a strategic alliance constitute the prime resources provided by partner firms.

The production technology, product design, expertise and training supplied by foreign partners of a strategic alliance are typically superior in quality and efficiency to those available locally. The government may place limits on ownership of equity shares in a strategic alliance and regulate prices of the production output. Capital investment in new facilities invested by strategic alliance partners should enhance capacity, efficiency and quality. New facilities should further contribute to international strategic alliance performance by providing the opportunity to recruit and train employees *de novo* from the market rather than have people transferred to the strategic alliance that are already employed in existing facilities by the local partner, since existing employees from the local partner firms are more liable to bring their attitudes and work practices from the old feather-bedded 'iron rice bowl' regime.

Industrial units and equipment supplied by the local partner as a capital contribution are likely to constitute a performance liability. The external transactions of an international strategic alliance are perceived as complex economic phenomena that some partner firms may decide to handle directly in order to reduce uncertainty, and in this way enhance the performance of its international strategic alliances. The integration of input and output transactions between an international strategic alliance and its partner firms also offers channels for mutual learning and adjustment between the two parties. Direct supply permits knowledge transfer from partner firms to an international strategic alliance through the provision of technical designs and other know-how, as well as through the support of a partner firm's staff that is likely to be the recipient of the direct supply arrangements. These are all known as potential advantages of 'internalization' of partner firms' ownership and they are expected to improve an international strategic alliance's performance.

Corporate governance

The on-going performance of a strategic alliance has important feedback effects on the partners' relative bargaining power and the existing structure of corporate governance. Superior performance creates an additional power bargaining counter for partners in a strategic alliance and may reinforce extant control patterns together with their influence on corporate governance. The processes and outcomes of corporate governance in a strategic alliance are directly related to its performance. When the partners' control and power is even, each partner's perception of the performance of a strategic alliance, as assessed from its own perspective, is the same. When control and power is unevenly shared between the partners, the prediction of performance is less straightforward. The on-going performance of the partnership exerts an important feedback effect on the partners' bargaining power, the pattern of corporate governance and the quality of the co-operative relationship between the partners.

China is a huge country that has experienced dramatic changes in its political and economic scene since the 1980s. It has a mixed economy where certain sectors of the economy face more government influence than others. Government leaders' perceptions of a particular industry are pivotal to an understanding of the structure of corporate governance of an international strategic alliance in terms of characteristics such as the size, the equity share of partners and other structural features. Local managers, unfamiliar with business operations under competitive market conditions or current global business standards, are seen as ill-equipped to compete against managers from global firms that are far more experienced in designing effective strategies for a strategic alliance. Strategic alliances must institute effective corporate governance to create a competitive advantage in a global economy. Performance measures are fairly simplistic and involve organizational ranking by the board of directors of the strategic alliance management. The strategic role of the board of directors results in a need for accurate descriptions of corporate governance at the national level and an understanding of the performance measures used to evaluate success in a strategic alliance.

A strategic alliance where one partner dominates the corporate governance role will be more successful because it approximates a unitary firm, which is easier to manage. Corporate governance offers an ability to determine the most effective use of whatever strategic resources a partner firm is prepared to share with its international strategic alliance. There is an argument in favour of leaving an international strategic alliance's governance in the hands of the partner that supplies the most critical resources, as this partner is likely to have the greater expertise. Corporate governance provides a set of rules under which strategic alliances are permitted to use strategic assets from partner firms as these strategic assets will contribute positively to an international strategic alliance's performance. Benefits will accrue to the international strategic alliance where the board of directors institutes a role for strong corporate governance.

Corporate culture

Corporate culture is necessarily multidimensional in an international strategic alliance but there is still little guidance for choosing which dimension to include or exclude from these corporate cultural perspectives. Researchers tend to use customized performance measures that may allow for specific comparisons among management practices in a strategic alliance. It has been noted that this lack of ability to generalize the cultural criterion hinders the validity of many predictors of strategic alliance performance. Recent role theory provides an explanation as to why corporate culture should be based upon multidimensional perspectives. Role theory has been successfully used by researchers in psychology, social psychology, sociology, organization behaviour and human resource management. Researchers from various organizational fields have concluded that role theory plays an important part in explaining social structure and has been recognized as central to the understanding of partner investment behaviour in a strategic alliance. In role theory, individual partner roles are influenced by both their partner-related resource attributes and the market context in which a strategic alliance operates. Role theory represents a major advance in the explanation of performance as it combines a psychological, a national cultural and a sociological perspective where the strategy and organizational behaviours that are defined by an international strategic alliance should relate to a specific organization that may exhibit all situational contexts.

Corporate culture is included in this study as one of the fundamental contextual factors that influence performance. The power factor and the senior organizational roles present in managerial actions are relevant in the socio-cultural milieu of hierarchical relations. Ethical environmental factors are also relevant in attracting local and foreign investments to the new economic environment of China. Concentrations of power, information and decision-making among local firms are not conducive to the implementation of growth strategies. However, the non-hierarchic, egalitarian sharing practices of the more competitive foreign firms are having their impact on strategic alliances in China. After economic reform, these egalitarian managerial values have become endemic in most local firms and entail a normative shift from the paternalistic and authoritarian managerial style to a supportive style. The great problem for an international strategic alliance in China is how to rapidly earn the public trust and credibility that most Chinese see as the consequence of working together for many years.

The establishment of corporate culture in a strategic alliance should be measured through a comprehensive assessment of 'corporate culture roles' taken as inputs from the strategic alliance partnership. Organizational principles and social norms established in a strategic alliance provide a clue to the discovery of which partner roles should be measured at work. Varying forms of corporate culture may be used to encourage other types of role-related behaviour, including promotion systems used to reward managers for career accomplishment and pay systems used to emphasize a career role for the skill-based employees. Corporate culture provides partners' management participation in training and new skills acquisition. This increased recognition of the organizational role in a strategic alliance places emphasis on the joint career responsibility of partner firms and makes the organizational role an important one to consider when evaluating performance achievement.

Organizational learning

Organizational learning theory suggests that the more partner-related knowledge and market-based skills that firms acquire, the more their management processes can be expected to improve performance. The use of this reasoning helps to explain why previous business experience when forming a strategic alliance has been found to increase a firm's propensity to learn from the broad-based market in which the strategic alliance operates. A firm's previous experience has the potential to confer benefits on performance. Organizational learning implies that the longer an international strategic alliance has been operating, the more opportunity there will have been for its members to learn how to achieve congruence between partner goals. This includes the establishment of a 'strategic fit' for the strategic alliance and accommodating 'culture fit' and other partner-related differences. A longer operational history should denote that an international strategic alliance has been able to avoid or resolve severe conflicts over both the attainment of partner goals and the way the alliance is managed. Unless it fails at a relatively early stage, an international strategic alliance is likely to move along a learning curve where previous business experience should have a positive effect on strategic alliance partners' goals. Evidence from many strategic alliances in China suggests that a critical period comes after about two or three years, as by this time any unsatisfactory relationships should have become evident. The evidence suggests that strategic alliances of longer standing tend to achieve better performance.

Organizational learning is a process that should help local managers and employees to work more effectively in order to develop their capabilities and commitment. It can also provide a means to enhance learning about an opaque local context that might include ways of securing adequate resources for local business operations. The resource deficiency that most local Chinese firms still experience, especially in capital, advanced technologies and marketing services, represents a further performance challenge. If local partner firms can reduce or compensate for these resource deficiencies, the performance of the strategic alliance may be expected to benefit. Strategic alliance partners learn from each other by what has come to be known as obsolescence bargaining whereby the knowledge transferred by learning means that it can no longer be used as a lever for bargaining power and the effective learner in an international strategic alliance can raise the 'price' for its continued participation in the partnership. However, our findings suggest that the local partners do not significantly gain bargaining power through effective organizational learning because the foreign partners are cautious when transferring their technologies to their strategic alliances and keep the key technological secrets firmly in their own hands. Alternatively, if these technologies are low in transparency, high barriers to learning will be created.

Over time, an international strategic alliance in China accumulates its own bases of knowledge and skills and becomes less dependent on its partner firms. If this learning accumulation is accomplished in an unbalanced manner, by the acquisition of knowledge or skills only from one partner firm, then this partner firm's contribution will eventually be devalued. Both partners have inherent and often conflicting motivations for a strategic alliance increasing local content, as the local partner wants to cultivate domestic suppliers whereas the foreign partner wants to reduce cost but both partners want to save foreign exchange. If material sourcing is changed from the foreign partner on whom the strategic alliance depended for imported materials to a local supplier, this change will diminish the bargaining power of the foreign partner. Changes in a strategic alliance's local environment, particularly in government policies, can trigger structural reconfigurations in a strategic alliance in China; for instance, when relaxations of the conditions on direct foreign investment in China enabled strategic alliances to acquire sales and services from foreign parents, rather than forcing them to use inappropriate local supplies.

An international strategic alliance partner may have a portfolio of international business experience including international trading, technology transfer, joint ventures or wholly-owned subsidiaries. Only the last two imply experience of managing investments in a foreign country, but lessons can be learned from other types of international experience across the national boundary. Since an international strategic alliance is formed through partnerships it is relevant to take the experience of both partners into account, and yet many previous academic studies have not examined the effects on improved performance of local partner attributes or even registered that an international strategic alliance's local partner's previous international business or investment experience might contribute to an alliance.

Recent results suggest that previous experience is likely to be of particular significance to strategic alliance performance in a developing country context such as China's, where cultural differences and under-developed institutional frameworks present major problems that can otherwise seriously unsettle a strategic partnership. It appears to be helpful for foreign firms entering developing countries to work with a strategic alliance partner who not only provides local knowledge and connections but who also has some experience of international business and can therefore communicate on the same wavelength. Researchers frequently take the performance of an international strategic alliance into account when investigating such organizational phenomena as learning, as this emphasis is in accord with the need to develop a normative theory of organizational learning in the context of international strategic alliance formation.

Building main themes for foreign investment and corporate governance

Primary consideration must be given to the pooling of foreign investment and control priorities that are heterogeneous in the measurement of a strategic alliance's performance. Even when access is available to such information from a large sample of strategic alliances, there is greater risk of error from the variance in accounting procedures of each strategic alliance. It is recognized that the development of a strategic alliance is one of crucial strategic concerns and yet measuring the performance of a strategic alliance continues to pose problems, both from the standpoint of practitioners and of researchers of international business studies. The collaborative nature of a strategic alliance places constraints upon the strategic actions any one partner can take and even the sincerity of a partner's long-term commitment to the collaboration may be in doubt. In the case of international strategic alliances, the influence of different corporate cultures adds to the risk of misunderstanding and failure in business co-operation. Five indicators for the relationship between the foreign investments and corporate governance are summarized in Table 11.1.

The quality of ownership resources put into an international strategic alliance at its formation by partner firms has a highly significant bearing upon their performance. An international strategic alliance in China needs to establish its own forms of work organization and to independently recruit and train its own personnel in line with its own criteria, rather than inheriting standards from the local partner in a country in transition from socialism. The policy implication is that it is wise to resource a

Table 11.1 Five indicators for a research framework for the relationship between the foreign investments and corporate governance

Research framework →	**Theoretical perspectives →**	**Research indicators**
Formation model	Ways of forming strategic objectives	Strategic goals versus economic goals
Ownership model	Ways of investing in ownership resources	Capital versus non-capital resources
Governance model	Ways of controlling ownership resources	Strategic role of the board versus management of strategic alliance per se
Corporate culture model	Ways of making decisions	Decisional thinking versus cultural feeling
Learning model	Ways of taking in information	Technical, system and strategic learning

strategic alliance in ways that avoid getting locked into outmoded technologies and the heavily institutionalized working practices that are endemic in state controlled industries. This provision includes adequate capital to establish new plants and facilities, and the direct supply of high quality components and other production inputs where appropriate. The introduction of advanced technology and new production facilities appear to provide an important basis for the achievement of superior performance. From a macroeconomic perspective, the use of an international strategic alliance as a means of internalizing the operational resources of parent firms appears to be beneficial to the developing country.

A further international strategic alliance ownership issue that is an impediment to the achievement of decent performance arises from the resource deficiencies that most local partners still experience, especially in respect of capital, advanced technology, training and access to sophisticated subcomponents. If an international strategic alliance's performance can benefit a local partner, its resource deficiencies can be reduced. An international strategic alliance in China is expected to bring additional dimensions of international management, advanced technology and superior quality of supply networking into play in comparison with purely local firms. The relationships to be managed are more complex, because of the hybrid organizational nature of an international strategic alliance per se and the mix of ownership resources and learning styles that each partner brings. Extra managerial competencies are required, including a broader strategic vision to reflect partner firms' strategic objectives, a capacity to handle cultural and institutional differences and an ability to transfer hard and soft technologies from partner firms to the international strategic alliance. The local Chinese partners in most strategic alliances expect from the outset that management will be eventually shifted from the foreign partner firms to themselves over time through the process of organizational learning. As a result, in order to maintain their strategic and operational control, the foreign partner will have to continually make resource commitments to maintain the original balance of bargaining power. In a strategic alliance, valuation of ownership investments and the right to set 'control priorities' are perceived as the core of maintaining business control in the long term, and continuing renegotiations between the partners should be expected around such issues. The maintenance of resource complementarities between partner firms is perceived as an effective way for international strategic alliance partners to enhance their learning about an opaque local context. The experience of working with international strategic alliance partners in China will also enhance the ability to learn from, and adapt to, new and evolving contexts.

Effective corporate governance only becomes a significant predictor of an international strategic alliance's performance when strategic inputs of the board and partner firms' management involvement are taken into account. This suggests that, in a developing country, it becomes a positive benefit to an international strategic alliance if the local partner is brought into its management process provided that the foreign partner can provide an adequate resource base. If the resource base is not adequate, additional foreign managerial intervention is required to compensate for inadequacies. The alternative that leads to better performance is where there is less foreign control in combination with the provision of greater resource quality by that partner. These observations on corporate governance in relation to ownership investment are clearly specific to an international strategic alliance in which the technical competencies of one partner are inferior to those of the other. In such circumstances, a transfer of knowledge and expertise is both an objective of the junior partner and a necessity for the effective operation of the international strategic alliance itself. Such configurations can be found in international strategic alliances between developed country firms and local Chinese partners. In this respect, if partners shared corporate governance rather than there being domination by one partner of an international strategic alliance, that is likely to lead to achieve better management of their resources, knowledge and capabilities.

The partner firms given to their strategic alliance for training purposes or performance improvement should evaluate the excellence of the corporate culture. This is necessary if a strategic alliance is to continue to adapt to an increasingly competitive and global business environment. China is seeking to modernize and transform its national institutions without sacrificing its commitment to economic progress, socio-cultural heterogeneity and traditional social hierarchic values. The achievement of performance has been shown to be crucial to the sustenance of corporate culture for most strategic alliances in China as they mainly rely upon their strategic objectives, organizational principles, and social relation norms to provide internal performance measures. Recent cultural analysis of management practices and corporate culture highlights corporate culture as a relatively important factor in the development of strategic alliance performance in general, and can enhance organizational performance, especially specific managerial values related to power, decision-making, ethical priorities and ethical work climate that pose great corporate cultural problems.

Empirical studies of partners' management values when running strategic alliances are rare and differentially emphasize corporate culture, management principles and professional values rather than national cultural values. Local managers imbued with traditional Chinese cultures who work in a strategic alliance tend to underplay the use of power and are more likely to emphasize loyalty, belongingness and caring. Of course, local managers' attitudes vary selectively with age, education, occupation and industrial sector but, on the whole, managers in an international strategic alliance are participative, consultative and accessible. Effective management practices that achieve useful organizational purposes are theoretically more likely if the local managers engage actively in open communication within their strategic alliance. These managers need to be encouraged to contribute their resource, knowledge and capability inputs to the performance evaluation process by utilizing management information to ensure that procedural and substantive justice is done and seen to be done. An appropriate leadership style and the establishment of an organizational ethics system in a strategic alliance will enhance the alliance's reputation.

The problems facing a foreign firm investing in a strategic alliance are even greater when it is located in a developing country such as China as there are normally significant resource deficiencies and an unfamiliar environment. These considerations imply that an international strategic alliance's success requires considerable competence and knowledge inputs, some of which can be learned from previous or on-going experience. Three aspects of learning such as learning from experience, formation learning and operational learning are likely to have particular relevance to the specific case of an international strategic alliance in China. The amount of organizational learning required is likely to be greater when the strategic alliance's business crosses national boundaries, especially if the host location is a developing transition economy such as China, in which the environment is dynamic and many local partners have had little previous experience of working with foreign counterparts.

Summary

This chapter suggests that performance measures based upon 'goal, system and constituency' models provide useful information on the performance evaluation of a strategic alliance in China. Successful strategic alliances in China have been found to rely on formal corporate governance systems for monitoring performance to expand their markets. Performance measures can also be of great value to the strategic alliance as a means of improving communications, raising the level of trust between partners and increasing investment confidence between parent firm and strategic alliances. Performance indicators can be used as a way of linking a strategic alliance's performance to valued research paradigms such as strategic alliance formation, ownership investment, corporate governance, corporate culture and organizational learning. If these performance assessments are used properly they will provide feedback for foreign investors about current strategies, learning and special training requirements.

Appendix I: Major Tax Payments for Foreign Firms in China

1 **Value-Added Tax**

Value-added tax (VAT) is a type of turnover tax that is levied on the increase in the value of commodities at different stages of production or circulation or on the value added to commodities. All enterprises and individuals engaged in the sale or import of goods or the provision of processing, repair or maintenance services in China have to pay VAT.

(a) VAT payers in China, are divided into general taxpayers and small-scale taxpayers depending upon the scale of their operation and the ability of their accounting and auditing system to deal with the different methods of tax computation.

(b) Small-scale taxpayers are taxpayers who do not have a sound accounting and auditing system and whose taxable value of sales is below the prescribed standards.

General taxpayers are enterprises whose annual taxable sales value exceeds the limits prescribed for small-scale taxpayers. Small production enterprises with a proper accounting and auditing system may be classified as general taxpayers. However, individuals, non-enterprise units, and enterprises that do not regularly engage in taxable operations are classified as small-scale taxpayers even if their annual taxable sales value exceeds the standard limits for small-scale taxpayers.

(c) Taxable Items and Tax Rates

There are two VAT rates in China: a basic rate of 17% and a lower rate of 13%. The sale and importation of the following commodities are subject to VAT at the lower rate of 13%: grains, edible vegetable oil, drinking water, heating, air-conditioning, hot water, coal gas, liquefied petroleum gas, natural gas, methane, coal products for domestic use; books, newspapers and magazines; feedstuffs, chemical fertilizers, pesticides, agricultural machinery, agricultural plastic sheeting, and other commodities as specified by the state.

(d) Export Tax Exemption and Rebate

China has a zero VAT tax rate on exports. There is no export-related tax, and tax payments made in respect of the stages preceding export will be refunded.

(e) Special VAT Invoices

General taxpayers may purchase special VAT invoices from the tax authorities. Small-scale taxpayers and non-VAT taxpayers may not purchase or use such invoices. General taxpayers selling taxable items must issue special VAT invoices to the buyer. However, for the sale of taxable items to consumers and the sale of duty-free goods or goods for export, no special VAT invoices have to be issued. It is not mandatory to issue special VAT invoices for the sale of taxable items to small-scale taxpayers. Special VAT invoices that do not meet government specifications may not be used to claim deductions or an exemption from input VAT.

(f) Tax Liability and Payment Period
In the supply of goods or taxable services, the VAT liability arises on the day the taxpayer receives full payment for the transaction or issues an invoice for the transaction. In the case of import goods, VAT liability arises on the day of customs declaration.

2 **Consumption Tax**
Consumption tax is tax payable on the sales value or volume of taxable consumer goods sold in China by enterprises and individuals engaged in the production, subcontracted processing or importation of any of the following 11 categories of goods: cigarettes, alcoholic drinks and alcohol, cosmetics, skin-care and hair-care products, fine jewels and precious stones, firecrackers and fireworks, gasoline, diesel oil, motor vehicle tyres, motorcycles, and small motor cars. It is levied on consumer goods on top of VAT and is applied before VAT is calculated. Consumption tax is included in the transaction price and is only payable on the production, subcontracted processing and importation of taxable consumer goods. Since consumption tax is included in the transaction price, it is not payable in subsequent stages such as wholesaling and retailing. The tax is ultimately borne by consumers.

(a) Taxpayers
Payers of consumption tax are enterprises and individuals engaged in the production, subcontracted processing and importation of taxable consumer goods.

(b) Taxable Items and Tax Rates
Consumption tax is payable on 11 taxable items at 25 different tax rates (tax amounts), ranging from 3% to 45%. It is levied by value at the production stage; but for yellow spirits, beer, gasoline and diesel oil, it is imposed by volume (specific duty). Taxable consumer goods for export are exempt from consumption tax unless otherwise stipulated by the government.

(c) Tax Liability and Payment Period
In the sale of taxable consumer goods, the consumption tax liability arises on the day the taxpayer receives full payment for the transaction or issues an invoice for the transaction. In the import of goods, it arises on the day of the customs declaration.

3 **Excise Duty**
Excise duty is levied by Customs on commercial commodities or articles entering or leaving China's national boundaries or customs territories.

(a) Taxpayers
Payers of excise duty on commercial commodities are consignees of imports and consignors of exports. The former have to pay import tariffs while the latter have to pay export tariffs. Excise duty is payable on articles by the following people: incoming passengers carrying personal luggage and articles, service attendants on different modes of transport carrying personal articles,

owners of gifts and personal articles that enter China through other means, and addressees of incoming personal mail.

(b) Tariff Rates

China adopts a two-tier tariff for imports: a general rate and a preferential rate. The general tariff rate applies to goods from countries and regions that have not signed reciprocal tariff agreements with China, while the preferential tariff rate applies to goods from countries and regions that have signed such agreements with China. Specific duties, compound duties and sliding tariffs are levied on a selected number of imported goods. The current average import tariff rate of China is 11%. For exports, excise duty is not split between general or preferential rates. There are 5 tariff ranges between 20% and 50%.

(c) The dutiable value of imported goods in general is their cost, insurance and fright price while the dutiable value of exports is their free on board price.

(d) Payment of Excise Duty

Taxpayers or their agents should make payment at designated banks within seven days from the date of issuance of the excise duty demand by Customs.

4 **Business Tax**

A business tax is a kind of turnover tax levied on the revenue generated from the provision of taxable services, such as communications and transportation, construction, finance and insurance, post and telecommunications, culture and sports, entertainment and other services, as well as the transfer of intangible assets and the sale of immoveable properties within the territory of China.

(a) Taxpayer

Payers of business tax are enterprises or individuals engaged in the provision of taxable services, transfer of intangible assets or sale of immovable properties in China.

(b) Taxable Items and Tax Rates

There are nine applicable rates for business tax, ranging from 3% (for communications and transportation) to 20% (for entertainment).

5 **Income Tax on Foreign Firms**

(a) Object of Taxation

Foreign enterprises have to pay income tax on their income derived from production, business operations and other sources within the territory of China. As Chinese 'residents', foreign enterprises are required to bear full tax liabilities and pay income tax on all income derived from sources inside and outside China. However, foreign enterprises which are not Chinese 'residents' will only bear limited tax liabilities and pay income tax on income derived from sources inside China.

(b) Taxpayers

Foreign firms established in China include equity joint venture, contractual joint venture and wholly foreign-owned subsidiaries.

(c) Taxable Items and Tax Rates

Foreign firms that have establishments or venues in China have to pay corporate income tax of 30% and local income tax of 3% on their incomes from production and business operations and on profits (dividends), interest, rentals, royalties and other incomes derived from sources both inside and outside China that are effectively connected with such establishments or venues. Foreign firms that have no establishment or venue in China but derive profits, interest, rentals, royalties and other incomes from sources in China, or although they have establishments or venues in China the said incomes are not effectively connected with such establishments or venues, have to pay income tax of 20% on such incomes.

6 **Individual Income Tax**

Individual income tax is levied on the incomes derived from sources both inside and outside China by individuals that who are domiciled in China, or although without domicile have resided for one year or more in China; and on the incomes derived from sources within China of individuals not domiciled or resident in China, or individuals not domiciled but who have resided in China for less than one year.

(a) Taxpayers and Tax Liability

Resident taxpayers are Chinese citizens and foreign nationals residing in China. They are individuals domiciled in China (who, by reason of their permanent registered address, family or economic interests, habitually reside in China); or foreign nationals, overseas Chinese, and Hong Kong, Macau and Taiwan compatriots who have resided in China for a calendar year in a tax year. Resident taxpayers have unlimited tax liabilities and have to pay individual income tax to the Chinese government on incomes from global sources.

Non-resident taxpayers are foreign nationals, overseas Chinese and Hong Kong, Macau and Taiwan compatriots who are neither domiciled nor resident in China, or foreign nationals, overseas Chinese, and Hong Kong, Macau and Taiwan compatriots who are not domiciled in China and have resided in China for less than a calendar year in a tax year. Non-resident taxpayers have limited tax liabilities and are required to pay individual income tax to the Chinese government only on incomes from sources inside China.

(b) Taxable Items, Tax Rates and Deduction Standards

Income from wages and salaries

Income from wages and salaries is taxed at progressive rates ranging from 5% to 45%.

Taxable income: for people working in China, the taxable income is the balance of their monthly income after deducting Rmb800. For personnel recruited from outside China, the taxable income is the balance of their monthly income after deducting Rmb4,000.

(c) Filing of Tax Returns

Tax returns may be filed by taxpayers themselves or by withholding agents.

7 **Land Appreciation**

(a) Taxpayers
The taxpayers of land appreciation tax are organizations or individuals who transfer state-owned land-use rights, buildings and their attached facilities and derive income from such transactions.

(b) Tax Rates and Deductible Items Appreciation amount
The appreciation amount is the balance of proceeds received by the taxpayer on the transfer of real estate, after deducting the sum of deductible items.
Deductible items
Deductible items for the transfer of state-owned land-use rights include amounts paid for the acquisition of land-use rights, costs and expenses for the development of land, taxes and fees related to the transfer of real estate, and other deductible items as stipulated by the Ministry of Finance.

(c) Filing of Tax Returns
Taxpayers should file their tax returns together with the necessary documents to the tax authorities at the place where the real estate is located within seven days of the signing of the real estate transfer agreement. The necessary documents include the real estate title deed and land-use right certificate, land transfer or real estate sale and purchase agreement, real estate evaluation report, and other relevant documents.

8 **Urban Real Estate Tax**
Urban real estate tax applies to foreign enterprises, as well as enterprises established by Hong Kong, Macau and Taiwan compatriots and overseas Chinese. Two tax rates are applicable: 1.2% of the value of the property or 18% of the rental income. Real estate purchased by foreign nationals, Hong Kong, Macau and Taiwan compatriots, and overseas Chinese for non-business purposes are exempt from this tax for the time being.

9 **Stamp Duty**
Documents subject to stamp duty include contracts or documents in the nature of a contract in regard to purchase and sale transactions, contracted processing, contracted construction projects, property leasing, goods transportation, warehousing, loans, property insurance, technical contracts, documents of transfer of property title, business account books, certificates and licenses, and other documents determined by the Ministry of Finance to be taxable.

10 **Vehicle and Vessel Usage Licence Tax**

11 **Central Government Tax Revenue**
Central tax revenue: domestic Consumption Tax; Customs Duties; VAT and Consumption Tax collected by Customs on behalf of the government.

12 **Local Government Tax Revenue**
Local tax revenue: Individual Income Tax; City and Township Land Use Tax; Farmland Occupation Tax; Fixed Assets Investment Orientation Regulation Tax; Land Appreciation Tax; House Property Tax; Urban Real Estate Tax; Inheritance Tax (not yet legislated); Vehicle and Vessel Usage Tax; Vehicle and Vessel Usage Licence Plate Tax; Deed Tax; Slaughter Tax; Banquet Tax; Agriculture Tax and Animal Husbandry Tax and their local surtaxes.

13 Tax revenue shared between the Central and local governments

(a) Domestic VAT: 75% for central government and 25% for local government.

(b) Business Tax: the parts consolidated and paid by the railway department, the headquarters of various banks and the headquarters of various insurance companies, and the additional 3% Business Tax paid by financial and insurance enterprises Resource Tax belong to the central government; and the rest is assigned to the local government.

(c) Enterprise Income Tax: income tax paid by central enterprises, income tax paid by local banks and non-bank financial institutions, and the part consolidated paid by the railway department, the headquarters of various banks and the headquarters of various insurance companies belong to the central government; and the rest is assigned to the local government.

(d) Income Tax on enterprises with foreign investment and foreign enterprises: the income tax paid by foreign funded banks belongs to the central government. All other revenues are assigned to the local government.

(e) Resource Tax: the central government portion is the tax paid by offshore oil enterprises, and the rest is assigned to the local government.

(f) City Maintenance and Construction Tax: the part consolidated and paid by the railway department, the headquarters of various banks and the headquarters of various insurance companies belongs to the central government; the rest is assigned to the local government.

(g) Stamp Tax: 94% of the Stamp Tax revenue collected on stock transactions is allocated to the central government; the remaining 6% is assigned to the local government.

(h) Security Exchange Tax.

Source: Adapted from HKTDC Research Department (2003).

Appendix II: Interview Questionnaire for Forming an International Strategic Alliance

Name of the company:
Name of interviewee:
Position of interviewee:
Is the interviewee a member of the board of directors?
Number of years the interviewee has worked for the foreign company:
Nationality and ethnic background of conducted:

Name of interviewer (s):
Date of interview:
Duration of interview: _____ hours
Was the interview tape-recorded? (yes/no)
Language in which interview was interviewee:

Stage I: International Strategic Alliance at Formation

1 **Initial business contacts in China**

i. When was the first business visit to China? (Month, year)
ii. How many persons were involved in this visit?
iii. Which regions of China did they visit?
iv. What was their first impression of China as a prospect for business development?

2 **How much importance did your company attach to the following when it established its first international strategic alliance in China?**

Objectives

Not at all important — Extremely important

|----------------|----------------|----------------|----------------|-----------------|------------|

1 — **7**

Factors	*Scale (1–7)*
Line of business	....
Scope of current operations	....
International business activities	....
Objectives in the local market	....
Current and future market	....
Sales estimate by sector	....
Foreign and domestic distribution	....
Local industry conditions	....
Past product imports	....
Anticipated competition in the host country	....

Approximate input requirements for all materials	....
Present sources of supply	....
Availability of utilities	....
Transport routes planned	....
Communication system for accessing sector information	....
Environmental protection plan	....

3 **How important were these partner-related and non-partner-related factors of where to locate the international strategic alliance?**

Not at all important — Extremely important

|---------------|---------------|---------------|---------------|---------------|---------------|

1 — 7

Factors	*Scale (1–7)*
Choice of product range	....
Line of business	....
Resource commitment	....
Size and scope of current business operations	....
Location	....
Financial performance	....
Marketing experience	....
Compatibility of partners' management	....
The control of majority capital ownership	....
Management participation	....
International activities	....
A long-term commitment to the partner	....
Distribution of profits	....
Technological improvement	....
Technical expertise	....
Operational experience	....
Task-related influence	....
Culture-oriented influence	....
Management participation	....

4 **How important were the following criteria in achieving (1) strategic fit (2) cultural fit (3) operational fit when choosing your partner?**

Not at all important — Extremely important

|---------------|---------------|---------------|---------------|---------------|---------------|

1 — 7

Criteria	*Scale (1–7)*
Strategic Fit	
Description of technology and equipment to be used	....
Scope of production	....

Products ....
Market segment ....
Financing requirements ....
Technology transfers ....
Land-use arrangement ....

Cultural Fit
Infrastructure improvements required ....
Production/operations plan ....
Cost estimate including technology transfer fees, royalty rate ....
Layout of proposed equipment and costs ....

Operational Fit
Organization overhead costs
Organizational structure ....
Estimated manpower requirements ....
Estimated annual output/turnover ....
Transport and local storage requirements ....
Estimated total investment cost (working capital) ....
Proposed capital structure ....
Quality of product/service ....

5 **How important were the following inputs to be provided by your international strategic alliance partner in influencing your selection?**

Not at all important Extremely important

|---------------|---------------|---------------|---------------|-----------------|------------|

1 **7**

Criteria	*Scale (1–7)*
Local market knowledge	....
Knowledge of local culture	....
Links with major buyers	....
Distribution channels	....
Labour	....
Regulatory permits	....
Materials/natural resources	....
Capital	....
Product	....
Production knowledge	....
Technology	....
Local brand names	....
Other (please specify and score)	....

Strategic Motives for Chinese Managers

6 **How much importance does your company attach to the following strategic motives for forming an international strategic alliance?**

Benefits

Not at all important Extremely important

|---------------|---------------|---------------|---------------|----------------|------------|

1 7

Inputs	*Scale (1–7)*
Technology transfer	....
Benefit from tax incentives	....
Obtain foreign cash investment	....
Help upgrade suppliers' technology	....
Learning management expertise	....
Develop export opportunities	....
Help expand in China market	....
Opportunity to train Chinese staff	....
Establish strong business presence	....
Assistant diversification of products	....
Opportunity for good long-term profit	....
Ability to import superior components	....
Gain a strategic position	....
Import substitution	....
Employment creation	....

Strategic Motives for Foreign Managers

How much importance does your company attach to the following strategic motives for forming an international strategic alliance?

Benefits

Not at all important Extremely important

|---------------|---------------|---------------|---------------|----------------|------------|

1 7

Inputs	*Scale (1–7)*
Create a strategic position	....
Opportunity for good long-term profit	....
Attraction of the Chinese market	....
Establish strong business presence	....
Low labour cost	....
Facilitate international expansion	....
Learning how to do business	....
Benefit from tax incentives	....
Low cost sourcing	....

Opportunity for quick profit	....
Advantageous transfer pricing	....
Diversification of products	....

7 **Did the contract or separate contracts specify any of the following:**
(Ask for details and circle *two* as appropriate: Y/N and whether in international strategic alliance or separate contract)

Technology supply (who and/or when)	Y/N
Use of production/process technology	Y/N
Use of product technology/design	Y/N
Utilization of brand name/trade mark	Y/N
Transactions (import and export targets)	Y/N
Management	Y/N
• board composition	
• appointment of Chief Executive Officer and executives	
• labour management and department positions structure design	
International strategic alliance tasks and targets	Y/N
• production capability,	
• annual production volume,	
• sales targets and business development	
Marketing and distribution systems	Y/N
Specification of suppliers	Y/N
Supply of basic services (power, water, etc.)	Y/N
Provision of management & professional services	Y/N
Termination arrangements	Y/N
Duration of international strategic alliance contract	_____ Years
Duration of technology contract (if any)	_____ Years
Total of investment capital: _____ ($)	

Stage II: Corporate Governance

8 **Which control mechanisms are employed in the international strategic alliance?**
(Ask the extent to which each of the following approaches to control are used in the international strategic alliance, scoring along the following scale.)

Hardly used at all — Used to a very large extent

|---------------|---------------|---------------|---------------|---------------|----------------|------------|
1 — 7

	Scale (1–7)
Control through direct personal contact	....
Formal systems, procedures and rules	....
Performance-related rewards, career advancement	....
Shaping attitudes	....
Other control mechanisms?	....

9 **Satisfaction with international strategic alliance performance**
Please use the scale to indicate the extent to which you are satisfied with the strategic alliance's performance on the following criteria:

Not at all satisfied at all — Fully satisfied

|---------------|---------------|---------------|---------------|---------------|------------|

1 — 7

	Scale (1–7)
Profitability	....
Growth of sales	....
Market share	....
Percentage of output exported	....
Percentage of inputs purchased within China	....
Quality of supplies	....
Production efficiency	....
Production quality	....
Technological development	....
Development of local managers	....
Development of local employees	....
Development of expatriate managers' understanding of doing business in China	....
Quality of relations with governmental authorities	....
Quality of collaboration between partners	....

10 **Operational trends of the ISA**

	1999	2000	2001	2002	2003
Total employees	....	....	....	....	....
No. of foreign staff	....	....	....	....	....
Sales turnover (US$)	....	....	....	....	....
Proportion of sales exported by value (%)	....	....	....	....	....
Proportion of inputs supplied within China (localization %)	....	....	....	....	....
Operational profit before tax (US$)	....	....	....	....	....

11 **General background of the company's management**

a. How many Board members are there?
b. What are the nationalities of the Board members?
c. Which owners or interest groups are represented on the Board?
d. What is the nationality of the general manager?
e. From which organization did he come?
f. Who appointed the general manager?

Stage III: The Corporate Culture

12 **Strategic versus financial orientations displayed by international strategic alliance**
Please use the scale to indicate the extent to which you are satisfied with the strategic versus financial orientations displayed by strategic alliance on the following criteria:

Not at all satisfied — Fully satisfied

|---------------|---------------|---------------|---------------|----------------|------------|

1 — 7

	Scale (1–7)
Strategic orientations	....
Gain strategic position in China	....
Establish strong business presence in China	....
Opportunity for long-term profit	....
Learning how to do business in China	....
Financial orientations	....
Low-cost sourcing	
Low labour cost	
Benefit from transfer pricing	
Benefit from tax incentives	

Please use the scale to indicate the extent to which you have adopted human resource management practices undertaken by internaional strategic alliance on the following criteria:

Not at all satisfied — Fully satisfied

|---------------|---------------|---------------|---------------|----------------|------------|

1 — 7

	Scale (1–7)
Formal recruitment versus relationship	....
Reliance on contracts	....
Formalization versus personalization	....
Emphasis on training	....
Integration between parent and affiliates	....
Reliance on formal reward system	....

Stage IV: Organizational Learning

13 **Please use the scale to indicate the extent to which you are satisfied with the organizational learning achieved by strategic alliance on the following criteria**:

Not at all satisfied — Fully satisfied

|---------------|---------------|---------------|---------------|----------------|------------|

1 — 7

	Scale (1–7)
Learning from Working with Counterparts	
• Industry-based learning	....
• Competence in understanding management	....
• Competence in understanding marketing	....

- Communication within or between departments ....
- Dealing with information ....

Inter-partner Learning ....
- Ways of approaching the government ....
- Strategic decision-making ....

Learning in a Strategic Alliance ....
- Company values and objectives ....
- Personal relationships and trust ....
- Language barriers ....

14 **Please use the scale to indicate the extent to which you are satisfied with the (1) strategic learning (2) system learning (3) operational learning by international strategic alliance on the following criteria:**

Not at all satisfied Fully satisfied

|----------------|----------------|---------------|----------------|-----------------|------------|

1 7

Learning Outcomes	*Scale (1–7)*
Strategic Learning	
Attraction of industry characteristics	....
Economic conditions	....
Government function	....
Resources allocation	....
Technology transfer	....
Socio-cultural factors	....
System Learning	
Economic scale	....
Corporate tax	....
Brand development	....
Information processing	....
Learning how to export	....
Learning management expertise	....
Upgrading Chinese suppliers' technology	....
Operational Learning	
Organizational objectives	....
Division of labour and function	....
Required activities	....
Required actions	....
Required attitudes	....

15 **What were the main complementarities you were looking for between what your partner and your company could bring to the strategic alliance?**

16 **What were the main complementarities you have *actually achieved* between what your partner and your company have brought to the strategic alliance?**

17 **What was the rationale for the way the strategic alliance was linked into the corporate organization?**

18 **Perception of inter-partner consensus on the international strategic alliance's overall mission and strategy.**

19 **Mutual perceptions**

How do you think foreign and local managers in your international strategic alliance differ:

(i) their management style:

(ii) in their attitudes:

20 **Managing in international strategic alliance**

To what extent have you experienced the following difficulties in managing your strategic alliance?

Please answer for each item by marking the appropriate point on the scale. If there have been serious problems under any of the following headings, please give details or illustrate.

No problem Major problem

|----------------|----------------|----------------|----------------|-----------------|------------|

1 **7**

	Scale (1–7)
1. Differences between partner's objectives or priorities	....
2. Problems due to different practices	....
3. Government laws and regulations	....
4. The behaviour of government authorities	....
5. Infrastructure limitations	....
6. Supply problems	....
7. Marketing and distribution problems	....
8. HRM problems	....
9. Attitudes or behaviour of foreign managers	....
10. Attitudes or behaviour of Chinese managers	....
11. Competence or training of expatriate managers	....
12. Competence of training of Chinese managers	....
13. Cultural differences	....
14. Problems of communication within the international strategic alliance	....
15. Problems of communication with Chinese parent company	....
16. Problems of communication with foreign parent company	....
17. Language barriers	....
18. Any other major problems, such as corruption?	....

References

Agarwal, Sanjeev and Ramaswami, Sridhar, N. (1992) Choice of foreign market entry mode: impact of ownership, location and internalisation factors. *Journal of International Business Studies*, 23: 1–28.

Allport, G. W., Vernon, P. E. and Lindzey, G. (1970) *A Study of Values*. New York: Houghton Mifflin.

Anderson, Erin and Weitz, Barton (1986) Make or buy decisions: a framework for analysing vertical integration issues in marketing. *Sloan Management Review*, 27: 1–26.

Argyris, C. and Schön, D. A. (1975) *Organizational Learning: A Theory of Action Perspective*. Reading, MA: Addison-Wesley.

Badaracoo, Joseph L. (1991) *The Knowledge Link: How Firms Compete through Strategic Alliances*. Boston, MA: Harvard Business School Press.

Barney, Jay (1991) Firm resource and sustained competitive advantage. *Journal of Management*, 17: 99–120.

Becker, B. E. and Huselid, M. A. (1998) High performance work systems and firm performance: A synthesis of research and managerial implications. *Research in Personnel and Human Resources Journal*, 16(1): 53–101.

Berle, Adolf A. and Means, Gardiner C., Jr. (1932) *The Modern Corporation and Private Property*. New York: Macmillan.

Blodgett, L. Longfellow (1991) Partner contributions as predictors of equity share in international joint ventures. *Journal of International Business Studies*, 22: 63–78.

Boisot, Max and Child, John (1996) From fiefs to clans and network capitalism: explaining China's emerging economic order. *Administrative Science Quarterly*, 41: 600–628.

Bottomore, T. B. and Rubel, M. (1956) *Karl Marx: Selected Writings in Sociology and Social Philosophy*. London: Watts.

Brown, A. D. and Starkey, K. (1994) The effect of organizational culture on communication and information. *Journal of Management Studies*, 31: 807–28.

Buckley, Peter J. (1988) The limits of explanation: testing the internalisation theory of the multinational enterprise. *Journal of International Business Studies*, 19: 181–93.

Busoni, S. and Prencipe, A. (2001) Exploring the links between product and knowledge dynamics. *Journal of Management Studies*, 38: 1019–1035.

Busoni, S., Prencipe, A. and Pavitt, K. (2001) Knowledge specialization, organizational coupling, and the boundaries of the firm: why do firms know more than they make? *Administrative Science Quarterly*, 46: 1185–1200.

Cherington, J. (1980) *The Work Ethic: Working Values and Values that Work*. New York: AMACOM (American Management Association).

Child, John and Yan, Yanni (1999) Investment and control in international joint ventures – the Case of China. *Journal of World Business*, 34/1: 3–15.

Child, John and Yan, Yanni (2001) National and transnational effects in international business: indications from Sino-Foreign joint ventures. *Management International Review*, 41: 53–75.

Child, John, Yuan, Lu and Yan, Yanni (1997) Ownership and control in Sino-foreign joint ventures. In Paul W. Beamish and J. Peter Killing (eds) *Cooperative Strategies: Asia-Pacific Perspectives*. San Francisco, CA: New Lexington Press.

Ciborra, G. (1991) Alliances as learning experiments: co-operation, competition and change in high-tech industries. In L. K. Mytelka (ed.) *Strategic Partnerships and the World Economy*. London: Pinter.

Contractor, Farok J. (1990) Ownership patterns of U.S. joint ventures abroad and the liberalisation of foreign government regulations in the 1980s: evidence from the benchmark surveys. *Journal of International Business Studies*, 21: 55–73.

Contractor, Farok J. and Lorange, Peter (1988) Why should firms co-operate? The strategy and economics basis for cooperative ventures. In Farok J. Contractor & Peter Lorange (eds) *Co-operative Strategies in International Business Studies*. Lexington, MA: Lexington Books.

Corones, S. (2000) Implied good faith and unconscionability in franchises: moving towards relational contract theory. *Australian Business Law Review*, 28: 462–469.

Cullen, John B., Johnson, Jean L. and Sakano, Tomoaki (1995) Japanese and local partner commitment to IJVs: psychological consequences of outcomes and investments in the IJV relationship. *Journal of International Business Studies*, 26: 91–115.

Das, T. K. and Teng, B. S. (2000) Instabilities of strategic alliances: an internal tensions perspective. *Organisation Science*, 11: 77–101.

Demsetz, Harold. (1991) The theory of the firm revisited. In Oliver E. Williamson and Sidney G. Winter (eds) *The Nature of the Firm*. New York: Oxford University Press.

Deshpande, R. and Webster, F. (1989) Organizational culture and marketing: defining the research agenda. *Journal of Marketing*, 53: 3–15.

Dodgson, M. (1992) The strategic management of R&D collaboration. *Technology Analysis and Strategic Management*, 4: 227–244.

Donaldson, Lex (1995) *American Anti-Management Theories of Organization: A Critique of Paradigm Proliferation*. Cambridge University Press.

Dunning, John H. (1977) Trade, location of economic activity and the multinational enterprise: A search for an eclectic approach. In B. Ohlin, P. O. Hesselborn and P. M. Wikman. (eds) *The International Allocation of Economic Activity*. London: Macmillan.

Dunning, John H. (1980) Toward an eclectic theory of international production: some empirical tests. *Journal of International Business Studies*, 11: 9–31.

Dunning, John H. (1988) *Explaining International Production*. London: Unwin Hyman.

Dunning, John H. (1989) The study of international business: a plea for a more interdisciplinary approach. *Journal of International Business Studies*, 20: 411–436.

Dunning, John H. and Rugman, Alan M. (1985) The influence of Hymer's dissertation on the theory of foreign direct investment. *American Economic Review*, 75: 228–232.

Dunning, John H. and McQueen, M. (1981) The eclectic theory of international production: a case studies of the international hotel industry. *Managerial and Decision Economics*. 2: 197–210.

Dyer, J. H. and Nobeoka, K. (2000) Creating and managing a high performance knowledge-sharing network: the Toyota case. *Strategic Management Journal*, 21: 345–367.

Eisenhardt, Kathleen M. (1989) Building theory from case study research. *Academy of Management Review*, 14: 532–550.

Eisenhardt, K. M. and Schoonhoven, C. B. (1996) Resource-based view of strategic alliance formation: strategic and social effects in entrepreneurial firms. *Organization Science*, 7: 136–150.

England, G. W. (1975) *The Manager and His Values*. Cambridge, MA: Ballinger.

Etzioni, Amitai (1964) *Modern Organizations*. Englewood Cliffs, NJ: Prentice-Hall.

Fagre, Nathan and Wells, Louis T. Jr. (1982) Bargaining power of multinationals and host governments. *Journal of International Business Studies*, 13: 9–23.

Fama, E. and Jensen, Michael C. (1983a) Agency problems and residual claims. *Journal of Law and Economics*, 26: 327–349.

Fama, E. and Jensen, Michael C. (1983b) Separation of ownership and control. *Journal of Law and Economics*, 26: 301–326.

Flamholtz, E. (1995) Managing organizational transitions: implications for corporate and human resource management. *European Management Journal*, 13: 39–51.

Furnham, A. (1990) *The Protestant Work Ethic: The Psychology of Work-related Beliefs and Behaviours*. London: Routledge.

Galbraith, Jay R. (1973) *Designing Complex Organizations*. Reading, MA: Addison-Wesley.

Galunic, D. C. and Rodan, S. (1998) Resource recombination in the firm: knowledge structures and the potential for Schumpeterian innovation. *Strategic Management Journal*, 19: 1193–1201.

Gatignon, Hubert and Anderson, Erin (1988) The multinational corporation's degree of control over subsidiaries: an empirical test of a transaction cost exploitation. *Journal of Law, Economics, and Organization*, 4: 305–336.

Geringer, J. Michael (1991) Strategic determinants of partner selection criteria in international joint venture. *Journal of International Business Studies*, 22: 41–62.

Ghoshal, Sumantra (1987) Global strategy: an organising framework. *Strategic Management Journal*, 8: 425–440.

Gomes-Casseres, Benjamin (1987) Joint venture instability: is it a problem? *Columbia Journal of World Business*, 22: 97–102.

Gulati, R. (1995) Does familiarity breed trust? The implications of repeated tics for contractual choice in alliances. *Academy of Management Journal*, 38: 85–112.

Guo, Aimin and Akroyd, Robert (1996) Overcoming barriers to technological transfers into China. In John Child and Yuan Lu (eds). *Management Issues in China: International Enterprises*. London: Routledge.

Hagedoorn, J. (1993) Understanding the rationale for strategic technology partnering: interorganizational models of co-operation and sectoral differences. *Strategic Management Journal*, 14: 371–86.

Hagedoorn, J., Link, A. N. and Vonortas, N. S. (2000) Research partnerships. *Research Policy*, 29: 567–86.

Hakansson, Hakan. and Johanson, Jan. (1988) Formal and informal cooperation strategies in international industrial networks. In Farok J. Contractor and Peter Lorange (eds) *Cooperative Strategies in International Business*, Lexington, MA: Lexington Books.

Hall, W. (1995) *Managing Cultures: Making Strategic Relationships Work*. Chichester: John Wiley.

Hall, Wendy and Eppink, Jan D. (1992) Strategic alliances in the airline industry. *Journal of Strategic Change*, 1: 341–348.

Hamel, Gary, Doz, Yves and Prahalad, C. K. (1989) Collaborate with your competitors and win. *Harvard Business Review*, 5: 567–75.

Harrigan, Kathryn R. (1985) *Strategies for Joint Ventures*. Lexington, MA: Lexington Books.

Hennart, J.-F. (1988) A transaction costs theory of equity joint ventures. *Strategic Management Journal*, 9: 361–74.

Hennart, J.-F. (1991) The transaction costs theory of joint ventures: An empirical study of Japanese subsidiaries in the United States. *Management Science*, 37: 483–497.

Hofstede, G. (1980) *Culture's Consequences: International Differences in Work Related Attitudes*. Beverly Hills, CA: Sage.

Hollows, J. and Lewis, J. (1995) Managing human resources in the Chinese context: the experience of a major multinational. In H. Davies (ed.) *China Business: Context and Issues*. Hong Kong: Longman.

Hong Kong Trade Development Council (2003) *Guide to Doing Business in China*. Hong Kong: Hong Kong Trade Development Council.

Inkpen, A. C. (1998) Learning and knowledge acquisition through international strategic alliances. *Academy of Management Executive*, 12: 69–80.

Inkpen, A. C. and Beamish, P. W. (1997) Knowledge, bargaining power, and the instability of international joint ventures. *Academy of Management Review*, 22: 177–202.

Janger A. R. (1980) *Organization of International Joint Ventures*. New York: The Conference Board.

Jensen, Michael C. and Meckling, William H. (1976) Theory of the firm: managerial behavior, agency costs, and capital structure. *Journal of Financial Economics*, 3: 305–360.

Kale, P., Singh, H. and Perlmutter, H. (2000) Learning and protection of proprietary assets, in strategic alliances: building relational capital. *Strategic Management Journal*, 21: 217–37.

Khanna, T., Gulati, R. and Nohria, N. (1998) The dynamics of learning alliances: competition, cooperation and relative scope. *Strategic Management Journal*, 19: 193–210.

Khanna, T. (1998) The scope of strategic alliances. *Organization Science*, 9: 340–355.

Killing, J. Peter (1983) *Strategies for Joint Venture Success*. New York: Praeger.

Kogut, B. and Zander, U. (1996) What firms do: coordination, identity, and learning. *Organization Science*, 7, 502–18.

Kogut, Bruce (1988) Joint ventures: theoretical and empirical perspectives. *Strategic Management Journal*, 9/4: 319–332.

Kroeber, A. L. and Kluckhohn, C. (1952) *Culture: A Critical Review of Concepts and Definitions*. Cambridge, MA: Peabody Museum.

Larsson, R., Bengtsson, L., Hendricksson, K. and Sparks, J. (1998) The interorganizational learning dilemma: collective knowledge development in strategic alliances. *Organization Science*, 9: 285–96.

Lazonick, William and O'Sullivan, Mary (2000) Maximizing shareholder value: a new ideology for corporate governance. *Economy and Society*, 29: 13–35

Lecraw, Donald J. (1984) Bargaining power, ownership, and profitability of transactional corporations in developing countries. *Journal of International Business Studies*, 15: 27–43.

Lorange, Peter and Roos, Johan (1992) *Strategic Alliances: Formation, Implementation, and Evolution*. Oxford: Blackwell.

Lyles, M. A. (1988) Learning among joint-venture sophisticated firms. *Management International Review*, 28: 85–98.

Macaulay, Stewart (2000) Relational contracts floating on a sea of custom? Thoughts about the ideas of Ian MacNeil and Lisa Berstein. *Northwestern University Law Review*, 94: 775–804.

Macher, J. T. (2001) Vertical disintegration and process innovation in semiconductor manufacturing: foundries vs. integrated producers. Georgetown University Working Paper. Washington, DC.

Madhok, Anoop (1995) Revisiting multinational firms' tolerance for joint ventures: a trust-based approach. *Journal of International Business Studies*, 26: 117–137.

Mallin, Chris and Rong, Xie (1998) The development of corporate governance in China. *Journal of Contemporary China*, 7: 33–42.

March, J. G. (1991) Exploration and exploitation in organizational learning. *Organization Science*, 2: 71–87.

Mariti, P. and Smiley, R. H. (1983) Co-operative agreements and the organization of industry. *The Journal of Industrial Economics*, XXXI: 437–451.

Marris, Robin L. (1964) *The Economic Theory of 'Managerial' Capitalism*. London: Macmillan.

Mintzberg, H. (1983) *Power in and Around Organizations*. Englewood Cliffs. NJ: Prentice-Hall.

Monks, Robert G. and Minow, Neil (1995) *Corporate Governance*. Oxford: Blackwell.

Mowery, D. C., Oxley, J. E. and Silverman, B. S. (2001) The two faces of partner-specific absorptive capacity: learning and cospecializing in strategic alliances. Discussion paper 01–064. Boston, MA: Harvard Business School, Division of Research.

Nelson, R. and Winter, S. (1982) *An Evolutionary Theory of Economic Change*. Cambridge, MA: Balkan.

Nonaka, Ikujro and Hirotake, Takeuchi (1995) *The Knowledge-Creating Company*. New York: Oxford University Press.

Nonaka, I. (1994) A dynamic theory of organizational knowledge creation. *Organization Science*, 5: 14–37.

North, Douglass C. (1990) *Institutions, Institutional Change and Economic Performance*. Cambridge: Cambridge University Press.

Ohlin, Bertil G. (1933) *Inter-regional Trade and International Trade*. Cambridge, MA: Harvard University Press.

Oxley, J. E. (1997) Appropriability hazards and governance in strategic alliances: a transaction cost approach. *Journal of Law Economics and Organization*, 13: 389–407.

Pfeffer, Jeffrey (1981) *Power in Organization*. Marshfield, MA: Pitman.

Pfeffer, Jeffrey and Salancik, Gerald R. (1978) *The External Control of Organizations: A Resource Dependence Perspective*. New York: Harper and Row.

Phillips, N., Lawrence, T. B. and Hardy, C. (2000) Interorganizational collaboration and the dynamics of institutional fields. *Journal of Management Studies*, 37: 23–43.

Pierce, Jon L., Rubenfeld, Stephen A. and Morgan, Susan (1991) Employee ownership: a conceptual model of process and effects. *Academy of Management Review*, 16: 121–144.

Pinto, J. (2000) Product development speed in the internet age. Controls Intelligence and Plant System Report, June: 4–5.

Porter, Michael. E. (1980) *Competitive Strategy: Techniques for Analysing Industries and Competitors*. New York: Free Press.

Porter, Michael E. (1985) *Competitive Advantage: Creating and Sustaining Superior Performance*. New York: Free press.

Porter, Michael E. (1990) *The Competitive Advantage of Nations*. Basingstoke: Macmillan.

Porter, M. E. and Fuller, M. B. (1986) Coalitions and Global Strategy. In Michael E. Porter (ed.) *Competition in Global Industries*. Boston, MA: Harvard Business School Press.

Powell, W. W. (1998) Learning from collaboration: knowledge and networks in the biotechnology ad pharmaceutical industries. *California Management Review*, 40: 228–40.

Prencipe, A. (1997) Technical competencies and product, evolutionary dynamics: a case study from the aero engine industry. *Research Policy*, 25: 1261–1276.

Renner, K. (1904) *The Institutions of Private Law and their Social Function*. London: Routledge and Kegan Paul, 1949. A translation of the 1928 revised edition.

Reynolds, John I. (1984) The 'pinched shoe' effect of international joint ventures. *Journal of World Business*, 19: 23–29.

Ricardo, David (1951) On the Principles of Political Economy and Taxation, in P. Sraffa (ed.) *The Works and Correspondence of David Ricardo*. Cambridge: Cambridge University Press.

Ring, P. S. and van de Yen, A. H. (1992) Structuring cooperative relationships between organizations. *Strategic Management Journal*, 13: 483–498.

Rothaermel, F. T. (2001) Incumbent's advantage through exploiting complementary assets via interfirm cooperation. *Strategic Management Journal*, 22: 687–699.

Rugman, Alan M. (1982) Internalisation and Non-equity Forms of International Involvement. In Alan M. Rugman (ed.) *New Theories of the Multinational Enterprise*. New York: St. Martin's Press.

Rugman, Alan M. and Verbeke, Alain (1992) A note on the Transational solution and the transaction cost theory of multinational strategic management. *Journal of International Business Studies*, 23: 761–771.

Schann, Jean-Louis (1983) Parent Control and Joint Venture Success: The Case of Mexico. Unpublished doctoral dissertation, University of Western Ontario.

Schaan, Jean-Louis (1988) How to control a joint venture even as a minority partner. *Journal of General Management*, 14: 4–16.

Schilling, M. A. and Steensma, H. K. (2001) The use of modular organizational forms: an industry-level analysis. *Academy of Management Journal*, 44: 1149–1168.

Schultz, Theodore W. (1961) Investment in human capital. *American Economic Review*, 51: 1–17.

Scott, John (1979) *Corporations, Classes and Capitalism*. London: Hutchinson.

Scott, John (1985) Theoretical Framework and Research Design. In Stokman, Frans N., Rolf Ziegler and John Scott (eds) *Networks of Corporate Power*. Cambridge: Polity Press.

Scott, John (1997) *Corporate Business and Capitalist Classes*. Oxford: Oxford University Press.

Scott, John and Michael Hughes (1976) Ownership and control in a satellite economy: a discussion from Scottish data. *Sociology*, 10: 21–41.

Shapiro, C. and Varian, H. R. (1999) *Information Rule: A Strategic Guide to the Network Economy*. Boston, MA: Harvard Business School Press.

Shleifer, Andrei and Robert W. Vishny (1997) A survey of corporate governance. *The Journal of Finance*, LII: 737–783.

Simonin, B. L. (1999) Ambiguity and the process of knowledge transfer in strategic alliances. *Strategic Management Journal*, 20: 595–623.

Smith, Adam (1961) *An Inquiry into the Nature and Causes of the Wealth of Nations*, E. Cannan (ed.) London: Methuen.

State Statistical Bureau of the People's Republic of China (2003) *China Statistical Yearbook*. Hong Kong: International Centre for the Advancement of Science and Technology.

Teece, David (1976) *The Multinational Corporation and the Resource Cost of International Technology Transfer*. Cambridge, MA: Ballinger Publishing.

Teece, David (1986) Transaction cost economics and the multinational enterprise. *Journal of Economic Behaviour and Organizations*, 7: 21–45.

Thompson, James. D. (1967) *Organizations in Action*. New York: McGraw-Hill.

Ting, Wen Lee (1988) *Multinational Risk Assessment and Management*. New York: Quorum Books.

Vachani, Sushil (1995) Enhancing the obsolescing bargain theory: a longitudinal study of foreign ownership of U.S. and European multinationals. *Journal of International Business Studies*, 26: 159–180

Vernon, Raymond (1966) International investment and international trade in the product cycle. *Quarterly Journal of Economics*, 80: 190–207.

Williamson, Oliver E. (1970) *Corporate Control and Business Behavior*. Englewood Cliffs, NJ: Prentice-Hall.

Williamson, Oliver E. (1975) *Markets and Hierarchies*. New York: The Free Press.

Williamson, Oliver E. (1985) *The Economic Institutions of Capitalism*. New York: The Free Press.

Williamson, Oliver E. (1988) Corporate finance and corporate governance. *Journal of Finance*, 43: 567–591.

Williamson, Oliver E. (1996) *The Mechanisms of Governance*. New York: Oxford University Press.

Yan, Aimin and Gray, Barbara (1996) Linking management control and inter-partner relationships with performance in US-Chinese joint ventures. In John Child and Yuan Lu (eds) *Management Issues in China: International Enterprises*. London: Routledge.

Yan, Aimin and Gray, Barbara (1994a) An empirical investigation of a negotiations model in American-Chinese joint ventures, paper given to the Conference on Management Issues for China in the 1990s., St. John's College, Cambridge, March.

Yan, Aimin and Gray, Barbara (1994b) Bargaining power, management control, and performance in United Stated China joint ventures: a comparative case study. *Academy of Management Journal*, 37: 1478–1517.

Yan, Yanni and John Child (2000) Effects of value chain in international joint ventures: the sectoral analysis. *Journal of Global Marketing*, 14: 37–55.

Yan, Yanni and John Child (2002) An analysis of strategic determinants in Sino-British joint ventures: does learning affect decision-making? *British Journal of Management*, 13: 109–122.

Yan, Yanni and John Child (2004) Effects of investors' resource commitments on information reporting systems: control perspectives on international joint ventures. *Journal of Business Research*, 57: 361–371.

Yin, R. K. (1994) *Case Study Research: Design and Methods*. Beverly Hills. CA: Sage.

Yuchtman, E. and Seashore, S. E. (1967) A systematic resource approach to organizational effectiveness. *American Sociological Review*, 32: 891–903.

Index